Praise for *What's the Economy For, Anyway?*

"Yes, *What's the Economy For, Anyway?* is tremendously exciting, thought-provoking, and essential to thinking about our survival. But for me, it's just plain fun to read! I've always been the hedonist of the Simplicity movement, so I know when something is truly enjoyable. And this book is. Read and enjoy!"
—**Cecile Andrews, author of *Slow Is Beautiful* and *The Circle of Simplicity***

"This book raises many fundamental questions that are rarely asked. Why should be people be unemployed when there is work to be done? Why do economists tend to view income as being more valuable than vacations and other forms of leisure? Our view of the economy tends to be far too narrow. *What's the Economy For, Anyway?* will help broaden our perspective." —**Dean Baker, co-director, Center for Economic and Policy Research**

"By focusing on economic growth, we get misery in the USA. But the authors suggest another world is possible, one that would be better for all. We will all do better for following their advice to build a house of health and achieving the good life that lasts forever." —**Stephen Bezruchka, M.D., University of Washington School of Public Health**

"Economics professors are good at answering 'how to' questions, but not so good with 'what for?' or 'so what?' questions. This clearly and simply written book strikes a powerful blow for economic sanity by asking the main 'what for?' questions, and giving cogent and specific answers. A wonderful voter's guide on economic issues for the 2012 election and beyond!" —**Herman E. Daly, professor emeritus, School of Public Policy, University of Maryland**

"The economy should be for us, but it's not. This smart, lively, and lovable book explains how we could move it in a happier and more sustainable direction."
—**Nancy Folbre, professor of economics, University of Massachusetts, author of *The Invisible Heart***

"At a time when a lot of insane ideas are in danger of being enacted in Washington, D.C., including a frenzy of bills to fleece the middle class and further pamper our economic elite, this book asks the most fundamental question of all: What in hell is the economy for, if not for a good and sustainable quality of life for all? And it offers some fresh ideas for economic progress based on common sense and the common good. Read, absorb, and take action!"
—**Jim Hightower, former Texas agriculture commissioner and author of *Swim Against the Current: Even a Dead Fish Can Go With the Flow***

WHAT'S THE ECONOMY FOR, ANYWAY?

Why It's Time to Stop Chasing Growth and Start Pursuing Happiness

JOHN DE GRAAF AND DAVID K. BATKER
FOREWORD BY JAMES GUSTAVE SPETH

BLOOMSBURY PRESS
NEW YORK · BERLIN · LONDON · SYDNEY

Published by Bloomsbury Press, New York

All papers used by Bloomsbury Press are natural, recyclable products made from wood grown in well-managed forests. The manufacturing processes conform to the environmental regulations of the country of origin.

LIBRARY OF CONGRESS CATALOGING-IN-PUBLICATION DATA

De Graaf, John.
What's the economy for, anyway? : why it's time to stop chasing growth and start pursuing happiness / John de Graaf and David K. Batker.
p. cm.
ISBN-13: 978-1-60819-510-7 (hardback)
1. United States—Economic conditions. 2. Economic development—United States. 3. Happiness—United States. I. Batker, David. II. Title.
HC103.D38 2011
330.973—dc23
2011017438

First U.S. edition 2011

1 3 5 7 9 10 8 6 4 2

Typeset by Westchester Book Group
Printed in the U.S.A. by Quad/Graphics, Fairfield, Pennsylvania

To Herman E. Daly, whose ideas
provide the foundation for a twenty-first-century economics.

In memory of Jonathan Rowe (1946–2011),
a brilliant advocate of new ways to measure progress.

Contents

Foreword

As cofounder of the Natural Resources Defense Council and the World Resources Institute, as a civil servant, and more recently, as dean of the Yale School of Forestry and Environmental Studies, I have watched the erosion of our environment and particularly our growing climate crisis with deep concern. It has become clear to me that these crises are exacerbated by the basic way we have organized our economy and made a priority of its growth above all else. Many potentially effective solutions to climate change are rejected because of their perceived impact on the economy. We find ourselves today in a strange place where in order to stave off a planetary catastrophe, saving the planet from climate disruption, we must show that it will not hurt the economy.

In the climate context and otherwise, our quality of life is being steadily sacrificed to a single goal—growth of the Gross Domestic Product, or GDP. It is time that Americans thought more deeply about this goal and its limitations.

This book brings a fresh and needed perspective to our common efforts by asking a simple but essential question: What is our economy for, anyway? It answers that question in a manner originally suggested by Gifford Pinchot, first chief of the U.S. Forest Service and a former Yale Forestry dean himself.

What's the Economy For, Anyway? goes beyond a challenge to the mythology of GDP and the primacy of economic growth, asking how our economy might be organized if quality of life, justice, sustainability, and that right to the pursuit of happiness enshrined in our Declaration of Independence were its goals. How might our economy look then? How might we measure its successes and failures? And how can we get from here to there?

The authors, one an economist and one a journalist, offer a critique of our current unsustainable system, but theirs is not a message of gloom and doom. With humor, solid evidence, common sense economic arguments and a truly patriotic spirit, they suggest solutions that can help restore our country's place in the world.

This is a time of fear, of loss of confidence in the future, of denial in the face of grave ecological danger, and of rapacious greed. But it is also a time of intellectual ferment and ideas that can, if we encourage them, bring forth a happier, healthier, fairer, and more sustainable future. This book provides a valuable contribution to that much-needed ferment, and does so in an accessible fashion, offering pragmatic solutions to our economic woes. It makes clear that the dangers of climate change, peak oil, species extinction, the ever-widening chasm between rich and poor, and the insecurity and pessimism that characterize our era demand that we seek more of what matters, and not simply more.

James Gustave Speth, professor of law at Vermont Law School, author of *The Bridge at the Edge of the World*, and former dean of the Yale School of Forestry and Environmental Studies June 2011

Introduction

The economy. It's nearly all anyone talks about these days besides reality shows, and not without reason. Much of our time is spent on economic activity—working, buying, selling, borrowing, lending, producing, consuming, volunteering, and retiring. The economy is enormously complex—amazing, really. Consider the items right around you—this book, for example. Knowledge and technology were needed to produce it. Inputs of energy, materials, capital, and labor have been marshaled and combined to make it. Elaborate systems from forests to transportation to retail outlets helped too. The economy is really an awe-inspiring human creation. It is also constantly being transformed, for better or worse.

By any measure, the U.S. economy is not in perfect health. Recently, it shook as if in an earthquake. Millions of Americans were thrown out of work, businesses closed their doors, houses were foreclosed upon, students lost scholarships, and services were cut drastically. The crisis raised one question to a crescendo: How can we get the economy going again?

Contradictory answers abound: Reduce wages. Raise wages. Cut lavish benefits. Provide more basic benefits. Regulate less. Regulate more. Increase stimulus spending. Reduce the debt. Raise taxes. Lower them. The debate is important because policy decisions actually do determine whether an economy improves or gets worse. For example, while hundreds of American banks collapsed following the recent financial crash, Canada experienced no banking crisis at all because that country had different banking policies in place.

Yet these discussions of reviving the economy have all proceeded without considering a more fundamental question: *What's the economy for, anyway?* What are our economic goals? What do Americans want from their economy? More stuff? Affordable college education? More leisure? Universal health insurance? Lower taxes with fewer benefits? Fairness?

A healthy and sustainable environment? A secure retirement? Happiness . . . ?

Surveys show Americans want more time for friends and family. Yet they are actually spending more hours working and commuting to work than the previous generation. An economy that requires longer work hours cannot deliver increased leisure time for friends and family. Moreover, despite working more, 80 percent of Americans are earning less real income than they did ten years ago. "You're lucky you have a job" has replaced the vision of rising middle-class prosperity.

People in other countries are beginning to notice what has been happening in the United States. Consider a recent ruckus in Sweden.[1] The famous Swedish furniture company, IKEA, opened a factory in Danville, Virginia. Workers at the factory earn eight dollars an hour. They work a lot of mandatory overtime, often on short notice, which disrupts their family lives. They have few benefits and what vacation days they receive are mostly chosen by the company.

The workers are mad. When Danville granted IKEA big tax breaks to move there, the people it hired expected wages and benefits like those provided to IKEA's Swedish employees. In Sweden, IKEA pays a *minimum* wage equivalent to U.S. nineteen dollars an hour. Workers receive at least five weeks of paid vacation and *all* overtime work is voluntary.

But while workers in the Danville plant complained, public officials there did not. They considered the poor salaries and meager benefits a fair trade for the jobs produced. Yet in Sweden, the story made the front page of Stockholm dailies. Many Swedes consider IKEA's treatment of its U.S. workers a betrayal of the company's reputation as a good corporate citizen. They argue that IKEA is treating American workers the way American companies treat workers in Mexico. "For us, it's a huge problem," declared one Swedish labor leader.

IKEA spokeswoman Ingrid Steen called the situation in Virginia "sad," acknowledging the huge difference in pay, benefits, and working conditions between what IKEA provides Swedish and U.S. workers. But, she added, "That's related to the standard of living and general conditions in the different countries." Ouch! Evidently, the United States is IKEA's destination for low-wage outsourcing, a third-world nation in its eyes.

Will Swedish do-gooders boycott IKEA for exploiting American workers? If so, perhaps American pundits will respond, "Maybe so, but

Swedes pay high taxes." And indeed they do. Yet even after taxes, IKEA workers in Sweden have larger take-home paychecks than their Virginia counterparts, and they get full health care, free college educations, and other benefits in the bargain.

American businesses say they couldn't possibly offer what the Swedes do and compete in the global economy. Yet according to the World Economic Forum, Sweden ranks second in the world in competitiveness, higher than the United States. What's wrong with this picture?

What kind of economy would Americans actually prefer? There are many aspects to this question, but consider one recent study. In a large-sample survey, Americans were offered three imaginary countries, and asked in which of them they would choose to live if they had the choice.[2] In country A, the top 20 percent of the population own 20 percent of the total wealth (complete equality). In country B, the top 20 percent own 35 percent, and in Country C, the top 20 percent of the population own 80 percent of the wealth. Four fifths of Americans polled chose Country B. Nearly as many Republicans as Democrats made that choice. More Americans actually chose Country A than chose Country C.

Country A is fictional. No nation in the world has, or ever had, complete equality. But Country B represents the situation in a real country— Sweden—and Country C represents that in another real country—the United States. When offered a choice between the two based on wealth distribution, Americans of all political persuasions overwhelmingly chose Sweden over the United States!

A generation ago, Swedes didn't earn more than Americans did, and they certainly didn't talk about the United States as a third-world country. That was before the massive shift in wealth from the middle class to the richest Americans. Greater financial inequality is one outcome the U.S. economy has certainly delivered. While the productivity of American workers rose dramatically in the last decade, their median incomes actually fell. But *somebody* must be better off. And indeed, American corporations chalked up their largest quarterly profits in history recently while, as we reveal later in this book, the incomes of the richest Americans skyrocketed.

America has seen worse: the Great Depression. Out of that period, we adopted a new economics (macroeconomics) and with it, new economic goals (full employment), new measures (Gross National Product), new policies (including banking regulations), and new institutions such as Social Security. From the wreckage of the Great Depression and World War

II, the United States reduced poverty, created the strongest educational system in the world, and built the largest middle class in world history. Life expectancy and health outcomes in the United States became the envy of most of the world, and our high-wage economy provided the highest-paying middle class jobs and a secure retirement for all workers.

Building a successful twentieth-century economy required changes in economic goals and policies to better reflect America's ideals and fulfill Americans' demands for a more just and prosperous economy. Yet today dozens of countries perform better than the United States in terms of health, education, economic security, and a host of other measures.

We're not in the twentieth century anymore. The world is running low on oil. The climate is changing, with potentially disastrous consequences. Useful water is less available, while floods are increasingly prolific. Unlike in the 1930s, when roads and indoor plumbing were scarce and forests, water, and wetlands were abundant, now roads are abundant and natural systems and their services, such as flood protection, are increasingly scarce and more valuable. Yet neither our economy nor our measures of economic progress reflect these realities. To be successful in the twenty-first century, economies must become sustainable. They must be built to prosper within the physical limits of the earth and local natural systems. Making that possible will require vast changes to our economy, including our energy, transportation, food, and manufacturing infrastructures.

Impressively, Americans have developed solutions to virtually every environmental and economic problem. But only by shifting investment, improving and carefully targeting economic incentives, and actually reflecting true costs and benefits in our markets can these solutions actually be implemented and a better, more sustainable economy realized.

About thirty years ago, the United States took a different economic track from most other industrialized nations, reviving a nineteenth-century economic philosophy called laissez-faire, the view that government policies hinder economic development. This ideological turn included deregulating markets, cutting taxes for the rich, and reducing government services. In the aftermath of the financial crisis, it is time to reflect on what those changes actually delivered, and to ask again what Americans want out of their economy and how their goals can be achieved. That's what this book tries to do.

Economic progress in America has always come through the efforts of people, working individually and together. Individual action devoted to improving personal capacity, paying attention to purchasing decisions, and rewarding work is critically important. But many improvements, social and economic, also require working together. Women did not get the vote through individual action. It took collective effort to change the U.S. Constitution. Additionally, our economy has often been viewed as a sector of society independent from others. But in fact, economic problems cannot be solved in isolation from other problems. Progressives in the United States came together one hundred years ago across class, race, gender, and other divisions to give women the vote, democratize the U.S. Senate, regulate food and drugs, institute progressive taxes, and eliminate child labor. Their accomplishments were possible because they worked together beyond the confines of narrow self-interest to invest in our common wealth.

The Big Question

The authors of this book have been activists for reforms that, in their minds, would make the United States a more livable, just, and sustainable society. As executive director of Earth Economics, Dave has been involved in the effort to identify, value, map, and model the economic benefits offered by nature. An economist, he has worked to improve real wages and banking policy in the United States and other countries. As executive director of Take Back Your Time, and as a producer of documentary films, John has tried to promote new ways of measuring happiness and to achieve such policy changes as a paid vacation law for Americans. And yet, for any economic, environmental, or social improvement either author has suggested, there seems to be a common rebuke: *What will that do to the economy?*

"If you can get them asking the wrong questions, you don't have to worry about the answers," writes Thomas Pynchon in *Gravity's Rainbow*. In our view, there is a question that should take precedence over *What will that do to the economy?* It's the question: *What's the economy for, anyway?* John began asking that question in a series of lectures about four years ago. The question turned into a campaign fueled by timely support from the Rockefeller Brothers Fund. It became a college class at the University of Washington and another at the Evergreen State College. The idea was refined during dozens of speaking events and conversations with students. Then John teamed up with Dave to produce the film *What's the Economy for, Anyway?* As interest increased, we decided to write this book to flesh out our ideas in greater detail.

What You'll Find in These Pages

We have structured this book to ask a fundamental question and explore some answers that make sense to us.

In Chapter 1, we examine our nation's primary economic measurement, the Gross Domestic Product, demonstrating its failure to tell us what we need to know about how well our economy is actually working. We question the goal of our economy: What should it really provide— mountains of more stuff, or something else?

Chapter 2 suggests an answer, offered long ago by a prominent American, and a different way to measure progress developed in the tiny Himalayan country of Bhutan.

Chapter 3 examines the basic needs that every economy should deliver: How should we provide food, shelter and clothing?

Chapter 4 dissects our health system, essential to a good quality of life. While expenditures on sickness are a ballooning portion of the economy, we're actually less healthy than countries that spend much less. We ask why that is and offer some answers.

Security is the subject of chapter 5 as we examine debt, unemployment, crime, retirement, and some impressive solutions from Europe.

In chapter 6, we discover that Americans are time starved. Yet time is the key to better health and happiness, closer friends and family ties, and stronger communities. Americans once enjoyed shorter working hours and more vacation time than workers in any other country in the world. Might we regain that distinction?

Chapter 7 is about fairness. Equality matters, and the gap between rich and poor in the United States has become the widest in the industrial world.

Chapter 8 examines opportunity for social mobility, once seen as an American birthright, but now sadly lacking in comparison to many other countries. How is our education system failing, and what can we do to make it a beacon for the world once again?

One of the greatest economic challenges of our time is ecological sustainability, the subject of chapter 9. This chapter focuses on the pivotal role of the economy in environmental quality, the tremendous number of solutions available to solve our ecological problems and the policies required to implement them.

With chapter 10, we take a peek at history, exploring the astounding improvement of the American economy between 1900 and 1968 and the inspiring and instructive lessons Americans learned as they rejected the laissez-faire economics of the late 1800s, and replaced them with policies that regulated markets, built infrastructure, created a middle class, and developed the world's most powerful mixed economy. We see how Democrats and Republicans alike supported the transformation until the old economic ideology rose again in a new form.

Chapter 11 explores the re-emergence of laissez-faire economics during the last thirty years, and how this has led to a weakened economy and a more polarized America.

Chapter 12 examines the recent financial crisis and its impact on the wealth and well-being of all Americans. It highlights how bad policies can destroy economies, the urgent need for change, and improvements clearly within our reach.

Our final chapter, 13, pulls together a positive overview of solutions that can help us create a sustainable economy capable of delivering happiness to all its citizens.

The Big Picture

Some caveats: this is a Big Picture book (albeit without many pictures!). It offers a broad look at the economy and economic policy. For any specific area of economic performance, it is generalized and necessarily incomplete. Stories that are exceptions to what we point out can certainly be found, but we believe that the trends outlined here are broadly representative.

But no picture in a book like this can ever be as big as the real picture. So there are some things this book does not explore, in particular, the broad issue of globalization. Globalization is a dominant factor in shaping modern economies, including the American economy. However, economic policy in the United States is largely determined at the national scale, and our primary question is focused on what Americans want from their economy.

One pat answer to "What's the economy for, anyway" is "whatever markets provide." Laissez-faire economists say markets provide what people want since they vote with their dollars (though some voters cast a billion votes . . .). We believe that markets are essential and provide some but not all of what Americans want from an economy. Greater market intrusion into our lives can even impair the achievement of some of our goals, reducing our quality of life and requiring larger government to provide effective market oversight. Successful economic policy in this century requires attention to non-market economic values such as quality of life, fairness, and sustainability. We believe the idea that an *unfettered* market will deliver basic needs, opportunity, sustainability, and broad prosperity is based on a false nineteenth-century ideology, disproven in practice and regularly rejected by Americans over the last century.

We have tried to keep up with the latest statistics. These change rapidly in any economy, and more so during crises. In 2005, for example, France's unemployment rate was nearly double that of the United States. By 2009, the rates were virtually equal. We're sure you'll find in this book specific points or facts with which you quibble, but we believe our big picture approach points the way to the questions we all *should* be asking. It is our hope that it will inspire you to want to make our economy more humane, livable, prosperous, and sustainable.

As we write this introduction on May 22, 2011, the end of the world, predicted for yesterday by evangelist Harold Camping, has been unexpectedly delayed. Its coming was headlined in newspapers and trumpeted by millions of dollars in advertising, including full-page ads in *USA Today* and thousands of scary billboards. Mr. Camping has now offered a new date for the apocalypse—October 21, 2011, around the date of the publication of this book. So if you are reading it, it probably didn't happen. If it did, please don't blame our publisher.

Of course, most people considered Harold Camping crazy. Few expected his predicted rapture to actually occur. Most of us believe in facts and evidence. And yet, with regards to our economy, myths still abound. For some of our political leaders, the solution to the crisis that hit us in 2008 is to do more of what caused it, only faster. That those leaders can still push these myths and be taken seriously means that a real understanding of how our economy works, what we want from it, and how we might reach our goals, remains to be won. We hope to contribute a little bit to that ultimate victory.

Happy reading!
John de Graaf and David Batker
May 2011

CHAPTER 1

The Grossest Domestic Product

I want too much!

—RAFAEL BATKER, AGE THREE

The main message is to get away from G.D.P. fetishism and to understand the limits of it. There are many aspects of our society that are not covered by G.D.P.

—JOSEPH STIGLITZ[1]

"It's the economy, stupid," James Carville once wrote on the wall of Bill Clinton's presidential campaign war room. But maybe those words should be scrambled. Maybe "it's the stupid economy" sums things up better. How to describe a nation nearly twice as rich as it was a generation ago, but actually paying its median workers less than it was then?[2]

How is it that with so much wealth, so many people are so desperate? So unhappy? So stressed and strapped for time? Vanishing jobs, benefits, and retirement don't help. Where's the progress in that? How do we compete more aggressively? By paying people a dollar a day? Or by producing and consuming even more stuff?

Just what is "the economy"? What's it for? Is it working for us, or are we working for it? Can it work better? We'd better hope so. We'd better make it so.

Wasting Coal

Wherever you work, study, or play, you likely have experience with measures that matter. Length is measured by inches. Academic performance is indicated by grades. Measures are generally direct physical gauges quantified in specific units, such as tons of coal measured on a truck scale. Many things we want to track cannot be physically measured, so we also have indicators, intended to reflect a reality. Grades earned in school are intended to reflect knowledge learned. The terms *measure* and *indicator* are often used interchangeably.

Before he became an economist, one of the authors of this book, Dave Batker, was a geologist who worked in a coal mine. He ended up studying economics because one day, while working at the face of the Big Seam in Washington State's Centralia Coal Mine, he broke off a cobble of coal and wondered, "How is the economic value of coal measured?" Coal has many qualities, and no one measure covers them all. There is the heat it generates, measured in British thermal units (BTUs). The cost to recover it and the price it fetches are also important measures. And there are others: hardness, luster, density, and content including carbon, mercury, amber, and sulfur.

Coal also has qualities that are not measured. In a lump of coal cleaved off the seam face you can often see the delicate structures of fossilized trees or plants that lived millions of years ago, now ready to light the darkness for but a moment. They are exquisite, but to the coal company and consumer, fossils count for nothing. Millions of years in the making, they become fire, ash, and gas for the economy.

Likewise, we measure some aspects of our economy and ignore others. Economies are less tangible than lumps of coal. So economists have developed more than forty indicators that are intended to tell us about the economy and how it is doing. We check such things as inflation, employment, interest rates, housing starts, durable goods orders, retail inventories, stock and bond prices, trading volumes, and money supply. Each describes part of the economy.

But the king of all economic indicators is the *Gross Domestic Product*, or *GDP*. Trumpets please! The higher GDP gets, the better we assume the economy to be. Fattening King GDP is more important to most of our leaders than reducing unemployment, controlling inflation, stabilizing interest rates, reducing debt, or paying attention to a host of lesser economic dukes, barons, or other measures. They all bow to the GDP. But these days, more and more critics are suggesting that King GDP has no clothes. Yet naked or not, the measure that steers our decisions is the measure that rules.

When Dave worked as a geologist at the mine, he met another imperial measure: *quarterly profits*. Critical to every coal mine is the "life of the mine" calculation, an estimate of the date when the coal will run out. Though the Centralia Coal Mine was the fifth largest in the United States when Dave was working there, only three of its ten seams of coal were actually mined. Seven seams of valuable coal were completely wasted, treated as "overburden," dug up and plowed back into the pit, mixed with dirt, silt, sand, and rock.

Wasting seven seams of coal meant the mine would have a shorter life, about forty years rather than 140 years if the coal from all ten seams was recovered. Dave questioned the logic of mining only three seams. The mine's financial officer provided an explanation: "We make one percent more in profit by mining only the three best seams." Astonished, Dave argued the point: "But that's one percent more profit over forty years versus one percent less profit over 140 years. The owners will make more over the long run by mining ten seams." With a condescending smile, the financial officer replied, "But we want to maximize returns *this* quarter." He shrugged, turned, and walked away.

That brief conversation helped to change Dave's life forever. Troubled by economic decisions that made little sense, at least to him, he decided to dedicate his life to solving problems in economics instead of geology. He left the mine in 1985 to go to graduate school in economics at Louisiana State University. In time, he became an ecological economist, one who studies the impact of the economy on our planet. With his mentor, the renowned Herman E. Daly, he worked for a time at the World Bank (cue the boos from left-wing readers). After that, he worked as an economist with Greenpeace (cue the boos from right-wing readers).

Meanwhile, slope instability caused the Centralia Coal Mine to close in 2007, earlier than expected, leaving much of the best three seams unearthed. A total of 650 workers were laid off, and profits fell far short of expectations. Trains now bring Wyoming coal to the 1,400-megawatt power plant that was built only half a mile from the coal mine "for efficiency." For the short-term-profit-obsessed owners, it appears that long-term reclamation of the mine and lands will be far more expensive than they had anticipated. And maximizing profits from a coal mine is infinitely more difficult when it is not producing any coal.

Today, the mining company's goal is limiting corporate losses, placing the local community and larger public at constant risk of picking up the tab for the damage caused by shortsighted thinking in the first place. We now know that burning coal is a major source of atmospheric carbon dioxide (CO_2). Like a car with windows rolled up on a hot day, carbon dioxide allows light through, but retains heat, warming up our planet. Thus renowned climate scientists believe avoiding a climate meltdown requires leaving tremendous quantities of coal underground, unburned.[3]

Just like the quick profit calculus that prevailed in the mine, the single-minded goal of GDP growth rules our national economic policies. The focus of President Barack Obama's $787-billion stimulus package wasn't reducing unemployment, fixing the mortgage crisis, or building a twenty-first-century economy free from dependence on fossil fuels. It was to get King GDP through a financial hangover, and fattening as quickly as possible. Similarly, right after September 11, 2001, President George W. Bush went on television and told people to go shopping. He wanted them to buy more, so the economy, as measured by the GDP, would weather the storm.

What Is the GDP?

By any measure of measures, including frequency of reporting in the media, mention by political leaders, or, most important, influence on government policy, King GDP rules.

But what is the GDP, actually?

Economists offer a simple answer: *the GDP is the total market value of all final goods and services produced in a country in a given year.* Enunciate each word clearly and in a monotone, as countless economics professors do each year: *the GDP is the total market value of all final goods and services produced in a country in a given year.*

The GDP measures the quantity times the price of *final* goods and services sold. In the case of the Centralia Coal Mine, the final good was the electricity sold to consumers. Every expenditure is at the same time someone's income. This is why the GDP and associated indicators are called the *National Income Accounts.*

Our GDP measures the value of stuff produced and sold in the United

States. It is often confused with a similar, older indicator called the *Gross National Product*, or *GNP*. The GNP was developed in the 1930s, a time when the United States was self-sufficient in nearly everything and companies in this country were overwhelmingly owned by American citizens, not foreigners. Production in the United States by a foreign company is not counted as part of the GNP. On the other hand, American-owned production *is* counted in the GNP even when it takes places in other countries.

By 1991, foreign-owned companies were making many products in the United States, confusing how imports were counted. At the same time many U.S. companies were making more products in other countries. Imports and exports had also become very substantial portions of the total economy. Trying to dissect U.S. production overseas and foreign-owned production here with a labyrinth of joint ventures and other arrangements became impossibly complicated. The United States and global economies had changed dramatically. Globalization made the GNP virtually impossible to accurately calculate. So, in 1991, the American government officially abandoned the GNP as its most important economic measure and crowned the GDP king. The GDP measures domestic production, no matter who owns the company. It excludes the complicated web of overseas production by American-owned companies and joint ventures.

Technical details for calculating the GDP and all other National Income Accounts can be obtained from the Bureau of Economic Analysis housed within the U.S. Department of Commerce (www.bea.gov). That's the agency that collects and assembles data on the National Income Accounts. The Bureau of Economic Analysis (BEA) is understandably proud of its work in providing the American economy's preeminent measurement. According to the BEA Web site: "The GDP was recognized by the Department of Commerce as its [the Bureau of Economic Analysis's] greatest achievement of the 20th century and has been ranked as one of the three most influential measures that affect U.S. financial markets."[4]

So how did we get the GDP, and how did it rise to such importance?

From Micro to Macro

New economic indicators develop because economies don't just grow, they also transform. When the United States became a nation, most Americans were self-employed on self-sufficient farms. Some Americans were slaves, sold in markets as property. Overall, the monetary or market-based economy was small relative to the self-sufficient household economy. At that time, there were few services provided by private firms, public utilities, or government agencies, particularly compared to today's economy. A market-based GDP would have measured little of the early American economy.

What we want from the economy also changes over time. Thus the way we measure the economy's performance must also change. For America's first 150 years, no one worried about how much, as a whole, our nation produced. Then came the Great Depression. With people and factories idle nationwide, the government developed new national programs to boost production and put people to work. It needed a way of measuring the success of these *national* programs.

Prior to the Great Depression (roughly 1929–40) there was no GNP or GDP, no measure of total national economic output. We had no idea how much stuff our country made, and no one cared. There were no reliable national measures of inflation, unemployment, consumption, or money supply. Economists refer to the study of the economy at the scale of the nation (and state) as *macroeconomics*. But prior to the Great Depression, there was no real study of macroeconomics. The focus instead was on *microeconomics*, the study of supply and demand, economics at the scale of markets, firms, and households.

There was little in the way of macroeconomic theory either. The American economy rode the wild rapids of spectacular booms and busts. Mass bank failures and widespread foreclosures erupted every decade or so between booms. Economists just called it *the business cycle*.

But when the Great Depression hit, the business cycle became a steady downward spiral, dragging employment, production, exports, prices, and everything else down, down, down. People were out of work and hungry. Factories were idle. Farms were foreclosed. Prices tumbled. Stocks crashed. But without macroeconomic indicators, it was hard to know just how bad things really were. Indeed, in 1930, President Herbert Hoover declared, "The Depression is over," without knowing how many Americans were unemployed or whether overall production was rising or falling (it was falling). But to his credit, Hoover did authorize the first count of unemployed Americans on a national scale in the 1930 census.[5]

It is hard to solve a problem if you have no theory for how a system works, and no appropriate measures for either the problem or the solution.

In the 1930s, economists had no theory about how the national economy worked and no national-scale economic indicators. Microeconomics, focused as it was on firms, households, and markets, and the fuzzy idea of the business cycle, was incapable of solving the Great Depression. Macroeconomics was created to solve tangible economic problems stemming from a national-scale depression. Much of the crisis revolved around the issue of aggregate demand at the national scale; too few products were being purchased, which depressed prices and reduced incomes. With less demand, factories closed and laid people off so they had even less money to spend. Virtually every American suffered. Tens of millions lost jobs, farms, and homes or just went hungry.

The Birth of the GNP

As the need for national economic indicators and more comprehensive economic theories grew more pressing, the Bureau of Economic Analysis asked the Russian immigrant and University of Pennsylvania economist Simon Kuznets to figure out how to measure national income and expenditures as well as the total value of all the goods and services produced in the United States each year. In 1934, Simon Kuznets unveiled his Gross National Product.

The comprehensive nature of the GNP was breathtaking. It gathered specific data from every economic sector—from sausage sales to plastics production—then aggregated the whole of U.S. economic production into one number based on a common "currency" or unit of measurement, the dollar. Simon created an important measure where there had been none. It was a measure focused on national "aggregate production and aggregate demand." This was essential when our nation faced the problems of underproduction and underconsumption, when oil and forests were plentiful, and manufactured goods, like indoor plumbing, were rare.

The creation and adoption of the GNP was also a milestone in the most formidable economic ideological struggle in American history. The struggle wasn't between communism and capitalism, because Americans have always overwhelmingly supported capitalism. But for more than a century, they have debated two visions of capitalism.

One is laissez-faire economics, trusting the "invisible hand" of a largely unregulated market to deliver the best possible outcomes. The proponents of laissez-faire advocate minimum government beyond such services as the military, police protection, and the courts. For them, government policies are seen as hindering economic progress.

The other vision is of a mixed economy in which government is an active player, providing services, overseeing and regulating markets, preventing monopolies, and managing economic policy. In this view, government can play a significant and positive role in improving the economy. During the Great Depression, this new view took precedence over laissez-faire, a position it would not relinquish for half a century. The GNP and other macroeconomic measures were developed to provide information for the federal government to implement active economic policy-making at a national scale.

Seven years after Kuznets created the GNP, the shocking attack on Pearl Harbor plunged a mostly unprepared America into World War II. Dramatically shifting and increasing production for the war effort became the paramount national objective. Thanks in no small part to Simon Kuznets, the United States had the best economic tools of any nation on Earth to facilitate such a dramatic economic transformation. The detailed data collected with regard to how much aluminum, steel, electricity, rubber, copper, engines, cars, and other goods the nation produced was critical to assisting government planners in figuring out how many ships, planes, bombs, tanks, tires, and guns could be built and how to allocate resources to build them. Private and public investment were mobilized as never before, and production surpassed levels that seemed unimaginable in December 1941. Unique national-scale economic indicators and production data that the United States had developed contributed significantly to both solving the Great Depression and winning World War II.

Developing the GNP was a critical part of creating a macroeconomics for the twentieth century, one that could deliver a better life to people. It was a tremendous accomplishment, and we wish to acknowledge that. Nearly every nation on Earth now uses the GNP to indicate economic output. Simon Kuznets was justifiably proud of his measure. But like many creators who understand their inventions more deeply than those who will use them, he knew its limitations and offered a word of warning about making too much of the GNP: "The welfare of a nation can scarcely be inferred from a measurement of national income."[6]

But Kuznets is history.

Not the GNP, though. After World War II, the goal of full employment was replaced by growth in GNP as the primary economic goal. Presidents, congresses, the media, economists, and the general public missed the yellow light. Though Kuznets warned against it, the GNP (now the GDP) is generally assumed to measure how well our economy and our nation are doing. Increasing the GNP/GDP came to dominate economic policy decisions in the United States under every administration. It still does.

Bobby Kennedy's Warning

There were dissenting voices. Many academics, economists, and especially environmentalists echoed Kuznets's warnings. But for the most part, our leaders ignored them, with one very important exception. On March 18, 1968, early in his presidential campaign, Senator Robert Kennedy, the brother of assassinated president John F. Kennedy, stepped to the podium at the University of Kansas. His words seem as appropriate today as they were then, and they are worth quoting at length.

> For too long we seem to have surrendered personal excellence and community value in the mere accumulation of material things. Our Gross National Product now is over 800 billion dollars a year, but that Gross National Product counts air pollution, and cigarette advertising, and ambulances to clear our highways of carnage. It counts special locks for our doors and the jails for people who break them. It counts the destruction of the redwoods and the loss of our natural wonder in chaotic sprawl. It counts napalm, and it counts nuclear warheads, and armored cars for the police to fight the riots in our cities. It counts Whitman's rifle and Speck's knives and the television programs which glorify violence in order to sell toys to our children. Yet, the Gross National Product does not allow for the health of our children, the quality of their education, or the joy of their play. It does not include the beauty of our poetry or the strength of our marriages, the intelligence of our public debate or the integrity of our public officials. It measures neither our wit nor our courage, neither our wisdom nor our learning, neither our compassion nor our devotion to our country. It measures everything in short except that which makes life worthwhile. And it can tell us

everything about America except why we are proud that we are Americans.[7]

Only ten weeks later, after winning the California Democratic presidential primary, Senator Robert Kennedy was dead, felled by an assassin's bullet. In the four decades since, hardly a single political leader has gone where Kennedy did not fear to tread. He was far ahead of his time, but he had zeroed in precisely on the problems with GNP and GDP. It counts as positive a lot of things that make our lives worse, and it doesn't count at all so many things that make them better.

What Counts in the GDP?

Here are some of the things that count positively toward the GDP.

- *Pollution.* If groundwater is polluted, and we have to buy bottled water at a thousand times the price of tap water, the GDP rises. Because of enormous cleanup and legal costs, the oil belched by the BP Deepwater Horizon well in the Gulf of Mexico will contribute far more to the GDP than had that same oil actually made it to the refinery and been sold as gasoline, diesel, and other products. (The *Exxon Valdez* oil spill had a similar effect on the GNP two decades ago.) Cleaning oil off the beaches and wildlife can cost tens of thousands of dollars for every $100 barrel of oil cleaned up.[8]

- *Crime.* GDP increases as property loss claims arrive and people buy replacements for stolen goods. It increases as they install alarms and bars or hire guards. New prison construction, prison operating costs, and other crime costs all add to the GDP. We're actually better off with safe communities where such "defensive" expenditures are unnecessary. Crime requires defensive expenditures, which should be subtracted from the GDP. A recent Iowa State University analysis showed the social costs of a murder at $17.25 million.[9]

- *Health damage.* Another "defensive" expenditure includes many health care costs. For example, over 350 billion cigarettes were sold in the United States in 2006, adding to the GDP.[10] During the same year over $10 billion was spent treating lung cancer in the

United States, which also added to the GDP.[11] Instead of subtracting the cost of smoking-related cancer, the GDP treats it all as a positive benefit, the same as wheat production.

- *Family breakdown.* Divorce may not be good for families, but it is good for the GDP. A divorce can cost from $7,000 to $100,000.[12] That total usually includes the lawyers' fees, the establishment of separate households, and often the cost of therapy.

- *Debt, foreclosure, and bankruptcy.* When people or the government borrow too much and personal or national debt rises unsustainably, the GDP climbs. Even bankruptcies and foreclosures count positively in the GDP, since they incur legal costs, moving expenses, and replacement of lost housing or possessions. The average bankruptcy cost in 2010 was between $700 and $4,000,[13] and with an estimated 1.5 million Americans declaring bankruptcy that year, it adds up.[14]

- *Paper transfers and bursting bubbles.* New "financial products," such as derivatives and credit default swaps, were at the heart of the 2008 financial crisis, driving worldwide recession. These "products" count highly positively in the GDP because they increase the incomes of insurance companies and investment banks. Yet their value can just as suddenly vanish, as happened in 2008 when packages of subprime loans suddenly had no buyers. The financial services account was the fastest growing part of the GDP, as income from the sales of bundled mortgages and derivatives ballooned. Such bubbles are seen as great economic successes when they should more properly be measured as harbingers of disaster. American International Group's income from selling credit default swaps soared in 2006 to hundreds of millions of dollars, adding to the GDP. By 2009 the company lost over $61 billion due to the same credit default swaps.[15] Even the Bureau of Economic Analysis is considering changes.[16]

- *Increasing scarcity.* Depletion of natural resources is a cost to future generations. Yet scarcity is often reflected positively in the GDP. For example, as U.S. and global oil reserves have been depleted, gas prices have risen, increasing the GDP even while raiding the wallet of anyone with a gas tank to fill. The GDP gives no clue as to whether the rise in final market sales value is due to scarcity, productivity, or market manipulation. Paying four dollars for a gallon of gasoline at the pump adds twice as much to the GDP as paying two dollars per gallon. Sure feels good adding more to the GDP.

- *Risk.* The GDP does not take into account the risk of catastrophic costs. Retail electricity sold from nuclear power plants counts positively in the GDP. Expenditures attempting to minimize or clean up the Fukushima nuclear disaster also count positively. Due to the tremendous longevity of deadly nuclear isotopes, such as plutonium, the Environmental Protection Agency ruled that nuclear waste must be safely contained for one million years.[17] The associated unknown risks and costs count for nothing in the current GDP.

Now, consider a few important things that the GDP *does not* count.

- *Nature.* Natural resources are the basis for many of our most productive economic assets. Seattle's drinking water, for example, is filtered by the forest of the upper Cedar River watershed. Its quality far exceeds drinkability standards. This saves the city $200 million in costs for a needless filtration plant. The valuable service of natural water filtration does not count in the GDP. But building a filtration plant and raising water prices to pay for it would count. Building a levee for New Orleans counts, but the greater value of hurricane protection provided by natural coastal wetlands does not. Buying a boat to catch fish counts. The habitat that produces the fish does not count. The obvious economic goods and services that nature provides every year to Americans do not count in the GDP.

- *Sustainability.* The GDP says nothing about sustainability and does not discern whether activities contributing to the GDP are sustainable. The Atlantic cod fishery was the world's largest food fishery for over five hundred years. A few decades of overfishing caused the fishery to collapse. Overfishing counted more positively in the GDP in a single year than fishing at a lower sustainable rate. The GDP is incapable of distinguishing between the unsustainable demolition of a fishery and a sustainably managed fishery, such as the Alaskan salmon fishery.

- *Exercise.* We all know it's good for our health, but it only counts if we pay to go to the gym or otherwise spend money. That daily walk we try to take may be good for our health, but it's a waste of time as far as the GDP is concerned.

- *Social connection.* It's the most important thing we can do to be healthy and happy. But unless money is spent, friends and family are also a waste of time. The time Dave and John spend with their sons contributes nothing to GDP. Unless they are buying the kids something. That counts.

- *Volunteering.* It's the glue that holds communities together, and it will be increasingly important as budgets for social services tighten. But if it's unpaid, it counts for nothing. It's just another GDP waste of time.

- *Housework.* Domestic work isn't counted, at least not by the GDP. Hire a nanny; that counts. Hire a maid; that too. Hire a gardener or carpenter; you're contributing to GDP. Do it yourself, and you're slacking in your duties to our nation's preeminent measurement.

- *Price and quantity effects.* The GDP does not separate between price effects and quantity effects. For example, if a company doubles the price of a car, it shows up in the GDP just as it would if the company built and sold two cars at the former price. This means the GDP is deeply flawed even as a measure of production, its original purpose.

- *Quality.* One of the long-standing critiques of the GDP was the lack of a quality adjustment. Without adjusting for quality improvements, the GDP overvalues lower quality higher priced goods and undervalues goods of higher quality and better performance. The dumber, slower, more expensive computer added more to the GDP than a smarter, faster, cheaper computer. Recently, the BEA implemented corrections for quality improvements for some goods including computers, software, and in 2011, communications equipment. This is done using a quality-adjusted price index calculated by the Federal Reserve Board. Yet for the vast majority of goods and services, quality improvements, which benefit both producers and consumers, still reduce GDP.

Just imagine you're stuck in a traffic jam, burning gas and choking on exhaust, requiring you to pull off and fill up the tank. The traffic jam has added to the GDP. If you got into a wreck, totaling your car and increasing the cost of your insurance while the wreck caused an even bigger traffic jam for everyone else, the GDP would rise even more. And if you were injured in the wreck and sent to the hospital for weeks of recovery, the GDP would rise still higher. And if you'd had an expensive divorce that morning, and your house burned down that evening, requiring legal fees, insurance claims, and more new purchases, you would have had a completely stellar GDP day! Congratulations!

A Gathering Storm

Skepticism about the GDP is out there and contagious. Herman E. Daly began adjusting GDP measurements in the 1980s to subtract real costs like pollution, and his work culminated in the Genuine Progress Indicator (GPI) created by John Cobb Jr., Ted Halstead, and Jonathan Rowe. Beginning with the GDP, but adding the value of things such as housework and volunteering, while subtracting others, like pollution, family breakdown, and accidents, the GPI showed that quality of life in the United States had actually declined since 1973, while the GDP had more than doubled. As Rowe stated bluntly before the U.S. Congress in 2008, "Any measure that portrays an increase in car crashes, cancer, marital breakdown, kinky mortgages, oil use, and gambling as evidence of advance—as the GDP does—simply because they occasion the expenditure of money, has a tenuous claim to being reality-based discourse."[18]

More recently, some government leaders have expressed agreement with that sentiment, joining the call for new measurements of progress. The World Bank announced a green accounting program in 2010.[19] The European Union has held a series of conferences exploring alternatives to the GDP, while in 2009 the conservative French president Nicolas Sarkozy declared the GDP obsolete and minced no words about his agenda. "France will put this on the agenda of all of the international meetings and all the discussions that have for an objective the creation of a new order," he said.[20]

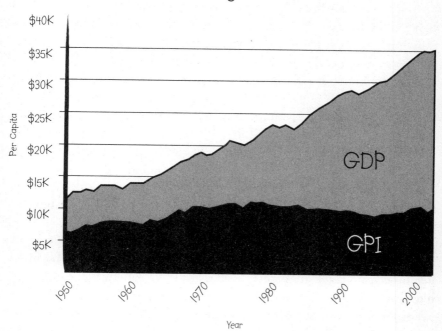

Gross Domestic Product
vs
Genuine Progress Indicator

In February 2010, President Sarkozy created the Commission on the Measurement of Economic Performance and Social Progress, chaired by the Nobel Prize–winning economists Joseph Stiglitz and Amartya Sen. Sarkozy asked them to present their findings before the year ended.

The commission delivered on September 14. Its report noted that "there are long recognized problems in GDP as a measure of economic performance, but many of the changes in the structure of our society have made these deficiencies of greater consequence."[21]

As the Declaration of Independence assailed King George III for arbitrary tyrannical governance, the report went about as far as polite, introverted, academic economists could go in calling for revolution against the world's most powerful monarch of economic measures: "Those attempting to guide the economy are like pilots steering a course without a reliable compass. The decisions we make depend on what we measure, how we do our measurements, and how we interpret them. We are almost 'flying blind' when the metrics on which action is based are ill-designed. Today, there is a broad consensus that we need better metrics and that we need to understand the limitations and uses of existing metrics."[22]

As the commission's report points out, getting economic indicators right, and particularly our most important economic indicator, is critically important to the health of the economy, to people's jobs and well-being, and to our children's future. We should be focused on what actually makes people better off. As Stiglitz argued: "What we measure affects what we do; and if our measurements are flawed, decisions may be distorted. Policies should be aimed at increasing societal welfare, not GDP. Choices between promoting GDP and protecting the environment may be false choices, once environmental degradation is appropriately included in our measurement of economic performance."[23]

Or, as the late Jonathan Rowe put it: "Metrics are silent rulers, in both senses of the word. In defining the task, they also define the steps we must take to carry it out."[24]

If the GDP is mismeasuring the economy, we're bound to make some big mistakes. Reforms of banking regulation which allowed banks to manufacture new "financial products" and inject them right into the economy, like drugs without any testing, boosted the GDP. But what we really needed was a national-scale tornado warning from our premier economic measure. As the Stiglitz report politely noted, "Some economic reforms in recent years may have increased GDP, but their adverse effects on these other dimensions of Quality of Life are unmistakable."[25]

The New Key National Indicators System

For those looking for new measurements of American economic performance, great news came in the passage of the Obama health care bill in 2010. Tucked away in its pages was the appropriation of $70 million over the next eight years to develop and publicize the new *Key National Indicators System* (KNIS) for the United States. Administered by the National Academy of Sciences, the new system will provide comprehensive and easy-to-access data on at least three hundred indicators, with a few given priority like the meters on a dashboard.[26]

KNIS is the brainchild of Chris Hoenig, a former executive at both IBM and the government's General Accountability Office who was dis-

satisfied with the GDP and other indicators. With help from founda-
tions and several prominent Americans, including the former Harvard
president Derek Bok, Hoenig created a Web site (www.stateoftheusa
.org) that shows a prototype for the new system.

After he spent years quietly working on his project, Hoenig's ideas for
new measures were introduced as an amendment into the health care bill.
It passed the Senate with only one objection, showing broad bipartisan
support. Unlike the archaic GDP (wait for the quarterly announcement),
the Key National Indicators System will allow all of us on our home
computers to immediately access the best data for an enormous array of
indicators, with cross tabs for towns and cities, states and countries, ages,
genders, income, race, and other useful information. A modest, quiet
man, Hoenig has shown what a single individual with a goal can accomplish. His KNIS may mark the beginning of the end for the GDP.

Indicators are associated with goals, like the goal of avoiding an explosion by measuring the pressure of a car tire or nuclear containment
vessel. Understanding how the system works enables the use of indicators
to achieve goals or prevent disaster, like knowing when to stop a rise in
pressure. This connects measures to perhaps the most important concept
in economics: the relationship between costs and benefits.

The When-to-Stop Rule

Did you ever eat pizza and never stop? Of course not. Eventually (though
often not as soon as you should), you get full. Sometimes you eat too
much and regret it later. Balancing costs and benefits, and knowing when
to stop, is central to every part of daily life. More is not always better.

The ecological economist Herman E. Daly points out that one of the
central tenets of economics is the *when-to-stop rule*, based on the *margins*.
The margin is the next unit of something, like the next slice of pizza.
When marginal costs exceed marginal benefits, it's time to stop eating, or
for a company to stop producing. People, businesses, government all apply
this when-to-stop rule every day. Even if marginal cost and marginal benefit cannot be exactly calculated, we still decide when enough is enough.
It is fundamental to microeconomics. Businesses constantly apply this
rule with their best data and judgment in choosing when to stop hiring,
how many products to produce, how long to stay open, and so on.

It takes some life experience and training to apply the when-to-stop rule wisely. At the age of three, when Dave's son, Rafael, wanted more ice cream on the full ice cream cone he was being offered, he was told that any more would be too much. But the three-year-old insisted, "I want too much!" Just for the sake of experiment and a little lesson, he was given "too much." The ice cream soon landed on the grass, and Rafael responded with a downward look of stunned disbelief followed by a yowl. It was almost like Alan Greenspan's look as he was testifying before Congress after his "self-regulating" economy melted down. Such lessons are best learned in childhood. By adulthood, wanting too much is usually considered pathological.

But although the when-to-stop rule is essential to microeconomics, no such rule exists in macroeconomics. Unlimited GDP growth is the preeminent macroeconomic goal. Yet every economy, from household to planet level, has physical boundaries and thresholds where costs eventually surpass benefits. A body can only handle so much. We all need time to rest and relax.

Scientists tell us that 350 parts per million is the limit for carbon dioxide in the atmosphere if we wish to keep the climate from changing catastrophically. There are physical limits to our economy, which we will explore in greater detail in chapter 9. Macroeconomics needs a when-to-stop rule. The *problem* is that macroeconomics assumes that unlimited growth should be our primary goal, and our primary measure for economic growth is the GDP. *Both the measure and the goal are flawed.*

During a depression when we had no economic measures, and a world war when we really needed a gauge of how much we could produce, the GNP/GDP performed well. But eighty years on, as with the GNP, it is time to retire the GDP to the museum of antique indicators. We have new economic goals, better data, and a better understanding of how and what to measure. We need indicators that actually gauge our progress toward our most important goals.

Eyes on the Prize!

Behind every measure stands a goal. There is no need to measure something if no goal is associated with it. A good measure must indicate if you are getting closer to, or farther away from, your goal. If your goal is to make a door frame of a certain size, weighing the lumber doesn't do you any good. You have to measure length, width, and height, and cut boards to the dimensions needed.

Simon Kuznets did not create the GNP by thinking about how to fix existing measures. He came up with a new measure for a new economic goal. The U.S. government in the 1930s set new goals: increase output, lower unemployment, stabilize prices, and manage the nation's money supply. Then, the GNP indicated whether or not we were achieving the first of those.

The economy grew and changed. The GNP, impossible to calculate by 1991, was morphed into the GDP. Today, as an economic indicator, the GDP is obsolete: counting expenses on pollution, crime, and sickness as positive and discounting good health, family time, and much of what matters most to Americans. Faulty indicators aside and far more important, the overarching economic goal behind GDP is the wrong economic goal. Striving to produce more and more stuff, indicated by the rising value of market transactions (GDP), was a good goal in the 1930s but can no longer deliver a better economy or greater well-being to Americans. As the GDP has risen, median incomes have fallen. The prevailing economic advice is for the average American to sacrifice income, benefits, health, time, and ultimately happiness to achieve greater GDP growth. The Nobel laureates in economics Joseph Stiglitz and Amartya Sen point out that policy to promote GDP growth is degrading the quality of life in America. The primary inertia behind the old economic goal is that we've had it for eighty years.

It is time to ask, what's the economy for, anyway? What do we, as Americans, now want from our economy? In the next chapter of this book, we will explore other goals. When we've done that, we can examine accurate, reliable indicators that can tell us how the economy is performing and how we're doing in building a twenty-first-century economy that delivers what Americans actually want and value.

CHAPTER 2

The Pursuit of Happiness

We believe these truths to be self-evident: that all men are created
equal; that they are endowed by their creator with certain unalienable
rights; that among these are life, liberty and *the pursuit of happiness* . . .
that to secure these rights governments are instituted.

—THE DECLARATION OF INDEPENDENCE, 1776

By now, we hope you agree that simply increasing the GDP is not necessarily the best goal for the economy. But what should we measure instead?
What *is* the economy for, anyway? Our answer comes from a little-known
pamphlet written by Gifford Pinchot, then the first chief of the United
States Forest Service. Pinchot was no wild-eyed radical. He was a Republican with progressive views. One day in 1905, Pinchot penned a memo
offering his view of the job he'd been hired to do.

His task, Pinchot explained, was to manage the public forests of America to achieve "the greatest good for the greatest number over the longest
run."[1] The forests, he thought, should be used to benefit all Americans,
rich and poor. They should not be locked away. But they should be managed carefully, to provide all generations to come with lumber, clean water,
and recreation.

The *greatest good*.

For the *greatest number*.

Over the *longest run*.

We suggest that this trinity, Pinchot's mandate, should provide the
new goals for our economy. Yet even in Pinchot's day, they were not new

ideas. Utilitarianism, a movement started in eighteenth-century England by the economist Jeremy Bentham, had long argued that the first two elements in the trinity were the true purposes of an economy.[2]

But Pinchot worried about posterity. *The greatest good for the greatest number* might mean using up everything now to make everybody happy in the short run. And that wouldn't be very good for those who came later. So Pinchot added *the longest run*. But in practice, what do these terms— *the greatest good*, *the greatest number*, and *the longest run*—mean? We think they are synonymous with (1) a high quality of life, (2) social justice or fairness, and (3) sustainability. We'll get to justice and sustainability later in the book. But now, let's consider the following question: If *the greatest good* means a high quality of life, what are the elements of such a life?

The Greatest Good

We asked people on the street about this. They answered, "A job that you care about, good health, family life, security, and friends 'to get you through hard times.'" Though no one actually mentioned needing a lot of money, we suspect they didn't consider money irrelevant either. But one interviewee put things in the simplest of terms: "I want to be happy."

Indeed, a high quality of life is one that makes people *happy*. That's what Bentham believed, and he wasn't alone among Enlightenment thinkers. Thomas Jefferson famously enshrined "the pursuit of happiness" as a right in the Declaration of Independence, adding that to secure such rights, "governments are instituted among men."

Jefferson even went so far as to conclude that the "only orthodox object of the institution of government is to secure the greatest degree of happiness possible to the general mass of those associated under it." Likewise, the American Constitution declared that the new government was established to, among other things, "promote the general welfare" of the people. So Pinchot's ideas were not novel even in his time.

To see whether the economy is accomplishing this first goal—promoting the greatest good, or the happiness of the people—we need to know what makes people happy and how our economic policies either enhance or thwart our pursuit of happiness. This is a subjective matter, of course, but not nearly as subjective as many people think.

There is now a respected "science of happiness," and interestingly, its findings mirror the teachings of our great religions; it is, indeed, "better to give than to receive," for example. An entire legion of books on the topic has been written in the past few years, some of them insightful, some of them fluff. None of the books conclude that the economic route to happiness consists of endlessly widening the superhighway of accumulation.

The Organization for Economic Cooperation and Development (OECD) increasingly takes happiness studies seriously. The OECD (made up of representatives from thirty of the world's richest nations) is looking for a whole new set of indicators on which to judge the progress of member countries. Its new Global Project aims at collecting so-called best practices—social and economic policies that are clearly shown to increase life satisfaction.

Gross National Happiness

The newfound interest in happiness has a surprising origin, a tiny land-locked Himalayan country called Bhutan, believed by some to be the model for Shangri-La, the utopia in James Hilton's 1933 novel, *Lost Horizon*. Here, an old way of life continues. Beneath soaring, icy summits, shepherds tend their flocks amid impossibly green terraces of rice and potatoes. Prayer flags flutter above dramatically beautiful palaces and fortresses. Bhutan is still idyllic.

But this little country of less than one million people is home to a great, and modern, experiment. "Gross National Happiness is more important than Gross National Product," its then sixteen-year-old king, Jigme Singye Wangchuck, proclaimed upon his coronation in 1972.[3]

In most countries, and especially in ours, King Wangchuck's proclamation might have been greeted with a polite smile, a yawn, and a quick return to the business of making money. But not in Bhutan, where people take their king's pronouncements seriously.

So for nearly forty years, Bhutan has actually been implementing the idea of *Gross National Happiness* (GNH), seeking ways to measure its progress toward greater well-being and shape its institutions with that goal in mind. Especially in the past decade, the Bhutanese have brought many of the world's smartest happiness researchers to their country in an effort to apply scientific rigor to the task of making their fellow citizens happier. It almost seems like a fable: one of the smallest and poorest of nations teaching the rich and powerful how to live.

November 2009. The cavernous ballroom at the Rafain Palace Hotel in Foz do Iguaçu, Brazil, is full, for the Fifth International Gross National Happiness conference. The audience of eight hundred people, many of them jet-lagged from transcontinental flights and wishing they were soaking in the splendor of the world's largest waterfall only ten miles away, would be a tough sell for any speaker. But in his quiet, humble way, Karma Ura engages them. Ura, the director of the Center for Bhutan Studies in Thimphu, Bhutan, explains that years of research into Gross National Happiness have led the Bhutanese to consider nine "domains" for assessing happiness.

1. Psychological well-being
2. Physical health
3. Time use (work-life balance)
4. Community vitality and social connection
5. Education
6. Cultural preservation, access, and diversity
7. Environmental sustainability
8. Good governance
9. Material well-being[4]

Bhutan's king found out that good, democratic governance was one of the important pillars of well-being. He became determined to make Bhutan a democracy and traveled throughout the country promoting the change. He then abdicated his throne despite popular pressure to remain in power. In 2008, Bhutan peacefully elected its first parliament. Its constitution enshrines Gross National Happiness as the purpose of government.

Bhutan has developed questionnaires with which to measure life satisfaction in each of these dimensions. Officials use these in regular polls of the Bhutanese people. Included are such questions as: How often do you feel safe from human harm? Rarely? Usually? Always?

The Bhutanese now base major policy decisions in part on an analysis of how changes might affect each of these domains, for better or worse. At a minimum, any change should not diminish the overall satisfaction derived from the domains; at best, it should enhance many of them. Recently, when considering a proposal to join the World Trade Organization, Bhutan used the policy tool established to analyze legislation. Needing a score of 69 on this measure, the proposal failed miserably (with a 42), and Bhutan has not joined.[5]

Bhutan's GNH undergoes consistent improvement. In March 2011, the National Statistics Bureau of Bhutan invited Dave and colleagues Bob Costanza and Ida Kubiszewski to help conduct a workshop there about natural capital and ecosystem services, part of Dave's regular work with Earth Economics. Bureau director Kuenga Tshering outlined a five-year goal to improve Bhutan's environmental sustainability (one of its nine domains of happiness) with practical physical measures of the content and benefits of the nation's resources, from lowland wetlands to Himalayan glaciers. Participants also advocated designing measurements for climate change threats such as glacial outbursts, forest fires, and flooding. At the workshop, Kuenga Tshering explained the kind of happiness Bhutan seeks to measure, "Gross National Happiness is not about momentary happiness, as from buying something new. It is about contentment that comes from family, community, spirituality, education, yes, material things, but also good governance, good relationship with nature, good physical health. We think this is the best path for Bhutan. We hope other countries can find value in what we're doing."[6]

As part of Bhutan's GNH calculations, Tshering's National Statistics Bureau may develop the world's most robust natural capital accounting system.

It's necessary to make clear that we don't put Bhutan on a pedestal; Bhutan's happiness levels, life expectancy, and quality of life have improved greatly in recent years, but its human rights record regarding Nepalese immigrants earns criticism, much of it deserved. But to suggest, as some have, that we pay no attention to Bhutan's ideas about measuring and improving happiness because it is not Utopia would be like rejecting those of Thomas Jefferson because he had slaves.

Diminishing Marginal Happiness

Traditional economics holds that *marginal utility*, the value added by each new widget to life satisfaction, for example, decreases with each additional acquisition of the same item. Happiness scientists have found that the same thing holds true with overall material consumption. For poor nations, happiness tends to rise quickly when purchasing power and standard of living increase. But past a certain level of annual income, perhaps as low as about $10,000 per person, the curve of increased satisfaction flattens and eventually becomes a straight line. It may even begin to decline. So, for instance, in the United States, surveys of self-reported life satisfaction show a slight downward trend over the past half century, despite average incomes more than doubling.[7]

It is true that in virtually all societies, rich people are happier than poor people, a phenomenon that reflects status and power differences and the psychological fact that we tend to judge our success, and therefore rate our satisfaction, in comparison to others. Yet as an entire society's income rises past a minimum of modest comfort and economic security, overall levels of happiness do not rise with it.

This finding led the former Harvard president Derek Bok to a sensible observation: "If it turns out to be true that rising incomes have failed to make Americans happier, as much of the recent research suggests, what is the point of working such long hours and risking environmental disaster in order to keep on doubling and redoubling our Gross Domestic Product?"[8]

Good question.

But if rising incomes don't do the trick, is there any hope at all? Is economic policy totally irrelevant to happiness? Is it all merely a matter of personal attitude? We don't think so. A certain portion of happiness *is* genetic—perhaps 50 percent, according to researchers. Some people are born more cheerful than others. But genetics can't explain the wide variation between countries in measures of happiness. Environmental and social conditions matter too, and policy often shapes these conditions.[9]

Measuring Happiness

In his influential book, *Happiness: Lessons from a New Science,* the British economist Richard Layard catalogs the many methods psychologists now use to measure how happy people are. *Self-reported* happiness or well-being is generally quite accurate. It is usually confirmed by physical evidence from brainwave tests and by assessments from friends and associates. We actually have good evidence that psychologists' measurements of happiness not only are accurate but also operate effectively across cultures.

The Gallup-Healthways organization conducts regular polls of life satisfaction: a daily poll in the United States and annual surveys in about 150 other countries. The annual country survey tends to find that residents of Nordic countries are, by and large, the happiest people on Earth. While most of the nations at the top of the list are affluent, moderate-income Costa Rica is always high on the charts. The 2009 survey ranked Denmark number one (it usually is), followed by Finland, the Netherlands, and Sweden.[10]

And it's not just the pastries, cell phones, wooden shoes, or bikini teams.

A 2009 article in the conservative-leaning *Forbes* magazine explained what the top four countries all have in common: They are highly egalitarian, having among the world's smallest gaps between rich and poor; they pay great attention to work-life balance, having some of the world's shortest average working hours; and finally, perhaps shockingly to Americans, they pay some of the world's highest taxes! We'll explore exactly why these things matter later in this book.[11]

Lessons from the Happiest Countries

The University of British Columbia economist John Helliwell, considered one of the world's leading happiness experts, points out that "the happiest countries, like Denmark, are, first of all, countries with a higher sense of community. They give people opportunities to engage with each other. And they have higher levels of trust, which is so essential to happiness. If people lose a wallet in these countries, they expect it will be returned with everything intact, and it is, almost always."

Helliwell adds: "They are generous. Denmark ranks at the top in per capita foreign aid and expenses to fight global warming. Generosity is huge where happiness is concerned. We give students twenty bucks each and tell one group to spend the money on themselves and the other group to give it away. The ones who give it away always report higher happiness levels afterwards.

"The Danes also encourage everyone to participate. In their eldercare facilities, everyone works, not just the staff. The people who live there are treated as citizens, not clients. Their summer camps bring kids to spend time with seniors in eldercare facilities, and the kids don't want to leave." Helliwell notes that although Americans sometimes think of Denmark as a *nanny state*, with great restrictions on personal freedom, the Danes rank highest in the world when asked, "Do you have the freedom to make your life as you choose?"[12]

At a 2010 Gross National Happiness conference in Vermont, Line

Kikkenborg Christensen, a young Danish graduate student, explained why Danes feel free. "I feel secure for me and for my children, so I can follow my passion," she declared. The Danes' strong social safety net (including excellent free health care, free higher education, and generous unemployment insurance) means they feel less need to get the highest-paying jobs and can choose the work they find most satisfying.[13]

Jennifer Lail, a University of Washington graduate student, observed the Danish attention to social connection while she was studying in Copenhagen. Her experience was eye-opening. "It's not a cultural norm to work after five there," she says. "Outdoor cafés fill up, even in winter. There's lots of attention to health as well. Hiking maps are everywhere, and half of all trips are on bicycle. Neighborhoods have public sports halls that most people belong to, from childhood on." Despite working less, the Danes are very productive while working, and Denmark is a wealthy country.

> You always see many people in the streets, and there is this sense of people taking care of each other, trusting each other. It's common to leave babies sleeping in their strollers outside stores. Everyone feels safe doing that. They are also serious about the design of things. They have lots of ways to make cars slow down. You find tables and benches on ordinary sidewalks so people can stop to rest and chat awhile with friends or strangers. Before I came to Copenhagen, I thought I knew what livability was, but I didn't.[14]

"Happiness is about time with family and friends, trust in neighbors, attachment to place," says John Helliwell. "Atlantic Canadians are happier than people in Alberta or British Columbia, even though they have lower incomes. They have more social connection."[15]

Helliwell's observations were confirmed for John de Graaf on a recent flight from Seattle to Houston. He sat next to a vivacious young woman, an actress and singer from Beirut, Lebanon, named Milia Ayache. She was on her way from Vancouver, where she'd been visiting her grandmother, to enjoy Thanksgiving with other relatives in Texas.

Milia had learned what matters most in life from her experiences during bombing raids in Beirut. When Hezbollah or Israeli bombs fell on her city, her middle-class family fled their home for nearby mountains. She remembered her mother telling her she had only minutes to pack a small suitcase. What would she take, knowing that her home might be only rubble when she returned? In such times, it was clear what mattered most— not expensive electronic gadgets, but a few clothes and items of sentimental value, like photographs, connections to the people in her life.

Friends Are Fun!

Not only does social connection matter for long-term life satisfaction. As Derek Bok points out, it also brings the most immediate pleasure. Researchers have found that the following activities, ranked on a scale from 1 to 5, are among the most productive of positive emotions when subjects are asked how happy they feel throughout the day: intimate relations (4.74), socializing after work (4.12), dinner (3.96), relaxing (3.91), and socializing at work (3.75).

By contrast, the least enjoyable activities include the evening commute (2.78), working (2.65), and that mother of all downers, the morning commute (2.04). For most people, these are solitary activities.[16]

Research on well-being finds that people are often poor judges of what will make them happy. In the United States, we are often encouraged to seek material wealth; President Ronald Reagan once said that he hoped America would always remain a country where everyone had the opportunity to "get rich." Compared with the 1970s, a far higher percentage of college students now rank "making a lot of money" above "contributing to society" on their lists of what they hoped to gain from a degree. Yet the psychologist Tim Kasser found that people whose key motivation is material wealth wind up *less* happy than those whose goal is service.

"You can be rich and happy, especially if your original motivation was to make a positive difference in the world," Kasser says. "But you are far more likely to live an unsatisfied life if you go for the money first, if your *primary motivation* is to get rich."[17] If wealth is your goal, you are less likely to develop strong social bonds; and if you succeed in becoming wealthy, you may always sense that others are befriending you only to gain a share of your cash.

The Time Balance Problem

What social connection requires most is adequate time. (We examine this issue more thoroughly in chapter 6.) The Bhutanese have elevated the issue of *time balance* nearly to the top of their list of domains of Gross National Happiness. Bhutanese do pretty well in this regard. Karma Tshiteem, secretary of Bhutan's Gross National Happiness Commission, points out that Bhutanese have thirty to forty paid vacation days plus twenty-four paid national holidays a year, and they want to keep it that way![18] Yet time pressures present clear challenges to happiness in most countries.

Michael Pennock, a population health specialist and statistician at the Vancouver Island Health Authority in Victoria, British Columbia, was invited to Bhutan to help develop its happiness questionnaire, and spent several months in the mountainous kingdom. Bhutanese officials, he explains, wanted the survey to be detailed and comprehensive. Early versions took more than a day to administer. One woman fainted while taking it.

Apparently, the Bhutanese were patient enough for such a long survey. But Pennock knew people in Western industrial countries, growing up in a culture of instant gratification, instant oatmeal, and instant messaging, would never tolerate a long questionnaire. So he developed one that takes only about thirty minutes.

If you're interested, the new, shorter questionnaire is available online at www.sustainableseattle.org. The questionnaire has been used in a scientific sampling of more than 2,400 residents in Victoria by a group called the Victoria Happiness Index Partnership. The same results regarding time use prevailed: While Victoria residents gave their overall quality of life a high rating of 76 (out of 100—Denmark typically scores in the low 80s; the United States in the low 70s), their time balance score was only 46 (the lowest of all dimensions surveyed).

One finding from the survey was particularly revealing. Residents of Victoria scored highest in "freedom from deprivation" (92). Only 6 percent of them thought they'd be happier if they had more possessions. Yet 66 percent hoped for more financial *security*. They gave their financial security a 53 score; only time balance came in lower. Clearly, they were nervous about keeping their jobs and about what kind of safety net might await them if they were to be suddenly laid off work. This is a serious concern—and even more so for Americans who also stand to lose their health care when they lose their jobs.

"The results suggested that stress and problems of time-balance were the most important factors in limiting well-being across the regional population," surmised the Victoria survey report. Interestingly, the Victoria results seem representative for Canada as a whole. Victoria is a prosperous community. But even in the economically depressed coal mining and fishing town of Glace Bay, Nova Scotia, the results were similar.[19] People are satisfied with the amount of stuff they possess, but worried about their financial security and badly pressed for time.

Susan Andrews says that the time crunch is also a powerful limit to happiness in Brazil. Andrews is an energetic American who moved to Brazil in 1992 and now runs Future Vision, a model "eco-village" and environmental learning center near São Paulo. Andrews helped persuade a small Brazilian city, a university, and a large company to assess the life satisfaction of their citizens, students, and employees. Natura, a large natural cosmetics company, polled its workers using the Bhutanese survey. While majorities reported overall satisfaction in every other area, only 30 percent felt positive about their time balance.[20]

As the Italian economist Stefano Bartolini of the University of Siena points out in his new book, *Manifesto for Happiness* (not yet published in English), these findings suggest that focusing our economic strategies and priorities on economic growth may well be counterproductive since it is likely to lead to even more overwork and time stress, while the methods we have used to speed economic growth over the past generation—tax cutting and deregulation—have led to even greater economic insecurity. (We cover this topic in more detail in chapter 5.)

We are now measuring life satisfaction in a major American city. With encouragement from the city council president, Richard Conlin, citizens of Seattle are forming a partnership like that in Victoria, and using the Pennock survey to assess their own life satisfaction.

Sustainable Seattle (the first organization in the world to develop local indicators of well-being back in 1991) has been leading that effort. Laura Musikanski, executive director of Sustainable Seattle, says she wants "to see Seattle become America's first Gross National Happiness City." Once the survey is complete, town meetings will be held in Seattle neighborhoods to analyze the results and make policy recommendations to the city council. Repeating the survey every couple of years can then tell Seattle if it has made progress.[21]

The Problem of Depression

Most Americans *are* fairly happy, and nearly a third of them are *very* happy. Yet while the share of Danes calling themselves "very happy" increased by 22 percent from 1975 to 2005, the American results, as pointed out earlier, have been roughly stable for half a century.[22]

Even then, the scores sometimes seem removed from the mood in the land. Indeed, while overall life satisfaction in the United States is very high, Americans rank far down the list when it comes to measures of negative emotions. According to Gallup-Healthways, people in 144 other countries report being less stressed than Americans, people in 88 countries report less worry, people in 68 countries report fewer periods of sadness, and people in 74 countries are less angry than we are. A quarter of Americans report feeling the blues each day, while two fifths are stressed out.

John Graham, a former diplomat who founded the Giraffe Heroes Project, which honors Americans who "stick their necks out for the common good," warns of desperation beneath all the smile buttons.

> There was a brawl in a major league baseball game between the Cincinnati Reds and the St. Louis Cardinals. Fights happen in sports, and the only thing special about this one was the reaction on sports talk radio the following morning. The consensus among hosts and guests was that the brawl was a good thing, not just because it had helped revive flagging interest in baseball, but that it added juice to fans' lives. It became clear, listening, that both pundits and fans agreed that violent anger in sports generated excitement in fans when so little else in their lives did. Nobody expressed the thought quite this way, but the point of these commentators and their call-in guests was clear: we Americans have lost the passion and energy that makes life fun and exciting, and watching others lash out (and presumably lashing out ourselves) can pull us back from the land of the living dead.[23]

American rates of anxiety and depression have increased substantially during the past half century. Roughly a quarter of Americans suffer from mental illness, and some 16 percent will experience a major episode of depression during their lifetimes. These figures are among the highest in the world, and double to triple those in most other wealthy countries (about double the European average, for example).[24]

Treatment of depression costs the U.S. economy roughly $80 billion a year. Most treatment is pharmaceutical: Americans consume a staggering

66 percent of all the antidepressants used in the entire world each year—isn't that a depressing thought! For those who suffer, the pain is acute. Many cannot afford treatment and do not receive it.[25]

In all of our major cities, one sees this human catastrophe: lonely people mutter to themselves or curse others; many of them are homeless and consumed by drugs or alcohol, wasting away, desperate, and of little value to a society obsessed with market transactions. Indeed, Derek Bok suggests that one of the most important things we could do to increase American happiness levels would be to devote more resources to providing mental health services to those who need them.

The Battle over Happiness

Happiness is hot. Happiness studies have exploded on American campuses. It seems as if everyone is talking about it these days, even the economists. Federal Reserve chairman Ben Bernanke gave the 2010 commencement speech at the University of South Carolina. His title: The Economics of Happiness.

Bernanke suggested that the Gross Domestic Product is a not a reliable measure of economic welfare and warned students about focusing on making a lot of money after graduation. "Money is not enough," he said. "Indeed, taking a high paying job only for the money can detract from happiness if it involves spending less time with your family, stress, and other such drawbacks."[26]

In the past year and a half, some twenty-seven thousand books and articles about the science of happiness have been published. Some, like Derek Bok's *The Politics of Happiness*, are balanced, thorough, and profound. But others, such as Arthur Brooks's *Gross National Happiness*, are ideological and shallow. "The data," writes Brooks, support the conclusion that "government, important as it is, has inherent happiness-lowering tendencies . . . taxation is inherently coercive . . . as government grows—measured in the percentage of GDP it soaks up—the percentage of the population that is satisfied with life shrinks."[27]

Really? Brooks's "data" seem to have eluded most happiness researchers and the Gallup polls that consistently rank high-tax Nordic countries as the world's most satisfied. Even another conservative, the economist Bruce Bartlett, an adviser to President Reagan, acknowledges that "one would expect the happiest countries to be the lowest-taxed countries. In fact, this is not the case. Most of the world's happiest countries are high-tax countries." As a percentage of the GDP, Denmark, the happiest country, pays 49 percent in taxes; Finland pays 43 percent, the Netherlands 39 percent, and Sweden 49 percent. Americans pay 28 percent of total income in taxes.[28]

Moreover, Brooks's suggestion that higher taxes cause a decline in happiness conveniently ignores that Americans' taxes are the lowest they've been since the 1950s, while happiness has remained flat and depression increased. Brooks also argues that policies that would increase time balance, including time away from work, would actually *reduce* happiness, because "most Americans regret that they can't work *more*, not that they can't work *less*" (italics his). Though satisfying work is important for happiness, the idea that Americans, whatever their jobs, want to work more will no doubt come as a surprise to those who check out Gallup's daily happiness poll: Americans rate themselves 20 percent happier on weekends (and happier yet during holidays) than on workdays. What a surprise! Interestingly, these results are confirmed precisely by a method of analysis that tracks Americans' moods by the words they use on Twitter or on Facebook.[29]

Except in the case of the unemployed, Brooks's opposition to leisure runs counter to the study of American happiness during daily activities cited earlier in this chapter and other surveys: A 2008 poll found that 69 percent of Americans would favor a law mandating paid vacations, for example; more than 70 percent support a paid family leave mandate; and more than 80 percent favor a law guaranteeing paid sick days.[30]

Despite the fact that happiness researchers have generally come to conclusions opposite his, Brooks seems determined to wrap the idea of happiness in his ideology in order to convince people that his economic policies, those favored by the government in recent years, are as good as it gets.

We'll return to some of the (often contradictory) arguments and policies Brooks advances later in this book. Most have been tried and found wanting for at least a generation. Still, even Arthur Brooks understands the lack of connection between GDP and life satisfaction: "Economic growth is not, and never can be, a direct measure of our national happiness. A narrow focus on gross domestic product without a conversation about how it meshes with and enhances our culture and values, will not necessarily enhance our gross national happiness. In fact, it may take us in the wrong direction altogether."[31]

Amen to that!

So What Can We Do to Be Happier?

It should be clear by now that psychologists know quite a lot about what kinds of behaviors lead to greater happiness. So what can we do with our economy to improve well-being? We need to pay more attention to time balance, security, and social connection. As individuals we can focus more of our time on family and community, and on building trust. We can devote less attention to maximizing incomes and more attention to generosity. As workers, we can ask our employers for more time off instead of higher pay. Less stuff and less debt allow for a better life with less income, less stress, and more time. In our local communities, we can find ways to design more relationship-friendly places. Farmers' markets are one great example. Shoppers there engage in ten times as many conversations with other people as those in supermarkets.[32] In our cities, as in Denmark, we can design public and private spaces that facilitate social connection, instead of discouraging it, as our pattern of urban sprawl surely does. For more suggestions, you'll need to keep reading . . .

Meanwhile, let's get beyond the GDP and see how our economic policies affect the quality of our lives.

CHAPTER 3

Provisioning the Good Life

Long ago, Dave worked as a veterinarian's assistant. One day, as he was helping stitch up a horse's hind end, his employer, John Siemens, an outstanding and renowned veterinarian, asked him a question: "What's the most important thing in the world to you?" For Siemens himself, the answer was simple: "A happy home." He didn't always achieve his goal, but he ordered much of his personal economy to reach it, and he did well. Right goals help us prioritize well.

The economy is a practical tool. It exists to provision us with goods and services, education, skills, conditions, and opportunities for achieving a good life. Americans are practical people. Working with goals and purpose, we have built an impressive economy. It has been constructed by solving very practical problems through assembly-line manufacturing, public libraries, lightbulbs, vaccines, rural electrification, water utilities, parks, public education, software, hardware, satellites, cell phones. The list is seemingly endless.

Americans have worked hard to solve problems of scarcity by providing goods and services that people here and worldwide need and want. These include a vast array of what we might call comforts or luxuries. Yet without provisioning and distributing the basics—food, water, shelter, and clothing—no economy can be successful. We need to start there. No discussion of the greatest good can ignore basic goods.

What Do We Need?

Orthodox economics assumes that the more stuff a person buys and consumes, the happier that person will be. In theory, each of us tries to maximize *utility*, or satisfaction. Every individual knows his or her wants and needs and makes spending choices to best satisfy them. According to this theory, a person's *utility function* is largely a matter of income and purchases. When we earn and buy more, we get more utility, plain and simple. We are assumed to be better off. The happiness we receive or give to other people doesn't count for the orthodox economist. But as we understand from chapter 2, it counts for the rest of us. Yet if the orthodox theory of utility, of what matters to people and how they make choices, is incorrect, what should take its place?

An understanding of human happiness is an important first step. We often don't know what will really make us happy. A practical alternative economic theory should begin with a theory of human needs and an explanation of how an economy can best provide for them. Manfred Max-Neef, a Chilean economist, has been trying to figure that out for many years. Whereas orthodox economics blurs needs and wants, while assuming they are infinite and insatiable, Max-Neef argues that real needs are actually few, finite, and rather easily met.[1]

Max-Neef challenged the idea that an ever-increasing GDP really made people in Chile better off. Dissatisfied with the traditional definition of *development* that seemed to waste mountains of money without really improving most people's lives, he and his students set about compiling lessons from psychology, biology, economics, and personal interviews to understand the essential ingredients for improving the human condition and provisioning the good life.

They developed a "taxonomy" of human needs by which individuals and communities could assess both their "wealths" and "poverties," giving them a chance to see where scarcity is most pronounced and which of their needs require the most attention (see table on following page).[2]

Two years working and volunteering in the Philippines gave Dave an appreciation for Max-Neef's framework. One rural area, Mountain Province, would score poorly by GDP standards. However, Filipinos there have close-knit communities. Despite financial poverty, people are genuinely quite happy, happier than some Americans who are far more affluent. Dave saw that people in Mountain Province would benefit with better livestock, higher incomes, formal education, credit, health care, and safer drinking water. These were areas of scarcity in Mountain Province.

On the other hand, neighborliness, belonging, safety, trust, and social cohesion were "wealths" of great abundance, more so than in many parts

Fundamental Human Needs

	Being (qualities)	Having (things)	Doing (actions)	Interacting (settings)
Subsistence	physical and mental health	food, shelter, work	feed, clothe, rest, work	living environment, social setting
Protection	care, adaptability autonomy	social security, health systems, work	co-operate, plan, take care of, help	social environment, dwelling
Affection	respect, sense or humor, generosity, sensuality	friendship, family, relationships with nature	share, take care of, make love, express emotions	privacy, intimate spaces of togetherness
Understanding	critical capacity, curiosity, intuition	literature, teachers, policies educational	analyze, study, mediate, investigate	schools, families, universities, communities
Participation	receptiveness, dedication, sense of humor	responsibilities, duties, works, rights	cooperate, dissent, express opinions	associations, parties, churches, neighborhoods
Leisure	imagination, tranquility, spontaneity	games, parties, peace of mind	day-dream, remember, relax, have fun	landscapes, intimate spaces, places to be alone
Creation	imagination, boldness, inventiveness, curiosity	abilities, skills, work, techniques	invent, build, design, work, compose, interpret	spaces for expression, workshops, audiences
Identity	sense of belonging, self-esteem, consistency	language, religions, work, customs, values, norms	get to know oneself, grow, commit oneself	places one belongs to, everyday settings
Freedom	autonomy, passion, self-esteem, open-mindedness	equal rights	dissent, choose, run risks, develop awareness	anywhere

of the United States. Some communities had nightly meetings that anyone could attend—to talk about, work on, and resolve problems. There was plenty of laughter and fun at these meetings, too. And because they were held every night, problems were handled quickly, generally before they spiraled out of control. Everyone in the village knew everyone else, as in many rural communities in the United States. There was no jail in one village, just a railing where troublemakers could be handcuffed for a while. For example, drunks were sometimes sentenced to sober up at the railing. Max-Neef's system seems far superior to the GDP for actually understanding economies and how to advance them. It is also useful on a personal level.

Dave and his wife, Isabel, posted Max-Neef's taxonomy of needs on their refrigerator door. You can slap it down on your table and talk about it. Write on it. Scratch stuff out, add ice cream or your pet rock. That's what Dave and Isabel did. Rather than argue about other things with your partner or friends, you can argue about the things in Max-Neef's boxes, which seem to encompass everything else you'd argue about anyway while adding a dose of perspective.

It's actually fun. Isabel and Dave went through the list to grade their quality of life, discovering where they were a bit impoverished and where improvements could lead them closer to "the good life." They agreed they had both been working too much and needed a greater dose of the "party" and "peace of mind" categories at the intersection of "leisure" and "having." They went to a party and hosted one. They took walks with their kids each week in a different park, and this activity contributed to a more enjoyable and balanced life for both of them.

The Base of the Pyramid

Manfred Max-Neef's table is in some ways a more sophisticated version of an earlier, highly popular theory of needs developed by the psychologist Abraham Maslow during World War II. Maslow worried that the psychology of his day was focused on pathology, on what conditions led to neuroses and psychoses. Instead, Maslow believed that psychology should be asking what actions and what kind of societies improve mental health and human happiness. He developed a theory based on the satisfaction of actual needs that he believed would help every individual flourish, physically and mentally.

Maslow argued that human needs assert themselves in a "hierarchy," a pyramid in which the most basic needs are represented by the lower levels, and nonmaterial needs, or *metaneeds*, are represented by higher ones.[3] Maslow never believed that lower needs must be completely satisfied in order for higher needs to assert themselves. And he never believed that the higher nonmaterial needs could be fulfilled through the purchase of material products. But he thought it obvious that an individual who was starving to death would be more interested in obtaining food than in reading poetry or receiving compliments.

From bottom to top, Maslow's pyramid comprises the following five needs.

1. *Physiological Needs*: air, water, food, shelter, minimal clothing, etc.
2. *Safety Needs*: health, security from crime or other traumatic stress, etc.
3. *Belongingness Needs*: friends, family, love, affection, etc.
4. *Esteem Needs*: education, competence, respect from others, opportunities to be productive, etc.
5. *Self-actualization Needs*: opportunities for creative expression, access to beauty, nature, leisure, etc.

While Max-Neef is an economist concerned about what development is and how economies advance, Maslow was a psychologist and the father of modern business management. Overall, John prefers Maslow, while Dave prefers Max-Neef. Yet we agree that no single theoretical lens is sufficient for understanding human needs and wants.

Maslow's Pyramid

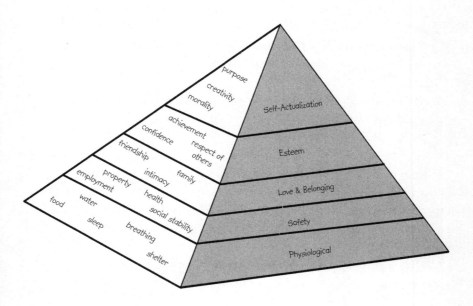

The Five Capitals

In order to effectively meet human needs, economies organize resources to serve people, more or less effectively. Economists often speak of "capital," when describing such resources. Movement of capital from place to place within the economy led in theory by market forces is assumed to rationally allocate resources toward the most efficient uses. When economists talk about capital, they are normally referring to two types of capital.

- *Built capital.* The physical infrastructure humans create from natural resources, including the technologies, machines, and other products that comprise the economy.
- *Financial capital.* Paper and electronic money and other representations of monetary value including stocks, bonds, retirement funds, and so on. These assets are all dependent on trust, and their value is realized when exchanged for real goods and services.

But there are other types of capital, which are equally essential for meeting the needs recognized by both Max-Neef and Maslow.[4] For example:

- *Natural capital.* Native plants and animals, topography, geology, nutrient and water flows, energy, and natural processes that nature provides. All built capital is created out of natural capital.[5]
- *Human capital.* A person's body, skills, knowledge, education, and such interpersonal skills as listening, cooperating, and communication.
- *Social capital.* The social organizations, laws, informal networks, markets, relationships, and trust that constructively enable people to live and work together.

These general capital assets are required to secure economic progress and a high quality of life. Each of these capitals is vital and complementary to the others. Soil, climate, seeds, a farmer's skills and knowledge, social systems such as markets, and money all fit together in the economy to grow food and put it on a plate.

What seems clear to us is that any theory of the economy based on *the greatest good for the greatest number over the longest run* should begin with an assessment of how our economy allocates resources and capital to meet the most basic of needs and move forward from there.

Because our forms of capital are so well developed, perhaps never in human history has procuring the basics of food, clothing, and shelter been so cheap in terms of human labor and time. The proportion of American household budgets dedicated to necessities has reached historic lows, at least for food and clothing. Yet many people in America still struggle to procure the basics.

Fat Food Nation

Some needs never change. We all eat. We *need* food. We also enjoy food. If your appreciation has waned, don't eat. Try fasting. It's cheap. It's an inexpensive one-day education worth the pangs, requiring no special talent, location, or electronic device. It is neither complicated nor difficult. Consider it a day of empathizing with your ancestors. For most of human history people fasted, mostly involuntarily. You may feel grumpy or enlightened, ravenous or cleansed, desperate or empathetic when you get really hungry, but you won't know unless you've experienced it. All the major religions and many health experts advise fasting on occasion.

Fasting for one day while writing this chapter did focus Dave's attention on food. His stomach grumbled. But he was also unexpectedly clearheaded. He got a lot of work done and drank a lot of water. He felt more thoughtful about food. And he grew more troubled about the economics of our food production system.

At one time, many Americans died of starvation or hunger-related diseases. The old graveyards of New England are inhabited by whole families buried in rows, their deaths separated only by weeks in a hard winter, snuffed out by malnutrition and diseases like tuberculosis (then called consumption). For a long time in America, producing and distributing enough food was a difficult problem. In some parts of the world it still is; nearly one billion people suffered from chronic hunger in 2010.[6]

By contrast, modern agricultural science, machinery, and trade have given Americans a cornucopia of food beyond the imagination of our great-grandparents. The average supermarket stocks forty-eight thousand items. Hundreds of brightly decorated boxes of different kinds of cereal compete for our attention. Food is cheap and fast and, increasingly, sweet and fattening.

Today, more Americans die from eating too much rather than too little. Obesity is at an all-time high, affecting over 30 percent of U.S. citizens. The United States is first in fat among all industrialized nations.[7] According to the U.S. Department of Agriculture, the number of daily calories that Americans ate rose from 2,234 in 1970 to 2,757 in 2003, an increase of 523 calories per day.[8] Consumption of corn sweeteners increased 400 percent. On average, every American consumes seventy-nine pounds of corn sweeteners each year.[9]

The economic and health costs of *over*eating are gargantuan. As one prominent critic of our food system, Michael Pollan, noted, "Our most significant health problems are all related to food: obesity, type II diabetes, heart disease, stroke, diet-related cancers." Pollan notes that these problems add $250 billion to our health care bill every year.[10]

In American drugstores, it's easy to find a diet product called Hoodia. It is one of the world's ironies that Hoodia, a cactuslike African plant, is used by the San people, or Bushmen, to fend off the pangs of hunger when they have too little to eat.[11] Now it is used to keep obese Americans from pigging out. It is a metaphor for a divided world in which millions die from too much food and millions more from too little.

Feeding Hunger

Ours is a land of economic extremes. Despite our progress, wealth, and humongous GDP, hunger still bites in every American city and its fangs are getting sharper. The *Washington Post* noted in late 2009 that "the nation's economic crisis has catapulted the number of Americans who lack enough food to the highest level since the government has been keeping track, according to a new federal report, which shows that nearly 50 million people—including almost one child in four—struggled last year to get enough to eat."[12] Poor and insufficient food stifles children's learning and skills development. Can a nation with so many children struggling for healthy nutrition really be considered prosperous?

Yet ending hunger in America is more complicated than adding soup kitchens or increasing incomes. Some Americans are not eating well due to irresponsible choices. Two children in Dave's neighborhood were recently removed from their father's custody because while receiving state support to feed, house, and clothe them, he blew cash on drugs and partying, skipped his rent payments, and apparently did not care if his children ate, bathed, or went to school.

But in many cases, competing needs drive lower-income Americans to pay less attention to proper nutrition. The researchers Richard Wilkinson and Kate Pickett point out that of the 12.6 percent of Americans whose incomes met the official U.S. definition of living in poverty in 2008, "80 percent have air conditioning and almost 75 percent own at least one car or truck."[13] They argue that "what this means is that when people lack money for essentials such as food, it is usually a reflection of the strength of their desire to live up to the prevailing standards. You may, for instance, feel it more important to maintain appearances by spending on clothes while stinting on food."[14]

Hunger and obesity degrade people's quality of life, productive capacities, and economic well-being, adding significant costs to society. Yet these problems are not just matters of individual choice. In many ways our economy discourages healthy eating. Fast-food restaurants populate our poorest urban areas, for example, while grocery stores offering healthier food are absent. Foods filled with fats and corn sweeteners are made cheap through multibillion-dollar state and federal agricultural subsidies, while healthier foods are unsubsidized and cost more.

Food Problems and Solutions

The farmer and author Michael Ableman advocates for and practices a kinder, gentler way of producing food, both for the land and the people who work it.[15] He runs Foxglove Farm, a thriving organic farm on Salt Spring Island in British Columbia, but his roots are in the United States. For years, he was the director of Fairview Gardens, an urban organic farm in Goleta, California, near the University of California at Santa Barbara. During his years at Goleta he observed what was happening to agriculture. His photos and writings documented the shift to ever-larger, more mechanized and chemicalized farms. In California's Central Valley, vast fields harbored lonely workers driving huge tractors or wearing gas masks while spraying pesticides on fields. His photos documented soil turned to hardpan, cracked earth, and windswept dust clouds carrying off tons of fine topsoil. He wondered, "Where are the people? There are no people."

Heavy machinery and chemicals displaced people, compacted soil, and annihilated weeds, bugs, birds, and wildlife.

Is such farming "efficient"? With heaps of subsidies it produces more food, marketed at a lower price, but at what full cost? Ableman saw rural communities and the livelihoods of countless family farmers collapse as debt (for industrial farm equipment and inputs) drove them from the land. Costs included tasteless vegetables, increased cancer among farmers and migrant farmworkers, frogs with extra legs, endless feedlots of animals wallowing in their own waste and force-fed with antibiotics. Overuse of such drugs has produced superbacteria, reducing the effectiveness of these same antibiotics for curing human illnesses.[16] These costs are all hidden by the low price of food. American agriculture is enormously productive, but with hidden and increasing costs to producers and consumers over the long run.

What Michael Ableman witnessed has been well documented in his books and those of other writers like Michael Pollan. But such writers have also documented a flourishing movement to smaller, more sustainable farms and local food production and distribution. In the last two decades, portions of states such as Iowa, Wisconsin, Washington, and Oregon have seen an enormous growth in small organic farms and cooperatives like Organic Valley, which market organic products. In Oregon, the percentage of the population involved in farming, which had fallen for decades, has doubled since the 1990s.

Dave is a supervisor for the Pierce Conservation District, dedicated to conservation and local farming. With farming in his family's background, he's seen both agricultural challenges and new promise. Pierce County, just south of Seattle, is the second most populous county in Washington State and hosts flourishing farmers' markets and specialty crops, including hops for local microbreweries. Community-based agriculture contributes sustainable jobs, efficient production, and high-value agricultural goods to the local economy. Today, residents can buy locally produced meats, seafood, summer fruits and vegetables, and organic grains from eastern Washington.

Small farms in America can be growth centers for jobs and economic value. Here is a summary of what can be done.

Improving markets. Farmers' markets are sprouting all over America. Once or twice a week, farmers sell their produce directly to the customers in public markets, providing healthy food and a sense of community. Market development often requires public investment. Cities are increasingly providing building and street space for public farmers' markets, bringing people into the city core. Improving farm cash flow also supports market development. Community Supported Agriculture organizations (CSAs) facilitate urban dwellers paying in advance for food shares. That provides the farmer with dependable preseason income to produce crops while citizens receive healthy, delicious, usually organic in-season food farms produce every week. Traditional agricultural extension services also improve efficiency and local crop value.

Saving fossil fuel. Our agricultural system is highly dependent on fossil fuel for fertilizer, pesticides, packaging, and transportation. An average spoonful of food eaten in America has traveled more than one thousand miles from farm to palate. Such energy-intensive agriculture requires about ten calories of fossil fuel to provide a single calorie of food. Locally produced food is less carbon intensive, provides local jobs, and diversifies and strengthens the local economy. Local food production reduces oil dependency and lowers carbon emissions.

Changing subsidies. Since the 1950s crop farm subsidies have expanded and focused on five crops: corn, wheat, rice, soy, and cotton, often based on quantitative production favoring larger farms. This large-farm bias has expanded agribusinesses at the cost of smaller local farms. As structured, these subsidies also impede achieving other goals such as a healthier population and more prosperous rural communities where small-farm income is locally retained rather than wired to agribusiness corporate headquarters. Corn subsidies reduce the price of corn products, for example. The market price of corn covers about 45 percent of the cost of production. Tax dollars cover more than the rest, ensuring profitability. Over 500 million bushels of U.S. corn were exclusively devoted to high-fructose corn syrup production in 2010.[17] This produced about 9 million dry-weight tons of high-fructose corn syrup selling at about thirty cents a pound. Subsidized high-fructose corn syrup is an ultracheap and unhealthy ingredient for anything. Fast foods, soft drinks, and processed foods can reduce product costs by adding corn syrup, while unsubsidized healthier fruits and vegetables are more costly. Shifting subsidies to promote the healthiest foods, and smaller farms, while taxing foods that damage human health makes better economic sense, providing *positive externalities* (extra benefits) and fewer *negative externalities* (costs to society not contained in the price of the product). Massive subsidies for corn ethanol have shifted agricultural land from food to energy production, increasing food prices. And, in the case of corn, the "return on energy invested" is marginal.[18] Shifting subsidies is no simple matter. Chopping subsidies off too quickly would put most American wheat farmers out of business. But a careful shift in subsidies would improve the quality of our food, the lives of most farmers, and our health.

Reducing environmental damage. Overuse of pesticides and fertilizers causes significant environmental degradation. Agriculture is the nation's largest water consumer and polluter. Agricultural runoff often contaminates aquifers, rivers, and marine waters. Fertilizers from Midwestern farms wash down the Mississippi River into the Gulf of Mexico, causing algae blooms that deplete oxygen in the water, killing fish and other life and creating a "dead zone" the size of New Jersey. Yet economic incentives still favor many of the most polluting industrial farming practices. Reducing farm inputs such as fertilizers and pesticides, while expanding wetlands which absorb fertilizers, filter and conserve water, can improve surface and groundwater quality, protect against flooding, and provide wildlife habitat and increase water availability. The use of no-till wheat farming conserves energy, soil, and water and increases farm incomes. New irrigation technology and soil moisture gauges can lower water usage by 50 percent or more. Reversing "distorting" policies, like tax exemptions for pesticides and costly organic farming certification, would level the competitive playing field and make the conversion to organic food production more farm friendly.

Protecting topsoil/acting on climate change. Agriculture is one of the largest contributors to global warming, And it will also be one of the sectors most affected by the increased frequency, intensity, and duration of droughts, freezes and floods, and climate chaos. Farming is also essential to solving the problem. Sequestering carbon in soils improves farmland quality. Utilizing farm animal wastes and methane for fertilizers reduces carbon emissions. Poor land use choices have wasted some of the nation's best agricultural lands. Every hour, for example, thirty-eight football fields of prime farmland are sacrificed to suburban sprawl. Land is considered to be of higher value when used for a shopping mall than when producing food. A factory that processes applesauce is valued as a capital asset, while the nation's soil, which actually produces our agricultural output, is not considered a capital asset or valued as such.

Soil carbon and fertility need to be treated as *natural capital* lest we lose them and suffer the costs. (We look closely at the subject of natural capital in chapter 9.)

Providing ecosystem services. Farms provide many "ecosystem service" benefits in addition to food, including wildlife habitat, floodwater reduction, and aquifer recharge. Consider flood protection. In 1993 the Mississippi River flooded millions of acres of land and major cities. Over $10 billion was spent building higher levees on the river, while farmers "tiled" farmlands, to more quickly drain water, previously infiltrated into the soil. Despite higher levees, catastrophic floods hit in 2008 and 2010, flooding cities like Cedar Rapids. The Army Corps of Engineers built higher levees, ignoring the flood protection provided by farmlands, which was lost as farmers improved marginal lands by piping water from fields to rivers, and resulted in floods damaging cities with the highest property value. Giving farmers a small economic incentive for flood control would have been far cheaper than conflicting investments in levees and farmland drainage. The city of Beijing, China, pays upstream farmers for the flood protection their farmlands provide and for other ecosystem services. This has increased rural incomes, funded construction of more schools, and reduced flooding costs in Beijing. The ecosystem services that farmlands provide need to be supported by real economic incentives.

Implementing progressive property taxes. The United States has an income tax because farmers demanded it and Americans passed a constitutional amendment to ensure it. At that time, a sizable portion of the farm population got tired of paying high property taxes while wealthy industrialists and bankers paid very little. The income tax is a *progressive* tax because the wealthy pay a higher tax rate than middle-income Americans or the poor. But we have no progressive tax on land. We might do well to consider a system where large corporate landowners pay a higher property tax rate than small farms. This would slow the monopolization of farmland and encourage greater local land ownership.

Improving health. Healthier food provides for a healthier population and lower health costs. It makes sense to tax cigarettes and alcohol because they harm people's health and increase health care costs. Increased prices for tobacco have changed behavior and reduced cancer rates and health costs. By the same token, targeted incentives could greatly increase the consumption of more healthy food and the percentage of American land that is used for organic production—now only about 0.5 percent of total agricultural land, as compared with 10 percent in Austria, for example.

Providing nutrition education. School gardens, local organic food in schools, better menus, nutritional education, and longer lunch breaks help children develop better eating habits. Cooking at home as a family using unprocessed foods improves the quality of food, family cohesion, and the health of the whole family.

Encouraging home gardens. Former first lady Eleanor Roosevelt promoted "Victory Gardens," and our current first lady, Michelle Obama, also champions home gardening. During World War II, home gardens raised about 40 percent of the nation's fresh vegetables. They can play a critical role in providing healthy food and reducing fossil fuel consumption. Providing even a small tax break for those who tend home gardens would easily pay for itself in better health and reduced energy use.

Increasing federal food supports. Subsidizing good food for poor pregnant women and families, using the Women, Infants and Children (WIC) federal program, has been successful in reducing infant mortality, while improving nutrition, health, and educational achievement. An expansion of this program and the federal food stamp program are necessary steps in the fight to reduce childhood hunger.

Training farmers. Training people to produce food sustainably, run small farms, build community businesses, and restore marginal lands would benefit the nation. These activities are more labor intensive and offer higher prospects of job creation than some other economic investments, including many contained in the recent stimulus package. There are thousands of young people who would relish the healthy, active, and meaningful life of producing quality food for America. A smart economy based on the greatest good for the greatest number over the longest run would massively expand efforts to increase the number of future farmers of America.

Food and agriculture are far more important to our economy than market measures such as GDP indicate. Nutritious food is closely linked to health, educational achievement, water quality, land use, energy consumption, even flood protection. Yet these values remain unmeasured. Climate change cannot be adequately addressed without improving agriculture. Water shortages and water quality in much of the United States are closely linked to agricultural practices. The everyday lives of all Americans could be greatly improved with more sensible economic policies for sustainable food production and distribution.

Cast into the Streets

Like food, housing is critical to health and quality of life. American shelter has improved vastly over the last century. Nearly all of our homes now include indoor plumbing, electricity, reliable heating, better insulation, communications, appliances, proximity to health care, and transportation access. Unimagined amenities spring forth from every room in houses, apartments, and condominiums. The average American home is more luxurious than most royal palaces of the past. Average house sizes doubled between the 1960s and the 1990s. Many new homes boast three-car garages.

For most Americans, home ownership represents their largest capital asset, a cornerstone of the middle class, an asset that fell in value in all fifty states after the 2008 financial crisis, a debacle from which the United States has not yet recovered (see chapter 12). At least 11 million mortgages were "underwater" by July 2010. The homes were valued at less than their buyers still owed on them. Some three hundred thousand homes were being foreclosed each month as of mid-2010. With high unemployment and cuts in unemployment benefits looming, the number of foreclosures will stay high.

Like food, housing cannot be separated from the rest of the economy. Income enables housing. Housing surplus, created by foreclosures, drives down housing values. As a leading financial magazine put it:

> As each month passes, it has become clearer that unemployment is the single greatest cause of high foreclosure rates and falling home prices. The correlation between cities with high jobless rates and extremely high foreclosures is stunning. The 10 worst real estate markets in the country each had unemployment levels above 12 percent in June [2010]. Two cities in California, Merced and Modesto, had jobless rates above 17 percent, nearly twice the national average of 9.6 percent.[19]

Dave visited Modesto in December 2010. This once-prosperous agricultural city is increasingly occupied by vacant houses and homeless people. Banks have become landlords, renting houses to the people who once held equity in them and still have jobs to pay the rent. Thirty years ago Modesto did not smell of feedlots with tens of thousands of cattle, because farms were smaller and more diverse. A crumbling economy and lost housing make for a vicious cycle of unemployment, foreclosure, and business closures.

In Cleveland, Ohio, one of the epicenters of the housing debacle, many people were evicted from their homes and became apartment renters. But then they were evicted again from their apartments, as the owners of those apartments could not make mortgage payments on the buildings themselves, so they were foreclosed. As vandals demolished empty houses block by block, the value of abandoned houses fell, pulling down the value of all housing in the affected neighborhoods. As housing values fell farther, even people with good jobs found themselves underwater.[20]

Unlike hunger, homelessness was rarely present in most of America until thirty years ago. Like hunger, homelessness has been getting worse recently. In many cities, homeless people include more children and families. Traumatized or disabled veterans, at times cursing or mumbling to themselves, frequent the downtown core. Business owners and shoppers find them bothersome.

Buddy, Can You Spare a Room?

In Seattle, Paul Carlson shows a ready smile that belies the decades he has spent working on this painful problem. Carlson is the Northwest coordinator of the U.S. Interagency Council on Homelessness, a division of the Department of Housing and Urban Development. He remembers that in the 1970s, homelessness, while it existed, was not a common sight in the United States. But in the early 1980s, he says, "a perfect storm increased the problem immensely."[21]

First, Reagan administration cutbacks in funding for mental hospitals resulted in "massive numbers of mentally and physically disabled people hitting the streets. But it wasn't all Reagan." Liberal groups, including the American Civil Liberties Union, successfully pressed the courts to release mentally ill people who were confined in hospitals against their will. Carlson points out that the blind devotion to ideology, both on the left and right, led to thousands of real-life tragedies, as mentally ill people were turned out homeless and without health care when the Reagan administration was also disinvesting in publicly funded housing. Gentrification in America's central cities also led to what Carlson calls *habitat destruction*, as hundreds of inexpensive single-resident-occupancy hotels (SROs) were razed to make room for expensive development.

"Here in downtown Seattle," Carlson remembers, "we had twelve thousand units of housing in SROs in 1980. They weren't pretty, but they provided very low-cost housing to disabled and poor people. Six hundred of them were destroyed just to build one Wells Fargo Bank in 1984. The residents had no place to go. By 1990, there were only three thousand SRO rooms left for people. We got something for it. Downtown became a more lively place, and middle-class homeowners saw the value of their houses appreciate continually. But we thought there was no cost to it. There was."

By the mid-1980s, some estimates put the number of homeless Americans as high as 3 million. Carlson says those estimates were too high, but the numbers are still shocking. "Most experts agree we now have about seven hundred thousand homeless, in shelters or on the street. Half to two thirds of them are mentally ill or otherwise disabled. A third are seriously mentally ill. We have a whole underclass of people whose life expectancy is fifty-five—lower than in Russia. Even in Seattle, a hundred of them die in the streets each year."

Carlson believes the United States has no housing shortage. "There are more than enough units to shelter everyone. But we are emptying houses everywhere due to foreclosures."

Often, the vacant residences fall into disrepair; whole rows of homes stand empty or become drug-dealing havens. One of the worst days of Dave's summer work in construction during high school was being assigned to evict three heroin addicts squatting in a small apartment building in the Hilltop area of Tacoma, prior to the building's renovation.

Two men and a woman, all emaciated, living in filth up to their ankles, called that ground-level apartment home. Appeals by the apartment building owner to the city and social workers met with no response. It is hard to find people leading more miserable lives than homeless heroin addicts. Far too weak and downtrodden to argue or fight, they cooperated as Dave rounded up their things and escorted them out of the building.

"I don't want to move you out," Dave told them, "but we'll be ripping all these walls and ceilings out tomorrow or the next day. You guys should really just go right to the hospital or the county rehab. You'll die if you live like this here or anywhere else."

"Mac, you're not making my life any better," one man responded. "If you want to help, give me some money for food. I don't need your advice."

Dave offered to buy them a burger at lunch. Two of them took him up on the offer. One, a Vietnam veteran, had a life story to tell and the willingness to tell it. His story was well worth listening to. His companion said very little. At the end of the lunch they thanked Dave. But that just didn't feel right, as a free meal hardly heals the loss of housing.

Even for someone used to recklessly bashing out walls and ceilings, in preparation for reconstruction, having to clean up the needles and feces of heroin addicts brings reflection, the drive to study harder in college, and zero interest in drugs. Unemployment, homelessness, rising health care costs for all, drugs, and crime are problems that cannot be solved with more unemployment, more homelessness, more jails, and less opportunity. See for yourself. Go to any hospital in any major American city and interview the homeless people waiting for treatment. Ask the health professionals how much treatment of the homeless costs.

For anyone who pays attention, the vicious cycle of bad individual choices, bad policy, and high costs is obvious. Two blocks north of the Earth Economics office, where Dave works, is the Pierce County jail. Three blocks west of the Earth Economics office is a halfway house for people being released from jail. One block south of the Earth Economics office is a homeless shelter and a kitchen where many of the residents released from the halfway house go next. Other countries treat homelessness differently.

Britain had about ten thousand chronically homeless people on its streets in 2005 (the percentage equivalent of about fifty thousand in the United States) when Tony Blair's Labour government decided to do something to find them homes. "Now the number has been reduced to eight hundred," notes Carlson. "It's quite a success story."

"Europe has a far greater housing shortage than we do," Carlson says with a frown. "But [Europeans] have far less homelessness. They put people into housing. They subsidize housing on a bigger scale." U.S. policies have often been penny-wise and pound-foolish.

Carlson continues: "We are really a third-world country that's in the first world. Our scale of poverty is much more profound than in any other rich country." However, he concludes, "We've learned from some of these things." The solutions to even complex problems like homelessness exist. First, sufficient low-cost single-resident-occupancy rooms need to be available. Second, there should be funding for social workers to interview homeless people and develop individual solutions to drug, health, housing, and employment problems. (When the second strategy was employed in the United Kingdom, it reduced homelessness by 92 percent and dramatically cut overall costs.) Allocating funds to secure solutions like sufficient housing "upstream" is cheaper and better than paying for the results of homelessness (for example, treating frostbite in the emergency room).

What are our housing goals? That a few people live in castles while more Americans than ever live on the street? Or that more Americans enjoy housing and home ownership?

Fashion Statement

Food, shelter, and clothing are basic needs. Americans used to make clothes. Now we import them at absurdly low prices. Unlike housing, the price of clothing has been plummeting for decades. Used clothes are now so abundant they are sold by the pound. Check out these bargains: You can buy wholesale "Grade A" clothing for forty cents a pound. "Grade A/B" goes for thirty cents. In July, you can buy winter clothes for fifteen cents a pound.[22]

Even new clothes are cheap. You can get a T-shirt for $3.99 on sale, or $1.99 in a "multipack." As Annie Leonard writes in *The Story of Stuff*, any T-shirt selling for $1.99 doesn't include all true costs in that price. For example, the cotton purchased by the average American in one year requires 176 cubic yards of water to produce. Cotton production requires 2.5 percent of the world's agricultural land, 25 percent of the world's fertilizers, and 25 percent of its insecticides. Just the pesticides sprayed on cotton plants cost about $2.6 billion every year.[23]

Leonard describes a trip to Haiti where she met with women who earned about two dollars a day while sewing apparel for Disney, while Disney's then-CEO Michael Eisner raked in $34,800 each day, and more than $100,000 a day if stock options and benefits were included.[24] Apparel workers around the world cannot afford to buy the new clothes they make. We, however, can afford the clothes. The average American now has three times as many clothes as thirty years ago. The former Harvard economist Juliet Schor reports that in 1991, Americans bought thirty-four items of clothing a year. Now, they buy sixty-seven, one every 5.4 days.[25] Few people wear three pairs of pants or six shoes at once however, so our drawers, closets, and houses are filling up with apparel.

One day at Dave's house, a loud POP! announced that a big cabinet, stuffed with clothes, had blown out, popping three screws on a side panel and disgorging the contents onto the floor. It was his wife, Isabel's cupboard. "Hey, don't blame me; you have too many clothes too," she replied when Dave ribbed her. "Why did I get the cheesy cabinet, anyway?" Isabel decided to get rid of half of her clothes, and Dave's whole family was inspired. They got rid of half of their clothes and never missed any of them. Drawers were empty, closets roomy. Vacant bins appeared out of thin air. Even the dirty clothes hamper somehow seemed roomier. It was so cathartic that Dave tried to reduce his clothes by half again. He put all the questionable clothes in a liberated bin, marked the date on it, and vowed, "If I don't wear these clothes within a year, out they go." After a year went by, he took the bin to Goodwill without ever opening the lid.

The whole process motivated Dave, Isabel, and their two sons to get rid of one third of the toys, clear out extra sheets, and unload unused tools.

For most of its history as a nation, the United States had import quotas on clothing. That ensured that some clothes would be "Made in the USA," at higher wage rates, creating jobs and raising the price of clothes. Those quotas were phased out in the 1980s and '90s. Clothing production moved almost entirely to countries with the cheapest labor, and the American textile manufacturing industry collapsed, taking whole towns in the Southeast with it.

It seems clear that except for the poorest, most Americans easily meet the basic needs of food, clothing, and shelter. Many of us, if we care to admit it, are overeating, drowning in a sea of clothing, and living in homes far larger than are actually comfortable. To ensure this profligacy, we borrowed to the hilt and made a religion of cheap, lured by the slogan of Walmart: Always Low Prices. Always. But the cost of this excess has been high, if hidden: debt, sprawl, environmental degradation, loss of whole industries and the livelihoods of countless thousands of American workers.

The U.S. economy, driven by its focus on the GDP, is an open mouth and bottomless stomach for new products (mostly made overseas). It delivers cheap goods. But, as we show in the next chapters, it delivers expensive *bads* as well. The trade-off is questionable. There's plenty of room for improvement, but not in the direction we've been going. Indeed, when it comes to quality of life, in a host of ways, the American economy is a dramatic underperformer.

CHAPTER 4

Unhealthy at Any Cost

It is one of the great and sobering truths of our profession that modern health care probably has less impact on the population than economic status, education, housing, nutrition and sanitation.

—THEODORE COOPER, ASSISTANT SECRETARY
FOR HEALTH UNDER PRESIDENT GERALD FORD[1]

Stephen Bezruchka calls it "America's best-kept secret." "We die younger than people in other rich countries," says Bezruchka, a craggy and fit mountain climber who also serves as an emergency room physician and a professor at the University of Washington's School of Public Health. "Thomas Jefferson may have said we have a right to life, but we don't have a right to a very long one. After World War II, we were the healthiest people in the world. Now we're not even close."[2]

Following the psychologist Abraham Maslow's hierarchy of needs theory, once we've obtained oxygen, water, and enough food, clothing, and shelter to keep from starving, freezing, or roasting, health and safety needs express themselves rather urgently; when you're sick as a dog, you can't think about much else except getting well, and if you're lucky and can stay in bed, that's where you go. Poor health can be life-threatening; you're way more likely to drop over from a heart attack or a stroke, or expire from cancer, than you are to die from accidents, crime, suicide, bee stings, lightning strikes, or terrorism (in descending order of probability).

So it's no wonder that health care—which, after all, is supposed to make us *healthy*—was, in 2009 and early 2010, consistently front-page-above-the-fold in our papers and at the top of our political agenda. From the reports of angry seniors demanding that government keep its hands off their Medicare, and fears of fictional "death panels," to the people carrying weapons to town-hall meetings, health care was headline news. Stories of underinsured families bankrupted by an operation or a hospital aspirin fed the sense that our medical system was dysfunctional. Though our former president, many Republican members of Congress, and the CEOs of American insurance companies still claim the United States has "the greatest health care system in the world," most Americans are a bit suspicious.

They have a right to be. But it isn't for lack of effort.

First of the Big Spenders

You might be surprised to know that by 2012, we Americans will be spending nearly $9,000 per person per year on our medical system, almost 18 percent of our whopping GDP. We're already spending $2.5 *trillion* a year on health care.[3] Soon, if present trends continue, we'll be spending one dollar out of every five on health, or rather, sickness, care alone.

We do get something for all that money. Recently, Dave had to go to the emergency room twice in the same day. His wife suffered acute pain and, it turned out, needed surgery to remove her gallbladder. Later that afternoon, his four-year-old son had difficulty breathing. It was pneumonia. The care they received was first-rate and the emergency room staff totally professional. But even though Dave had excellent health insurance, the day in the hospital ended up costing his family $7,000 out of pocket. Dave met many kinds of people in the emergency room. Some were there for frivolous reasons; one man showed up because he had a splinter in his finger! But others had real emergencies—a heart attack victim, a person in shock, people with broken bones or severe allergic reactions.

A nurse explained that many of those with real emergencies were there because they were among the millions of Americans who don't have health insurance or because other doctors wouldn't accept their publicly provided insurance. Some were sicker than they otherwise might have been because, lacking insurance, they hadn't seen the doctor when they suffered their first symptoms. The early care would have been relatively inexpensive, but they waited until their situation was desperate before seeking free emergency help. Each of them costs our medical system a lot of money. The United States wins the Health Care Spending Olympics hands down: We're not even 5 percent of the world's population, but we account for nearly half its total annual health care budget.[4]

So what about other rich countries; how much do they spend? T. R Reid, in his enlightening book, *The Healing of America*, tracks down the numbers. The Scrooges, such as Japan and the United Kingdom, spend only 7 or 8 percent of their budgets on health care, while profligates like Switzerland and France spend about 11 percent.[5] On average, the other developed countries spend about half what America does per person, and they all cover *everybody*, with universal health insurance. "Ah," you say, "there must be a catch." You get what you pay for, right? That's what our moms taught us, and that's what traditional economics teaches too. Using that logic, we find it hard to believe that Americans aren't the healthiest people on Earth. And, as Dr. Bezruchka points out, once upon a time they were; right after World War II, in fact. Back then, Americans' health and our health care were the envy of the world. But times have changed.

America Is Number Thirty-seven

First, there was that World Health Organization study done in 2000 that ranked the United States thirty-seventh in the quality of its health care.[6] Many experts think it has slipped a little farther down in the last decade, but lots of Americans don't trust the World Health Organization. Some argue that the WHO is part of the United Nations, which favors socialism, so it probably cooked the numbers. Never mind that the WHO commissioned American doctors to do the study; you really can't trust anyone these days.

But let's leave the possibly pinko WHO alone for a moment. What do other experts say?

The quality of health care models is a subjective thing, but what about *objective* health data?

Well, for starters, the Central Intelligence Agency's *World Fact Book* ranks the United States forty-ninth in life expectancy.[7] Simply put, that means that people in forty-eight other countries live longer on average than Americans do. We're talking about the CIA here, not the WHO. Forty-ninth: just above Albania. Now some experts take out the puny places—such as Andorra and Malta and San Marino and Singapore— that beat us on that list, getting us up to number thirty.

Even so, the only rich countries that give us a run for our money in the Life Expectancy Race to the Bottom are Portugal, Ireland, and Denmark. They rank just above the United States.

Whoops . . . did we say "run for our money?" Well, that's not exactly accurate, since America spends more than twice as much per person on health care as they do. And things are not looking up; to the contrary, the United States was eleventh in life expectancy as recently as 1980.[8] (More on the significance of that year in chapter 11 of this book.) Even more ominous: a new study finds that in 30 percent of the counties in America, women's life expectancy is now actually *falling*.[9]

Sadly, it's not just life expectancy that America is lagging in. It ranks forty-fourth in child mortality and forty-first in maternal mortality, again from the CIA's *World Fact Book*. (Its rate of deaths for moms giving birth has actually increased since 1990.) A new University of Washington study put U.S. men in forty-fifth place and U.S. women in forty-ninth place when it comes to the adult mortality rate—the percentage of people who die between the ages of fifteen and sixty. Every rich country does better. (The rate in Canada is nearly 50 percent lower than in the United States.) Even some poor countries also outperform America: Costa Rica ranks twenty-seventh overall, and Cuba, thirty-eighth, for example.[10]

According to the *Los Angeles Times* (October 2, 2007), an extensive study by the Emory University School of Public Health found that elderly Americans were much less healthy than Europeans of the same age.

> For example, heart disease was diagnosed in nearly twice as many Americans as Europeans 50 and older. More than 16% of American seniors had diagnosed diabetes, compared with about 11% of their European peers. And arthritis and cancer were more than twice as common among Americans as Europeans. "We expected to see differences between disease prevalence in the United States and Europe, but the extent of the differences is surprising," said lead author Kenneth Thorpe, a public health professor at Emory and former deputy assistant secretary of the U.S. Department of Health and Human Services.

Americans were also nearly twice as likely as Europeans to be obese. "We spend more on healthcare because we are, indeed, less healthy," Thorpe concluded.[11]

And if such evidence of failure isn't enough to cast doubt on our health care system, a recent Harvard study concluded that nearly forty-five thousand Americans die each year out of the 47 million Americans without health insurance.[12] Even in the hospital, U.S. patients face unusual dangers. More than one hundred thousand of them die each year from "health care" itself—errors or infections during treatment.[13]

We pay the most and get the worst results. Why are we putting up with that?

House of Health

So our health care system is sick. We took some steps to fix it in 2009, when the Patient Protection and Affordable Care Act passed Congress and was signed into law by President Obama. The new law will insure 32 million more Americans, prevent the denial of health care for "preexisting conditions," provide free medical checkups, and, according to the Congressional Budget Office, even reduce the deficit. It's progress. But fully fixing the system will require a far more holistic approach than has been discussed in the health care debate.

It's not obvious in the current debate, but no one would argue that good health *care* is our final goal. Who wants to spend time in the hospital, even the best hospital, even if the food wasn't so bad? The goal, of course, is *good health*. Health care is only part of that. Let's get metaphorical and consider American health as a house. Health care is merely the *roof*, the final protection against illness.

In our case, it's an expensive roof, gold plated, yet with millions of holes in it and a lot of other leaks—millions more who are underinsured, insurance companies that spend nearly as much finding ways to deny coverage as they do paying the bills, for example. Elizabeth Warren, chair of the Congressional Oversight Panel for the banking bailout, points out that half of American bankruptcies are due to unpaid medical bills—and 75 percent of those people have insurance.[14]

In other industrial countries, the roof is a simpler affair, asphalt shingles on a fiberglass mat maybe, but with hardly any leaks. Their health care systems rely more on prevention, less on high-tech treatment. Yet the people in the house below live longer, healthier lives. That's because *in those other countries, the foundation and the walls of the house are stronger, with fewer cracks to let in the cold.* If we patch up the leaks in our roof, but do nothing for the floor and the walls, the costs of health care will likely go through that roof.

As Stephen Bezruchka puts it: "It is not health care that makes us healthy. I say this as a medical doctor who has practiced for thirty-five years. During this period working in the emergency department, I have treated heart attacks, motor vehicle crashes, shoulder dislocations and stabbings. I could help many of these people. But when you add up all that medical care does, it still doesn't make that much of a difference."[15]

The Foundation

Let's start with the foundation. That's the head start toward health that children in most other rich countries receive. There's a stronger focus on prenatal care, for example. In part because of this, infant mortality in all other industrial countries is lower than in the United States. You've got a better chance of survival if you're born in Cuba.

Moreover, in every country in the world except, believe it or not, the United States, Liberia, Swaziland, and Papua New Guinea, mothers are guaranteed paid time off from work to take care of newborns.[16] Do you even know where Liberia, Swaziland, and Papua New Guinea are? In most rich countries, fathers also receive paid time off to bond with young children. In many cases, such *family leave* extends for up to a year or more.

That's even true right next door to the United States, in Canada, where parents can split a year of leave at 55 percent of their salaries. In the United States, by contrast, parents are only guaranteed unpaid time off—by the Family and Medical Leave Act of 1993—and then only if they work for companies with more than fifty employees. So American moms often return to work when children are only a few weeks old. Sharon Lerner, author of *The War on Moms: On Life in a Family-Unfriendly Nation*, writes that

> the effect of all this on babies can be serious and lasting: In an article published in *The Economic Journal* in 2005, researchers found that infants whose mothers had 12 weeks of maternity leave or fewer had lower cognitive test scores and higher rates of

behavior problems at age four than children whose mothers had longer leaves. In Europe, longer paid maternity leaves are linked to lower infant and child mortality . . . According to research by economists Sara Markowitz and Pinka Chatterji and published in 2008 by the National Bureau of Economic Research, women who return to work soon after the birth of a child are more likely to get depressed than other mothers. They're also less healthy: According to the study, longer maternity leaves are associated with improvements in mothers' overall health.[17]

Paid family leave, and the parental bonding it ensures, pays off in terms of children's health—fewer childhood illnesses, fewer problems with attention-deficit disorder, less obesity, easier socialization, better readiness to learn. Most countries find that such a social investment in early childhood results in lower health and other costs as children grow up. In Canada, where paid parental leave was recently increased from six months to a year, health care costs for children have dropped, leading to some interest in further extending the leave.[18]

A 2007 UNICEF study ranked the United States twentieth out of twenty-one rich nations in terms of children's welfare.[19] One factor in its low standing is obesity. American children are the world's leaders in that unhappy statistic. By the time they reach seventeen, only a quarter of young Americans can pass the physical and mental health tests necessary to enter the military.[20] Meanwhile, we still fill our TV screens with ads for junk foods targeting our children.

You might say that the foundation of our "health house" is weak or at least uneven. Metaphorically, the rich enjoy a house with a marble floor, and our middle class, a wooden one (with the floorboards sounding increasingly squeaky). Poor Americans, far less likely to be insured or to have maternity leave and other family benefits, have a dirt floor, with rain leaking through the holes in the roof. (More on that in chapter 7.)

And if the floor of the house is in trouble, what about the walls?

Wall Number One: Lifestyle

Liberal Democrats seem to talk almost exclusively about universal health care as the solution to our health problems. By contrast, Republicans tend to focus on wall number one: *lifestyle choices*. It's all a matter of *personal responsibility*, they say. Americans should simply stop smoking, eat properly, avoid overeating and excessive alcohol consumption, exercise regularly, and sleep enough. "Let Michael Moore slim down before he produces movies like *Sicko*," they declare, righteously wagging a finger. And, they argue, he doesn't need government to do this, nor do the rest of us.

That people should make good lifestyle choices is solid advice. Reducing smoking is good for health. Citizens of other rich countries generally exercise and sleep more than we Americans do, though there is some evidence that we dream more (just kidding). And non-Americans don't eat as much, so they are less likely to be obese.

But health isn't all a matter of personal responsibility. Our tax system subsidizes producers of sugars (have you ever read a label that didn't include *high-fructose corn syrup*?) and fats, and our culture relentlessly advertises fast, unhealthy foods. At the same time, Americans tend to work longer hours than people in other rich countries, leaving less time for healthy lifestyle choices. Policy changes are essential. Individual and social actions are both needed to improve lifestyles.

Europeans, for example, work 200–400 fewer hours each year on average than Americans do. Laws guarantee them sufficient time off, mandating a minimum of four weeks of paid vacation a year, curbs on overtime, and shorter weekly working hours. (More on this topic in chapter 6.) This leaves them more time to select foods carefully, eat more slowly—and, as a result, eat less—while exercising and sleeping more. Laws reducing work time enable people to make healthier choices and be healthier.

Wall Number Two: Stress Relief

It's no secret in the field of public health that stress is a killer. Dr. Sarah Speck, director of the Cardiovascular Wellness Program at Seattle's Swedish Hospital, calls stress "the new tobacco."[21] Sudden bursts of adrenaline worked to protect our early human ancestors against attack by savage beasts. But continued adrenaline response to the chronic stress of modern life leads to heart problems, obesity, hypertension, and weakened immune systems.

Several factors make American life particularly stressful. The United States is among the most competitive of wealthy capitalist countries and has the widest gap between rich and poor (see chapter 7). Fewer people on top; more on the bottom. Multiple studies (see especially Robert

Sapolsky's classic, *Why Zebras Don't Get Ulcers*) clearly show that whether it's humans or baboons, the lower your status, the higher your stress levels. CEOs don't have the greatest prevalence of heart attacks; it's the lower-level managers and grunts. More economically egalitarian societies, like Sweden and Japan, for example, are clearly less stressful and healthier. "About 880,000 deaths a year occur in this nation that wouldn't be there if we had a smaller income gap like the Western European countries," argues Stephen Bezruchka.[22] This is twenty-six times the total annual road fatalities in the United States.[23] Think of what federal, state, and local governments spend in road safety every year, while income inequality and stress kill us off at even greater rates.

Stress is also the result of insecurity. As our social safety net has been gutted in recent years (with more of us losing health and pension benefits, for example; more about this in the next chapter) and job protections have been reduced, life in America is riskier than it used to be. We are far more insecure than people in other rich countries, where strong social safety nets remain in place. Danes, for example, can be fired as easily as Americans, but then they receive generous unemployment benefits, job training, and government jobs if they are unable to find a position in the private sector. Insecurity often leads to anxiety. American rates of anxiety are double or triple those in western European countries.[24] Anxiety and other mental illnesses further impact physical health, creating a vicious cycle. Europeans say their social safety net gives them a feeling of peace of mind. It's certainly good for their health.

One of the most significant contributing factors to stress is debt. Debt and household finances are among the most commonly listed causes for divorce in the United States, another contributor to stress.

Finally, stress is also the result of time pressures and overwork. The extent of this impact was confirmed by a May 11, 2010, report from Kristen Hallam of *Bloomberg News*.

> Working 10 hours or more a day may harm the heart, according to a study of more than 10,000 British civil servants. People who added three or more hours to a seven-hour day had a 60 percent greater risk of heart attack, angina and death from cardiovascular disease than those with no overtime work, researchers from the U.K., Finland and France reported today in the *European Heart Journal*.

The results bolster evidence that suggests working overtime is linked to poor health and may play a greater role in heart disease than previously thought, wrote Gordon McInnes, a professor of clinical pharmacology at the University of Glasgow, in an editorial accompanying the study.[25]

More and longer breaks from stressful work are seen by Europeans as yet another way to improve health. Changing inequality in the United States is a long-term goal—there is no quick fix. But policies offering shorter work time and longer vacations, clear stress reducers, could be enacted more easily and quickly, and they should be. (More about this in chapter 6.)

Wall Number Three: Social Connection

It's another clear understanding in the field of public health that *social connection* strengthens immune systems and improves physical well-being. Studies even show that the more social connections you have, the less likely you are to get a cold when a virus is released into the room. In fact, connecting with others may be the most important single thing you can do to be healthier. On the other hand, being lonely is one of the worst things you can do for your health. Yet, despite Facebook and "social networking," America is an increasingly lonely country.

More and more Americans, especially older people, live alone, far more than in other rich countries. A recent study found that the average American has only two close friends he or she can turn to. A quarter of us have none at all.[26] Loneliness too often turns into depression. As with anxiety, Americans are two to three times as likely to suffer from depression as western Europeans. Depression further weakens immune systems and lowers physical health outcomes.

A National Institutes of Health study comparing frequency of chronic illness in the United States and the United Kingdom found that Americans are far more likely to suffer from heart disease, diabetes, and hypertension in old age. The study controlled for age, race, income, and gender differences and found, surprisingly, that poor Brits are as healthy as rich Americans.[27]

The study didn't find that eating fish and chips makes you healthier. And it wasn't drinking or smoking either. The Brits smoke a bit more than we do and drink a lot more. The major reasons for the difference were related to the fact that the Brits have more security and more free time, which they use to exercise more and, especially, to socialize more. Here again, public policies giving workers more time off the job would improve health, in this case, by allowing Americans more time to spend with family and friends. Clearly, this would also strengthen families and communities.

Wall Number Four: A Safe Environment

Americans, according to the UNICEF study of children's welfare, rank at the bottom in child safety, with the highest rates of accidents among children. This is partly due to time pressure on American parents, which leaves them less able to supervise their children. Other studies also show extremely high rates of accidents in American workplaces compared with those of other nations. Preventable death rates in the United States, including deaths from automobile accidents, are the highest among industrial countries. Republican senator John Ensign of Nevada acknowledges this, but says deaths from gunshots and traffic accidents shouldn't count in the mortality stats. "We Americans like our guns," he observes. "It's a cultural thing."[28] (We also like our fast food, so perhaps obesity shouldn't count either.) One can imagine Ensign in an earlier era saying that Americans shouldn't be considered bigoted because they like their segregation, but we digress.

On average, Americans breathe more polluted air than western Europeans, contributing to higher rates of child asthma. The European Union also has stricter controls on the release of toxic chemicals into the environment. Even children's toys are different in Europe. The Chinese, who make most of them, have been allowed to include various toxic plastics in those that are shipped to the United States, but are barred from selling the same unsafe toys to Europe.

Finally, and this is no small matter, every other industrial country guarantees its workers paid time off from work when they are sick; only the United States does not. Forty percent of American workers—and 86 percent of restaurant workers—get no paid sick days.[29] This is quite strange really, in light of the sermons from public officials telling Americans to stay home and keep their children home to prevent a swine flu epidemic, for example. You might not be able to afford food and your house might be foreclosed, but don't spread that flu around! In thousands of cases, parents, especially single mothers, are fired because they stay home from work to care for sick children.

In many other countries, as much as a month of paid sick leave is required by law and workers are allowed to use some of this time to care for sick children. These countries know that without paid time off, workers will come to work sick, as many American workers do. Their children will come to schools and day care centers sick. They will get others sick and stay sick longer, often requiring more expensive treatment for their illnesses. This line of thought is not rocket science. Most Americans get it immediately. That is why more than 80 percent of them favor a law that would guarantee paid sick days for workers.[30]

Health Improves During Recessions

There may be an upside to the recession that hangs over the United States. Health has actually improved during this period. As Stephen Bezruchka says, "Contrary to popular thinking, American health always gets better during recessions."

Christopher Ruhm, an economist at the University of North Carolina, Greensboro, estimates that for every 1 percent increase in unemployment during recessions, we're seeing a 0.5 percent *drop* in the adult mortality rate. "When I first got the results, I didn't particularly believe them," Ruhm said in an interview. "I made a picture that overlaid the national mortality rates and unemployment rates. I found that they were a mirror image. It was at that point that I really believed my results."[31]

This is counterintuitive; how can something so contrary be? Well, Americans are working less, and these findings are clear proof of how important that is for health. Among those who lose their jobs, the health impact is indeed mixed. Suicides have risen, and some turn to alcohol or abuse their spouses in reaction to their sudden sense of uselessness—"redundant," in the British expression. But others among the unemployed have used the time to exercise more, spend more time with family and friends, read, learn new hobbies, and generally pay more attention to their health.

For those who have not lost their jobs, the results are also complicated. A minority has seen hours and workloads increased, as they are expected to do the work of laid-off former colleagues. But overall, through furloughs, reduced schedules, and reductions in overtime, working hours for Americans are at their lowest in decades. People have more time and less money. They are using that time to sleep more, exercise more, and visit more with friends and family.

Since we are earning less, we are buying fewer drinks and cigarettes, eating fewer high-calorie, high-fat, high-salt restaurant meals, and driving less. While auto sales have fallen, sales of bicycles are up. As a result of reduced driving, traffic fatalities fell by nearly a quarter from 2007 to 2009. Less driving and reduced industrial output have also meant a drop in air pollution, reducing children's asthma deaths and improving overall respiratory health.[32] It's too early to tell whether these trends will continue if economic insecurity worsens further, but the preliminary findings are surprisingly positive for many Americans.

Interestingly, epidemiological studies show that health has improved in all recessions since the Great Depression. The positive impact of recessions on health is not nearly so dramatic in countries that already have shorter working hours and a stronger social safety net. But neither does their citizens' health suffer as much during economic expansions.[33]

This is not an argument for unemployment, but these findings raise a question: How can we return to full employment while not losing the health benefits that the recession has brought us? Here, the answer is clear: We should find ways to reduce working hours, share existing work, and trade productivity gains for free time instead of more production, even if it means that incomes will rise more slowly or not at all. There are many ways to do this; some will be explored later in this book.

What Else Can We Do to Improve Our Health?

Right now, our house of health has a foundation that is marble for the rich, rotting wood for the middle, and dirt for the poor. It has four walls that are a mixture of teak, balsa wood, and bamboo, all of them in sorry shape. And finally, it has a golden roof with millions of holes.

It is not enough to talk of making the roof all gold and eliminating the holes, though the health care bill helped in that regard. We need to eliminate the gold as well, taking the profit motive and costly complexity from the system and expanding a program like Medicare to cover everyone, potentially at less cost.

In 2002, John was hit by a motorcycle in Rome and quickly whisked away in a tiny (and we do mean tiny) ambulance to the polyclinic, where he received quick and efficient care. "The bad news from the X-rays is that your ribs are broken," the nurse informed him, "and we can't do much about that except tape you up and give you some pain killers." Before leaving the clinic, John asked what he needed to do about the bill. "No charge," the nurse said, smiling, "Italian hospitality." And, we might add (whispering the words, of course), "socialized medicine." When John returned home and went to his HMO to check things out, he was told that the Italians had done an excellent job and that he would be billed $300 from his HMO for that information.

So the roof does need to be fixed. *But fixing the roof is only a first step.* It's time for an extreme makeover. If we also pay attention to the foundation and the walls, we can ensure better outcomes at lower cost. We can:

- *Strengthen the foundation* by improving prenatal care and providing at least three months or more of *paid* leave to all parents of babies or very young children. We should make the Family and Medical Leave Act a paid provision and extend it to all workers. Early life lasts a lifetime.

- *Strengthen the wall of lifestyle* by encouraging healthy diets, teaching children the value of eating nutritious foods, eliminating subsidies to the purveyors of sugars and fats, and, especially, reducing working hours to give Americans more time for exercise, sleep, and healthy eating.

- *Strengthen the wall of stress relief* by reinstituting tax policies that narrow the gap between rich and poor, rebuilding our social safety net, and adopting policies like paid vacation time to give Americans periodic relief from the stress of hypercompetitive and long-hour workplaces. We must also provide more resources for the early identification and treatment of mental illnesses such as anxiety and depression.

- *Strengthen the wall of connection,* again by reducing working time, and by stimulating, through programs like national service, greater volunteer involvement with our neighbors and communities. Design of communities matters here too; our sprawling suburbs encourage disconnection, while urban village designs with smaller home sizes but more public space, from coffeehouses to car-free shopping districts, encourage it.

- *Strengthen the wall of safety* by improving OSHA and other protections for workers, building more pedestrian- and bicycle-friendly cities, and regaining the environmental zeal of the early 1970s, which led to much cleaner water and air for all Americans. Pass legislation—now in place only in San Francisco, Washington, D.C., and Milwaukee—that would require the provision of paid sick days. The late Senator Edward Kennedy's proposed Healthy Families Act would do this.

Most of these policies and provisions are taken for granted in other nations. Any or all of them will make the United States healthier, and almost certainly at *less* cost than our current system. Improving our health outcomes is less a matter of better science and more money than one of political will and *an ability to see the connections between things*.

How will our extreme health makeover affect the economy? Business leaders variously support and oppose these policies. In any case, most of the costs of such changes should not fall on business but be borne more generally by all of us. Fox News pundits will no doubt suggest that these reforms will cost too much and make us less competitive. But the cost of poor health is, and will continue to be, far greater than the price tag for such reforms. In their book, *Raising the Global Floor*, Jody Heymann and Alison Earle show clearly that the policies we recommend here do not make countries less competitive, nor do they increase unemployment rates. One thing more than any other makes it hard for American businesses to compete: the escalating cost of health care. Health care payments make producing an automobile far more expensive in the United States than in Canada, for example. Our failing health care system is actually making us less competitive.

Rules Matter

When it comes to health, rules matter more than sermons. Our most significant health gains have come when we required clean air, pure water, and safe food. Vaccination requirements and quarantines made an important difference in preventing epidemics. Cigarette and alcohol consumption declined when high taxes made the choice of such products less tempting. Seat belts, car seats, required safety improvements in auto structural design and road engineering all helped lower the number of traffic fatalities.

Whatever the health problems we Americans face, our health and our life expectancy today are now better than they were in our parents' or grandparents' time. But there are troubling signs. For example, childhood obesity has become a serious problem. Many doctors predict that the life expectancy of today's children will be shorter than that of their parents, reversing decades of progress. In light of this, the elimination of physical education (or in some cases, even recess!) in many American schools can be seen as misguided, if not criminally insane.

But what should truly concern us is that right after World War II, Americans were among the very healthiest people on Earth. Though our health has improved since then, more than forty other nations caught up to us and passed us. In fact, America is now far behind most of those countries. For nearly every measurable health outcome, the United States ranks *near the bottom* among the world's rich countries and below even some of the poor ones. This is only partly the result of our health care system. It is more the result of economic policies that have encouraged overwork, underconnection, poor diets, hazardous working conditions, and hell on the highway.

When it comes to health, it can hardly be argued that the American economy is promoting the greatest good for the greatest number or the longest run for any of us.

Doesn't it make you want to pop a pill? Instead, let's work for policy reforms that not only will improve our health but can actually make our businesses more competitive, not less.

CHAPTER 5

Risky Business

No man is an island, entire of itself.

—JOHN DONNE

Consider the full-page ad for Harley-Davidson motorcycles that ran in *USA Today* on August 27, 2009. IT'S A FREE COUNTRY, the headline proclaimed, BUT HAVE YOU FELT LIKE THAT LATELY? Then, in smaller print, but still in caps: IS IT STARTING TO FEEL CLAUSTROPHOBIC INSIDE THE SAFETY NET? It seemed to us like a strange ad to place at a time when the economy was reeling and polls showed Americans were feeling very insecure indeed. But in its own way, it beautifully summarized a dominant American idea: *freedom trumps security.*

Yet much evidence suggests that a sense of security actually *provides the foundation* for risk-taking, freedom, and individualism, much as discipline, patience, and knowledge of music fundamentals provide the basis for free-wheeling jazz. Happiness polls have found that in countries like Denmark, where the safety net is tightly woven, respondents are most likely to say that they feel "free to do the things I want to do."[1] Sure, it's possible to go too far and remove too much of the risk and adventure from life. No doubt that was the case in the former Soviet Union. But that's hardly the case in this economy, where the safety net has been getting weaker for the past thirty years.

Somewhere in the middle of his long reign, George W. Bush offered a glimpse of his vision for our future. Bush called it *the Ownership Society*.[2] In his view, John Donne was wrong, and probably a wimp. Indeed,

Bush declared in effect, "*Every* man *is* an island, fully responsible for himself." Every American, Bush made clear, should provide for his or her own social security, health care, retirement plans, and a host of other forms of insurance. Americans were told to say good-bye to the concept of social insurance and pooled risk, to the idea that they are all in this together.

Bush might have called it the *You're on Your Ownership Society*. But this idea didn't originate with him. It was the culmination of a generation of policies directed at stripping Americans of security guarantees they had become accustomed to since the New Deal.

"You know how to spend your money better than government does," said Bush.[3] Clever phrase; countless heads must have bobbed in affirmation. But when it comes to economic security, it's not as easy as it sounds.

Social Insurance: Buying in Bulk

The problem with on-your-ownership is a thing called a *risk pool*. Consider health care: When a government program like Medicare insures millions, prices can be kept low because actuaries know that only a small portion of the pool members will require hugely expensive treatment. But as a lone individual, solely responsible for your health care, you can't buy into a big risk pool like that.

You can buy into a smaller risk pool—a private health insurance plan. But because of their smaller size, private insurance providers and medical institutions must protect themselves against the calamity of too many of their claimants suddenly needing costly care. To cover this possibility, they jack up prices. If big costs occur, they are ready; if not, they make enormous profits. It's a win-win for them, but not for you. In cases like this, government *can* spend your money for you more efficiently.

Every red-blooded Costco shopper knows the value of *buying in bulk*; in effect, that's what government does when it comes to health care. Moreover, a big insurer like the government has the clout to negotiate prices, and you don't. That's why other countries with universal health care can cover everyone at much less cost and with consistently better outcomes.

Being insured against the vicissitudes of life is an important stress reliever and contributes mightily to happiness. When we asked random individuals about what the good life means to them, one young college student responded quickly: "Everything stable, nothing burning down financially," she said.

Indeed, security is an essential component of *the greatest good*. An economy designed to make people happy should make people feel *more* secure, financially and otherwise, over time. Ours does not.

Children at Risk

For too many Americans, insecurity starts in childhood.

A startling report, *Homeland Insecurity*, by the Every Child Matters Education Fund,[4] pointed out that as of 2007 (before the current recession made things even worse), 8 million American children were without health insurance, nearly 2 million had parents in prison, and 13 million lived in poverty. More than 3 million were abused and neglected each year. The United States' child abuse death rate is the highest among rich countries, three times as high as Canada's and *eleven* times as high as Italy's. According to the report, the effects of child abuse cost American taxpayers more than $100 billion annually.

The report suggests that American children don't share "homeland insecurity" equally. Ailis Aaron Wolf, analyzing the report in the *Boston Edge*, writes,

> Living in a "red" state appears to be more hazardous to the health of millions of American children . . . The factors weighed in the "Homeland Insecurity" ranking include such diverse indicators as inadequate pre-natal care, lack of health care insurance coverage, early death, child abuse, hunger and teen incarceration. Based on a diverse range of eleven child-related statistical measures, nine of the ten top states with the best outcomes for children today are "blue" states.[5]

Those states included Wisconsin, Iowa, New Jersey, Washington, Minnesota, Massachusetts, Connecticut, Vermont, and top-ranked New Hampshire, with Nebraska being the sole "red" state in the group.

Blue states were defined as those that voted Democratic in the 2004 presidential election, while *red states* voted Republican. All ten of the states with the worst outcomes were "red" states: Wyoming, Georgia, Arkansas, Alabama, South Carolina, Texas, Oklahoma, New Mexico, Louisiana, and, in last place, Mississippi.

According to Michael R. Petit, the former commissioner of Maine's Department of Human Services and lead author of *Homeland Insecurity*:

> The bottom line here is that where a child lives can be a major factor in that youth's ability to survive and thrive in America. The reason why this is the case is no mystery: "Blue" states tend to tax themselves at significantly higher levels, which makes it possible to reach more children and families with beneficial health, social and education programs. "Red" states overwhelmingly are home to decades-long adherence to anti-government and anti-tax ideology that often runs directly contrary to the needs of healthy children and stable families.[6]

"Blue" states also tend (with significant "red" exceptions, such as egalitarian Utah and the Dakotas) to have much smaller gaps between rich and poor, a subject we return to in chapter 7. They generally score higher in such key measurements of quality of life as life expectancy, educational levels, and freedom from violent crime, often approaching and sometimes even surpassing western European levels of success.

Risk Shifting

But America's risks don't end in childhood. In fact, the United States today is a far less secure place economically than it was a generation ago, thanks to what the Yale political scientist Jacob Hacker calls "the great risk shift."[7] Hacker points out that "over the past generation, the economic *instability* of American families has actually risen much faster than economic *inequality*" (italics his).[8]

Where the laissez-faire economist Milton Friedman once claimed that cutting back government left Americans "free to choose," Hacker contends that they have become *free to lose* instead, as a result of "a political drive to shift a growing amount of economic risk from government and the corporate sector onto ordinary Americans in the name of enhanced individual responsibility and control."[9]

Here are some of Hacker's gleanings from government data.

- Personal bankruptcies rose from less than three hundred thousand per year in 1980 to more than 2 million in 2005. (Half of the bankruptcies result from medical bills as companies cut back on health insurance.)[10]

- During the same period, mortgage foreclosure rates *quintupled*. (They are even higher now after the 2008 crash.)[11]

- Eighty-three percent of medium and large employers offered *defined benefit plans* in 1980. "Today," Hacker points out "the share is below a third." Defined benefits, such as pensions, provide a guaranteed level of payment when eligibility begins, as opposed to *defined contribution plans* which may be lost in the stock market. Defined benefits are inherently less risky for the recipients. (We provide more details on benefit plans later in this chapter.)[12]

- By 2005, the number of Americans worried about losing their jobs was triple what it was in 1980. (Sadly, many were right and lost their jobs in 2008.)[13]

- In 1970, only 7 percent of American families saw their income fall by more than 50 percent due to layoffs or other factors. Thirty years later, the figure was 17 percent.[14]

These last points are particularly significant. Losing something brings greater long-term reduction in happiness than gaining something adds to happiness. In general, people understand this and are "risk averse." According to a George Washington University survey, Americans are not exceptional in this respect: By a margin of more than two to one, they favor stability of income over risky opportunities to make more.[15] Yet despite such preferences, there has been a constant push to increase the economic risks of ordinary Americans in return for a shot at the golden basket. The result is a few big winners, but a multitude of losers, or at least people whose fortunes are ever more precarious.

Does Security Mean Greater Unemployment?

In general, the social safety net for working people is tighter in the capitalist democracies of western Europe than in the United States, where a tuna might easily slip through. Rates of poverty are lower by about half; the rich-poor gap is far smaller (more on this topic in chapter 7); all Europeans in every country are covered by national health insurance; retirement pensions are more available, more secure, and more generous; and unemployment and welfare benefits usually extend for longer periods. Europeans call their more generous welfare approach *the social contract*.[16]

Since the 2008 recession began, American and European unemployment levels have been similar, though levels in Europe generally have not risen as much as in the United States. In Germany, they actually *fell*. But before that, *official* unemployment levels in western Europe were higher than in the United States, especially in the larger countries. American conservatives charged that the social contract and more rigid rules protecting labor rights were responsible for the earlier gap and that greater job security here would actually lead to more unemployment as in Europe. But even before the crash, this argument was flawed; U.S. unemployment figures were systematically underreported.

Since early in the Clinton administration, the official unemployment rate in the United States has not included those workers who give up looking for a job. Even earlier, in the 1980s, an underclass of Americans, with few skills or opportunities for employment and without support from the welfare system, turned to illegal activities such as the sale of drugs. Many of them are now behind bars and also not counted in the unemployment figures. Counting those who have given up looking for work, and our prison population, would actually have added at least two points to the official unemployment rate, bringing it roughly to European levels even before the recession.

In their book, *Raising the Global Floor*, Jody Heymann and Alison Earle examine the impacts of generous social benefits for workers on unemployment rates.[17] Comparing the world's richest countries, they find no correlation between stronger safety nets and greater unemployment. It is true, as some conservatives argue, that in several European countries, especially Germany and France, rigid labor rules make it hard to fire or lay off workers. In such cases, employers may be more reluctant to hire. But it's not impossible to provide greater security for workers *and* flexibility for businesses under the social contract model.

Here, the world's happiest country points the way forward. The Little Mermaid in Copenhagen harbor knows a secret or two.

Prison Population Rates
per 100,000

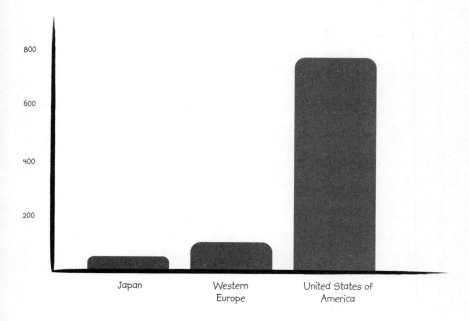

Flexicurity

Since as far back as 1899, the Danish government has provided generous benefits to its workers. But by the 1970s, high wages had made Denmark uncompetitive in foreign markets and led to balance-of-trade deficits and inflationary pressures. Yet austerity programs to cut wage demands and increase savings met strong public opposition, including repeated strikes and the frequent collapse of ruling coalition governments. High unemployment and harsh economic conditions followed, exacerbated by the 1970s energy crisis. Danish unemployment continued to rise, and Danish businesspeople complained of difficulties in remaining globally competitive until 1994, when the Danes first introduced their *flexicurity* model for the labor force.

Today, Denmark has one of the most competitive economies in Europe and one of the lowest unemployment rates in the world, while guarding and even improving its strong safety nets. In 2009, the European Council reported that "flexicurity is an important means to modernize and foster the adapability of labor markets."

The Danish concept of *flexicurity* rests on three legs.

1. *Flexibility in the labor market.* Danish businesses are given great leeway in hiring and firing workers. Regulations for starting businesses are relaxed. In 2008, the conservative *Forbes* magazine ranked Denmark as the number one country in the world for business. The equally conservative Heritage Foundation ranked it ninth, just below the United States, with this comment: "The non-salary cost of employing a worker is low, and dismissing an employee is relatively easy and inexpensive."

2. *A strong social safety net.* Though it's not hard for businesses to lay off or fire workers in Denmark, dismissed employees enjoy excellent benefits during periods of unemployment. They can be covered by unemployment benefits nearly equal to their previous salaries for two years or more. During this period, they receive thorough assistance in finding new work. After that, if they cannot find a job, they are offered one by the government. They must take it or lose their benefits. But such make-work jobs are rarely needed; most Danes find regular reemployment long before benefits run out.

3. *Lifelong training.* During periods of unemployment, Danish workers receive extensive training in new skills to make sure they are employable and to prepare them for technological changes in the economy.[18]

Thus flexicurity provides relief to employers from rigid labor rules and, at the same time, supplies income security, job-finding assistance, and useful education for employees. All of this does not come cheaply, however; the Danes pay among the highest taxes in the world, and of all rich countries, the percentage of GDP produced by the public sector is highest in Denmark. On the other hand, wages in Denmark are very high, with even the lowest-paid workers earning the equivalent of about twenty U.S. dollars per hour in 2010.[19]

Trust

With Denmark's high degree of social solidarity, reflected in its strong social contract and support for working families, Danes, along with citizens of other Nordic countries (Sweden, Finland, Norway, and Iceland), are among the most likely people on Earth to trust their fellow citizens. The sense that "most people can be trusted" enormously increases personal feelings of security.

The focus on equality in Nordic countries discourages status and consumer competition and encourages concern for community well-being. As a Republican state senator once told John, she discovered during a trip to Norway the feeling that "everybody isn't trying to get filthy rich." The Nordic "we're all in this together" ethic leads to a high valuation of honesty and sharing. Nordic countries understand the importance of both trust and generosity in improving levels of happiness.

Research shows the Nordics have good reason for their high levels of trust. Wallets filled with money left deliberately on streets in Nordic countries are more likely to be returned intact than anywhere else in the world, and residents know this. In surveys, they are more likely to say they expect their wallets and money to be returned than people elsewhere, about twice as likely as Americans, for example.[20]

But if trust and generosity are important contributors to happiness, unemployment most assuredly is not. Happiness researchers find that the loss of a job hurts far more than the drop in income alone. Productive work, with reasonable work hours, contributes greatly to self-esteem. That esteem takes a big hit when a job is lost. Not even the Danes can prevent job losses, but they view unemployment as an economic and social, rather than personal, failing. The social support and educational opportunities the Danes provide to their unemployed help to strengthen laid-off workers' sense of self-worth and minimize the blow to personal well-being.

Work-sharing or Kurzarbeit

Yet policies like those in Denmark are not as effective in maintaining well-being as programs that actually prevent the job losses in the first place. Perhaps the most successful strategy, especially in recessionary times, is the idea of work-sharing. In his inaugural addresss, President Obama congratulated workers who freely chose shorter hours and lower pay in order to prevent fellow workers from being laid off during the recession. But words are one thing and actions another. Obama might have done more by actively promoting a policy initiative pioneered in Germany.

The economist Dean Baker, director of the Center for Economic and Policy Research, argues that any further economic stimuli to reduce unemployment should include *Kurzarbeit*, or "short work," a German policy that encourages employers to reduce hours rather than lay workers off when times are tight, by making unemployment funds available even when workers do not lose their jobs.[21] Instead of cutting 20 percent of its workforce, a German company might reduce each worker's load by a day. Unemployment benefits kick in for the reduced work-time, so workers earn roughly 90 percent of their former incomes for 80 percent of the work.

Other countries have followed suit, and a bill sponsored by Democratic senator Jack Reed of Rhode Island and Democratic representative Rosa DeLauro of Connecticut would allow federal unemployment benefits to be used to top off salaries of reduced-hour workers in the United States. (Some seventeen states already allow this with their own unemployment dollars but cannot use federal unemployment funds to support such policies.) The business Web site 24/7 Wall St. ranked the idea number two in a recent editorial, "The Ten Things the Government Could Do to Cut Unemployment In Half."[22]

When the bill was discussed in Congressman Barney Frank's House Financial Services Committee, Dean Baker testified in favor—no surprise since he's a liberal—but so did Kevin Hassett, an economist with the conservative American Enterprise Institute. Hassett pointed out that even though the German economy tanked like ours did in 2008, Germany's unemployment rate didn't rise—thanks to *Kurzarbeit*. The law allows companies to retain workers instead of having to rehire later, he said. It's good for them, good for the workers, and doesn't really cost any more than traditional unemployment payments. It's a win, win, win. Nonetheless, not a single Republican has supported the Reed/DeLauro bill and not all Democrats do either, so it remains in limbo.[23]

Good-bye Golden Years

As noted earlier, we Americans aren't living as long as we could. However, we are living longer than we used to. Currently, we can expect ten years of retirement or more. But the security of that retirement is increasingly under threat.

In 2010, Social Security, perhaps the most popular of all government programs, celebrated its seventy-fifth anniversary. Most Americans can still expect to receive Social Security when they retire, but that money only goes so far, making up 30–40 percent of the income lost upon retirement. Retirees have had to supplement their Social Security with private pensions.

After World War II, most companies and government agencies began putting people on pension plans, deducting a small amount from their salaries to ensure a *defined benefit* payment after retirement. As with Social Security, working Americans had a good idea of how much they'd receive from their pensions.

In 1974, Republican senator Jacob Javits introduced the Employee Retirement Income Security Act. Its passage insured privately financed defined benefit plans and guaranteed that workers would receive their full pensions when they retired. ERISA was a law workers could applaud. With it, they felt far more secure. Only a generation ago, 80 percent of Americans could count on defined benefit plans to provide for them in old age. Today, less than one third of workers are covered by such plans.[24]

More of them now have 401(k) plans, which make *defined contributions* into pension plans that are invested in the stock market and rise and fall with it. An early hallmark of the Ownership Society, such plans were lauded as giving workers more control over their retirement and more opportunity to strike it rich as the stock market climbed in value.

But, as Jacob Hacker points, out, the plans were "dirt cheap" for employers, whose contributions to them were cut drastically from what they had been under the defined benefit plans. And the plans were risky. Sometimes, as in the case of Enron and WorldCom, the money was invested in the company's own stock. When these companies went belly up, workers saw near total losses of their pension savings. Hacker tells of one WorldCom employee who built up almost $1 million in his 401(k). After WorldCom's bankruptcy, precipitated by the illegal activities of its CEO, the employee received a final retirement check for $767.14![25]

Worse yet, as defined contribution plans became the rage, fewer companies offered any pension plans at all. And cutbacks in Social Security benefits actually resulted in an 11 percent *drop* in retirement wealth for the median family between 1983 and 1998, a time when the stock market was soaring.[26] During the same period, the American personal savings rate fell from more than 10 percent of take-home incomes to less than 4 percent. Today, at least 60 percent of American families feel unprepared for retirement. Millions more are overly optimistic about their own retirement prospects, not accurately estimating the amount of money they'll need when they stop working.

Michael Pennock, the statistician from the Vancouver Island Health Authority who developed Bhutan's happiness survey, recently returned to Canada from a visit to the Oregon coast. "It's just amazing for us Canadians to see the number of senior citizens, some of them very old, who are working as clerks at Walmart or McDonald's or other stores in the United States. You don't see that here in Canada. People that age have pensions to provide for them."[27]

Despite all this, when President George W. Bush announced his plans for the Ownership Society in 2004, a key plank was the privatization of Social Security. Conservatives claimed the Social Security system was near financial collapse, even though it was running a surplus that Republicans wanted to draw from to finance new tax cuts. Bush advocated shifting Social Security contributions into 401(k)s. Fortunately, public opposition stopped the idea in its tracks. We can only imagine what the retirement situation would look like for millions of Americans had their Social Security contributions evaporated in the stock market crash of 2008. But that hasn't stopped the Right from continuing to advocate privatization.

Social Security Plus

Steven Hill, the author of *Europe's Promise*, suggests an alternative that in our opinion would do far more to enhance the greatest good for the greatest number over the longest run. He believes that because defined benefit pensions are disappearing and other sources of savings such as home values and stock ownership have proven notoriously unstable, we must actually *strengthen* Social Security so that it pays *more*, not less, as many budget cutters have advocated.[28]

Hill says we should double Social Security benefits from about one third of annual income upon retirement to about two thirds, or roughly the European benefit level. He points out that 40 percent of Americans depend on Social Security for 84 percent of their retirement income. Even the top 40 to 20 percent of income earners depend on Social Security for a majority of their retirement income. Only the richest 20 percent can get along without it.

Hill's idea—he calls it *Social Security Plus*—would cost $650 billion a year, not chump change. Some revisions would be needed to keep Social Security performing effectively and securely in the black, while expanding its payout. The most obvious is to *lift the cap on required contributions.* Currently, Americans only pay Social Security taxes on up to $106,000 of their earnings, and none at all on income derived from interest and dividends. Collecting the Social Security tax on all incomes would bring in about $377 billion a year in added revenue and make possible improved Social Security payouts while helping ensure the system's health for many more years.

Moreover, Hill points out that if Social Security payouts were roughly doubled, those employers who do provide pensions would no longer need to do so. Currently, corporations receive $126 billion a year in tax deductions for these provisions, money that could go into the Social Security system. He also suggests eliminating some other tax deductions that overwhelmingly benefit wealthier taxpayers. Together, Hill says, "these three revenue streams would raise 100 percent of the revenue needed for doubling the payout of Social Security Plus."

Hill believes his plan would be fairer and more secure while making retirement benefits fully portable and eliminating a benefit provision that actually does make American companies less competitive. We agree.

Winding Down Work, Winding Up Retirement

Typically, Europeans retire earlier than Americans do, and on a much larger percentage of their previous salaries—about 67 percent, according to the OECD. Indeed, their situation is so generous that it has become too costly even for the European welfare states, some of which must provide five or ten more years of retirement benefits for workers than we do, since their citizens retire earlier and die later. Moreover, in Europe, even more than in the United States, an ever-larger group of seniors means greater demands on a smaller population of younger workers. So efforts to reduce pensions and increase the retirement age are at the top of the conservative agenda in Europe and have been passed in Germany and the Netherlands, though not yet in France, where thousands filled the streets to protest a raise in the retirement age from sixty to sixty-two.

But in our view, an economy concerned with the greatest good over the longest run would consider more creative solutions to this dilemma. Surely, the most reasonable is *phased retirement*. Instead of having workers fully retire at sixty or sixty-five or seventy, we should encourage them to retire in stages, with a larger portion of their retirement benefits kicking in at each stage.

They might first reduce work by one day a week, then in a couple of years, by two days a week, and so forth. Or their vacations might be lengthened—to two months, four months, six months, and so on. With workers in all countries living longer and in many cases staying fit longer into their lives, there is no reason they should be completely retired so early. Initially, this might cause some workflow confusion, so it will require some advance planning, but many companies and universities have found ways to do this effectively.

Partial retirement allows workers to stay attached to what is meaningful in their jobs and to the co-workers who are often their best friends. It allows room to be opened for younger workers to enter the company and the opportunity for older workers to mentor them. It allows older workers to find more time for exercise at an age when they need it most and to make new friends and find new hobbies outside the workplace. It can reduce financial pressures on the retirement system, be it Social Security or other pensions.

It is not for everyone—some workers can't wait to leave their workplaces completely, especially those "used up" by hard labor. But such an idea has wide appeal, and many businesses and institutions such as universities already take advantage of it. Targeted government incentives, including changes in tax policy and Social Security take-up rules, could spur greater use of phased retirement.

Incarceration Nation

Here's some good news on the security front. Rates of crime in the United States have mostly been falling over the past generation, despite what chronic television news viewers believe. Indeed, some crimes of theft, such as pickpocketing, are more common in European cities than here.

On the other hand, rates of violent crime in America are among the highest in industrial countries, and the United States has the dubious distinction of leading the murder-per-capita pack by plenty. Indeed,

Americans are about *five times* as likely to be murdered as residents of other rich countries.[29]

Availability of guns and a different cultural attitude toward their use may have something to do with the mayhem we're subjected to. So passionate are some about their guns (and so beholden are their politicians to the National Rifle Association), that we watched with a yawn while Oklahoma senator Tom Coburn attached a rider to a recent credit card oversight bill overturning nearly a century of law and allowing visitors to our national parks to carry loaded and concealed weapons, an idea considered crazy by almost everyone who works for the National Park Service, including Fran Mainella, former director of the NPS under George W. Bush.[30]

By contrast, the same Congress still feels no need to mandate any paid vacation time so Americans can actually *visit* their parks. (More on this in chapter 6.)

One answer to the murder rate, say conservatives, is the death penalty. On June 17, 2010, the state of Utah shocked the Western world when it executed a prisoner by *firing squad*. Texas, whose license plates might well read THE DEATH PENALTY STATE, has lethally injected 460 alleged murderers since 1982. The United States is alone among industrial countries in using the death penalty. But the results, as alluded to above, are less than stellar. Threat of death is no deterrent: Murder rates in America are actually *highest* in death penalty states.[31]

The decline in overall crime in the United States comes in part from a change in demographics: fewer Americans are in the age bracket most likely to commit crimes. But to be fair to the conservatives, it may also stem from the fact that we've locked so many people up.

"Never in the civilized world have so many been locked up for so little," reports the *Economist* magazine. Home to about a quarter of all the world's prisoners, the United States now holds 2.3 million people behind bars, more than half of them nonviolent offenders. The "war on drugs" and a flurry of "three strikes and you're out" legislation have resulted in a 500 percent increase in the prison population in the last three decades.[32] According to the *Homeland Insecurity* report: "Imprisonment has become a costly and ineffectual substitute for addressing substance abuse, poverty, mental illness, and educational failure. It also jeopardizes the life chances of millions of children who have a parent in prison."[33]

The United States locks up people at twelve times the Japanese rate, nine times the German rate, and about seven times the European rate overall, with about 750 prisoners per 100,000 Americans.[34] Free meals, free rent, free health care. It would be cheaper to put them all through college. Black males account for 44 percent of all U.S. prisoners, despite making up only 6 percent of our population. They wind up in prisons four times more often than black males did during the height of South Africa's apartheid regime.[35]

By contrast, many European countries have actually been shedding prisoners in recent years. France has fewer than it did in 1980, and in the Netherlands, the number of prisoners has fallen so fast, the Dutch had to close eight prisons and would have had to close more if they didn't import a few prisoners from Belgium. Forty percent of criminal trials in the Netherlands end up with community service rather than jail.[36]

The upside to the American "lock 'em up" approach is that some communities now *survive* on their prisons and spending for incarceration boosts the GDP significantly. When John spoke a few years ago at Sam Houston State University in Huntsville, Texas (population 35,000), he was surprised to find that the college employed nearly half the people in town, and Huntsville's eight (!) prisons—from minimum security to death row—employed most of the rest. The click of prison keys means the ka-ching of cash registers. In the upside-down world we inherit, more jails mean more GDP.

Global Security

For a couple of decades, especially during the 1980s, American insecurity centered on fear of domestic crime. It was almost an obsession, and politicians built careers on exploiting such fear. But ever since September 11, 2001, much of America's insecurity has been redirected toward fear of foreign terrorism. Increasingly, the world is a scary place—will Iran get the bomb; will the Taliban poison our water supply?

The United States' response to all of this is what you might call a Dirty Harry foreign policy. Americans will protect themselves through the use of overwhelming force, even, as they've discovered, against people who never harmed them in the first place. The United States has had troops in Iraq since 2003, and the war in Afghanistan is now the longest in U.S. history. Our nation has bases in dozens of other countries, including places like Okinawa, Japan, where the locals have long demanded that the Americans go home. All of these bases cost a bundle.

The current U.S. "defense" budget stands at nearly $700 billion a year (about the cost of Obama's stimulus package) and consumes over 20 percent of its total federal budget.[37] A portion of this money is actually spent for weapons even the Pentagon says it doesn't need. Direct costs for the Iraq and Afghan wars now exceed $1 trillion.

Ironically, many Republicans, who now recoil in terror at the prospect of deficit spending, never complained when Bush (and Reagan before him) massively increased war spending while slashing taxes for the rich, a one-two punch that produced the greatest deficit increases in American history. "Deficits don't matter," Vice President Dick Cheney said then. Now, apparently, they do. But advocating defense cuts to decrease the deficit is likely to get you called a traitor.

In his final speech as president, one such traitor, former general Dwight D. Eisenhower, warned us to beware the increasing power of the "military-industrial" complex and to consider that dollars spent on weapons came from the mouths of the hungry.[38] They still do.

A few years ago, John produced *Silent Killer*, a television documentary about ending world hunger. While researching the film, he learned that thirty thousand children die of hunger and hunger-related diseases every day, one every three seconds. This is a daily *holocaust*—ten September 11s *every day*. Experts say the hunger crisis could be ended *completely* for as little as $13 billion a year, less than what the U.S. military spends in one week.[39]

We know that generosity is an important contributor to happiness and that a world without poverty-stricken, desperate people, whose children die before the age of five, would be a safer world. A true national security policy would look to repairing a broken world where anger and resentment fester. It would transfer a significant portion of the dollars spent on bombs and guns to the provision of safe and adequate food, clean water, and the control of disease. It would seek the greatest good for the greatest number over the longest run.

For Americans ever to feel truly secure, they must build a world that is secure for all humans. But right now, as we have seen, it's not even secure for all Americans.

CHAPTER 6

The Time Squeeze

The nine-to-five is one of the greatest atrocities sprung upon mankind. You give your life away to a function that doesn't interest you. This situation so repelled me that I was driven to drink, starvation, and mad females, simply as an alternative.

—CHARLES BUKOWSKI

Consider the headline for a full-page story in the *New York Times* on July 31, 1910, more than one hundred years ago: HOW LONG SHOULD A MAN'S VACATION BE? PRESIDENT TAFT SAYS EVERY ONE SHOULD HAVE THREE MONTHS. We're not making this up. Three months! President Taft! A conservative Republican president best known for his appetite.[1]

"Two to three months vacation," Taft was quoted as saying, "are necessary in order to enable one to continue his work the next year with that energy and effectiveness which it ought to have." He suggested that men and women alike should have "a change of air where they can expand their lungs and get exercise in the open."

The article contained a subhead: WHAT BIG EMPLOYERS OF LABOR AND MEN OF AFFAIRS THINK ON THE SUBJECT. Leading industrialists and bankers of the day were asked their opinions regarding Taft's suggestion. Some actually thought it was a good idea. Not surprisingly, others thought it was crazy, but conceded that a month off wouldn't be a bad idea.

That was a century ago, when our economy was one tenth as productive as it is today. But woe awaits any modern American politician who advocates a month off each year (as in Europe), much less three. At least, that's what politicians think. Polls actually show fairly strong support for a paid vacation law in the United States—though most people think two to three weeks would be about right. But in our view, if our economy were really to serve the greatest good, a month off for everyone would be a no-brainer.

Why? Once we get past the basics—food, shelter, clothing, adequate health, and a sense of security and trust—what Abraham Maslow refers to as higher-level needs, or *metaneeds*, begin to assert themselves. Subsequent happiness increasingly depends on our ability to satisfy those needs. For Maslow, metaneeds include such nonmaterial needs as "belongingness," "esteem," and "self-actualization." Other needs researchers, including Manfred Max-Neef, challenge Maslow's view that needs assert themselves in a hierarchy of potency. But most happiness scholars agree that once basic security has been guaranteed, life satisfaction is derived primarily from the following, each related to the nine domains of happiness identified in chapter 2.

1. Social connection, including family and friends.
2. Value in the eyes of others, coming especially from productive contribution to the community.
3. Freedom to choose one's activities as much as possible.
4. Access to nature and beauty; what Maslow refers to as *aesthetic* needs.
5. Access to art and culture and a reasonable degree of "novelty."
6. Tolerance and appreciation of other cultures and lifeways.
7. The opportunity for creative expression: following one's "bliss."
8. Competence to care for oneself.
9. The opportunity to participate actively in the governance of society.

There is one common denominator for each of these contributors to happy lives.

Got Time?

A typical day for many Americans (especially those with children) now consists of rising earlier than a generation ago; rushing through or skipping breakfast; checking to see if any emergency e-mails or texts arrived during the night; urging the kids to get dressed for school or child care; dropping them off; commuting half an hour in heavy traffic to the workplace; dealing with the myriad extra demands of new "laborsaving" technology (e-mails, voice messages, texts); meeting ever-more-demanding deadlines with fewer staff; catching a twenty-five-minute lunch at one's desk while shopping online; mainlining coffee to keep from dozing in the afternoon; working later than expected, then fighting the still-snarled evening commute; picking little Jimmy up after six at day care (and paying the fine); popping dinner into the microwave while checking the BlackBerry; wolfing dinner down; fixing a plugged toilet; slumping in front of the television until it's time to put the kids to bed; dealing with an emergency phone call from a co-worker; checking last minute e-mails from work; and finally, stumbling into bed for six and a half hours fitful sleep.

Okay, you can breathe now. For many of us, it's like this five days a week, fifty weeks a year. At a minimum.

Aren't you exhausted just from thinking about it? No wonder Americans are 20 percent happier on weekends than on workdays! It's no wonder, either, that they've been reporting increasing levels of stress in recent years and that a quarter of them report feeling constantly rushed and another half often feel rushed, while barely a quarter report having time for all the things they want or need to do.

Life wasn't supposed to be this way.

John started the Take Back Your Time organization (www.timeday .org) because he still remembers a sociology class he took way back in the fall of 1968. Among the many social problems facing our country that year—the bloodiest of the Vietnam War, when American students were shutting down universities, when poor urban blacks were rioting, when both Martin Luther King Jr. and Bobby Kennedy were assassinated—was a surprising fear for the future.

A U.S. Senate subcommittee had predicted in 1965 that as a result of increasing labor productivity from automation and "cybernation"—the computer revolution we're all enveloped in today—Americans would be working only about twenty hours a week by the year 2000, while taking seven weeks or more of vacation a year. Even in the 1950s, newsreels showed the wonders of the laborsaving future: lawnmowers that figured out how to cut the grass so no one had to push them; miracle homes full of push-button appliances that saved Mom the inconvenience of baking a cake or even setting the table.[2]

We would, John's sociology professor explained, have more "leisure time on our hands than we'd know what to do with." John confesses that even then, it was a problem he thought he could deal with, a problem to look forward to. The "problem" gave birth to widespread efforts to help Americans figure out useful and enjoyable ways of using their leisure time besides watching television.

Overworked Americans

But "too much leisure time" turned out to be the problem that wasn't. By 1991, the sociologist Juliet Schor was arguing that the average American worker was putting in 163 hours *more* on the job per year than in 1973.[3] And since far more families had two parents working, the increase in working hours per family was much higher—500 to 700 hours more per year than in the 1970s.

Not everyone agreed with Schor's claims. Two prominent researchers, John Robinson and Geoffrey Godbey, using time diaries instead of Labor Department data, argued that Americans actually did have somewhat *more* leisure time than before, time they spent in front of the tube. But Godbey and Robinson agreed that Americans "felt" more pressed for time than before.[4]

Both Schor and Robinson/Godbey present strong evidence for their conflicting findings, and it's not necessary to decide who is most convincing. Some of the debate involves what we choose to call leisure and what activities we categorize as work. No one disputes that time spent preparing and consuming meals has been reduced, for example. If we define such activity as work, leisure time appears to grow. But in many families, cooking and eating together were times for socializing and strengthening bonds, and at the same time improving life satisfaction, a form of leisure in a way.

It should also be noted that increases in labor productivity are not "energy-free" advances for the workers whose productivity increases. In fact, the workers are required to get much more done and ever more quickly. Almost no studies have been conducted in this area, but we suspect they would find that working hours today are more mentally draining than in the past, while the hypercompetition of today's workplace makes them even more stressful.

Productivity for Whom?

Productivity, a hugely important term for economists, is itself a nebulous expression. Ironically, higher productivity now means that consumers perform a variety of pro bono tasks that companies once had to pay someone to take care of. We pump our own gas, make our own travel reservations, and use automated checkout lines at the grocery store. Productivity is said to have increased because the companies don't have to pay anyone to help us out anymore. Output per dollar spent by the companies goes up—that's what is defined as productivity by most economists. Automation can be a time saver—ATMs certainly are—but that's not necessarily the norm.

Often, we do the corporations' work for free, adding our free time to their bottom line. The total time spent doing the work doesn't really decline. Take automated operators, for example. For many of us, they are a time sink. Got a problem with your billing statement? Call the number on the statement. You're likely to go through something like this (forgive some exaggeration here to make the point):

First you hear irritating music. Then a recorded operator says: *Thank you for calling Consolidated Megacorporation, where we care only about you.* Yeah, sure, you think . . . *For English, press 1.*

You press 1. The operator continues: *Please enter your account number. If you wish to thank Consolidated Megacorporation for our awesome personalized service, press 1 . . . Press 2 . . . Press 3 . . . Press 6 . . . etc.* Your fingers are tapping on the table . . . *If you have a question about your billing statement, press 9.*

Relieved, you press 9. The operator returns: *Enter the last four digits of your social security number . . . Enter the last four digits of your maternal great-grandmother's social security number.*

Now, you're getting a bit frustrated.

You press hard on 0 several times. The operator scolds you: *You have pressed an incorrect key. To speak to one of our customer service representative, press 1.*

You pump your fist—"Yes!"—and press 1. *All of our representatives are serving other customers. Your call will be answered in approximately fifty-seven minutes. Do not hang up or you will lose your place in line.*

Sound familiar? Such demands on consumers' free time outside the workplace may mean it is insufficient for working hours to simply remain relatively constant; in light of these demands and the greater toll of speed-up on the energy of the workers, working hours need to be *reduced* simply to end the upsurge in workplace stress.

The American Way?

Why have American working hours been so stable in the past half century and even risen for many workers? For one hundred years, from the Civil War onward, hours had been falling, thanks in no small part to the demands of workers. As long ago as May 1, 1886, half a million of them filled the streets of America's major cities, demanding an eight-hour workday.[5]

On January 11, 1912, thousands of poor women speaking a babble of twenty-five immigrant languages left the textile mills of Lawrence, Massachusetts, to march in its icy streets, demanding an increase in pay of two cents an hour (from sixteen to eighteen cents) and a decrease in work hours of two per week (from fifty-six to fifty-four). Legend has it they carried banners reading: WE WANT BREAD AND ROSES TOO!

Bread (higher wages) and *roses* (shorter hours—time to smell the roses!) were the twin demands of the labor movement until after World War II, when the roses were left to wilt. The historian Benjamin Hunnicutt of the University of Iowa has shown clearly how important securing more leisure time was to the unions, and how labor leaders of the era made the case that shorter hours were needed so that workers could have the opportunity for cultural experiences, greater education, and the life of the mind.

By the 1920s, led by Jewish garment workers who wanted *their* Sabbath off too, unions had successfully won the two-day weekend. By the early 1930s, they were pushing for a thirty-hour official workweek as a job-sharing program to reduce unemployment during the Great Depression. They almost got it. On April 4, 1933, the U.S. Senate passed the Black-Connery Bill, establishing the thirty-hour week. But under pressure from the National Association of Manufacturers (NAM), President Franklin Roosevelt, an early supporter of the bill, got cold feet, and the bill was never approved by the House. In 1938, Americans got a forty-hour workweek instead, as part of the Fair Labor Standards Act.

While the National Association of Manufacturers opposed shorter hours in practice, it took credit for them in propaganda. A 1937 photo by the

famous Dorothea Lange shows a giant NAM-sponsored billboard on a
hardware store in California. The headline on the billboard reads: WORLD'S
SHORTEST WORKING HOURS: THERE'S NO WAY LIKE THE AMERICAN WAY!

Yet even without a law, many businesses adopted thirty-hour weeks
during the Depression. The Kellogg's cereal company was the most prominent, and its experiment was viewed by management and workers alike
as a huge success, until benefit packages after World War II made it
cheaper to hire fewer workers and require longer hours of them.[6]

After the war, interest in shorter work time waned in the United States,
even as a buffer against unemployment. Since federal jobs programs
helped lessen the impact of the Great Depression, and massive military
spending during World War II finally ended it, the ideas advanced by the
British economist John Maynard Keynes—countering recessions and unemployment by deficit spending on jobs programs—generally replaced
calls for sharing work during economic slowdowns (though Keynes himself, before he died in 1946, had become a staunch advocate of shorter
work time). The ascendant idea was to create jobs by promoting economic
growth, which would eventually produce new tax revenues and bring down
the deficits.

There were, however, momentary exceptions when political leaders once
again raised the possibility of shorter working hours. In 1956, Vice President Richard Nixon suggested that the time would come—and it was "not
too far distant"—when Americans would be working only four days a
week and "family life will be even more fully enjoyed by every American."[7]

During a recession in 1958, the AFL-CIO passed a resolution calling
again for job creation through shorter working hours: "The time has
come for wide-scale reduction in work hours so that more people may be
employed . . . We call upon Congress to take as rapidly as possible the
steps needed to amend the Fair Labor Standards Act to provide for a
7-hour day and a 35-hour week . . . The AFL-CIO also urges its affiliated
unions to press in collective bargaining for reduction in hours of work
with no reduction in take-home pay."[8]

Guns Instead of Hammocks

Nonetheless, not all labor leaders were cheering. Leon Keyserling, a
United Auto Workers consultant and former economic adviser to President Truman, was a strong opponent of shorter workweeks.

"Instead," writes William McGaughey, a coauthor with the late senator Eugene McCarthy of the book *Nonfinancial Economics: The Case for Shorter Hours of Work*, Keyserling "preferred increased military spending and production to meet the dual needs of a flourishing global economy and containing Soviet expansion." McGaughey's explanation of the connection between military spending and longer working hours is worth quoting at length.

> A National Security Council memorandum, NSC-68, written by State Department analyst Paul Nitze with Keyserling's help, argued that the United States could best achieve economic growth through an arms build-up to counter the Soviets. Preparations for war would produce a "growth dividend" so that the weapons program, he argued, would practically pay for itself . . .
>
> When the AFL-CIO Executive Committee announced in 1962 that a 35-hour workweek with no cut in pay would be its top priority in the 1963 bargaining sessions, representatives of the Kennedy administration announced their opposition . . .
>
> John Kennedy himself had said during the 1960 campaign: "In the face of the Communist challenge, a challenge of economic as well as military strength, we must meet today's problem of unemployment with greater production rather than by sharing the work."[9]

Besides the loss of enthusiasm for further shortening of hours, the postwar era, encouraged by the incessant messages of a new medium, commercial television, ushered in what came to be known as *the consumer society*. Expectations, for larger homes, cars, and shiny products, soared. Easier credit brought a cornucopia of stuff within easy reach of the middle class. At first, it seemed that Americans could have their bread, and roses too.

But by the mid-1970s, and especially after 1980, median wages weren't keeping pace with increases in America's capacity to produce. (We touched on this trend in the previous chapter, and explain it in greater detail in chapters 7 and 8.) Flattening incomes didn't derail the consumption train, however. Americans continued to buy more, in part by going deeper into debt, by having more members of the family enter the workforce, and by working more overtime. Juliet Schor refers to this phenomenon as the *work-spend cycle*.[10]

Indeed, debt made overtime hours, with their time-and-a-half-pay premium, a prize instead of a burden. Short on cash, many workers tried to grab all the overtime they could. In a twist of fate, a penalty that was supposed to keep working hours from expanding actually encouraged their expansion. By the boom times of the late 1990s, Americans were actually working more than the notoriously workaholic Japanese.

What Did the Other Guys Do?

The Europeans took a different path after the late 1960s. At that time, the average western European was still working a bit longer than his or her American counterpart. The Netherlands, for example, didn't end Saturday work until 1968. European technologies weren't as sophisticated. Some countries hadn't completely recovered from World War II damage. European hourly productivity lagged far behind that of Americans. The average western European workers produced only about two thirds as much in an hour of work. Consequently, they consumed far less as well; also about two thirds as much.

Fast-forward to 2005. During the intervening years, western European productivity per hour nearly caught up with America's. The hourly productivity of certain European countries even surpassed that of the United States in some years. And yet, despite prominent exceptions such as Norway and Luxembourg, western European per capita GDP, on average, is still only about two thirds as high as America's. So what gives? How is it that the Europeans caught up to Americans in hourly productivity but still lag so far behind in actual production and consumption? What in the world are they doing wrong?

Actually, we would argue that they've done something very right. Europeans, prodded by strong and active labor movements and social-democratic political parties, have taken a large chunk of their productivity gains in the form of more leisure time instead of putting all their apples into the barrel of increased GDP. They now work only 80 to 85 percent as many annual hours as Americans, and when you consider that fewer of them work and they retire earlier, the difference is even greater.

The nose-to-the-grindstone Brits average two hundred hours less paid labor each year than Americans do, while for the slacker Norwegians and Dutch the difference is twice as great. They put in ten to twelve full weeks less than Americans do each year. They've accepted their smaller houses and cars. In return, they've gotten six-week vacations, shorter workweeks, early retirements, and a host of other time-related benefits.

More Taxes, Anyone?

How did Europe turn out so differently? The Nobel laureate Edward Prescott of Arizona State University, a conservative, says taxes are almost the sole reason for the differences in hours worked. Those dumb Europeans, he suggests, have taxed themselves so much they discourage extra work—their taxes are a disincentive to long hours.[11] Prescott gives speeches in Europe, during which he tells the Europeans they should cut taxes so they can work more. Some German industrialists, who'd like to squeeze their workers as much as their American counterparts do, pay Prescott to preach his gospel. But most ordinary Germans laugh at this; they actually enjoy their free time. They like doing different things, not just the job they were trained for. It adds novelty to life and reduces boredom. And if not, they still get paid to visit the spas during their generous breaks.

The European disdain for attitudes like Prescott's was made plain to John when he participated in the *Economist* magazine's online debate in December 2009. The resolution: *This House believes that Europeans would be better off with fewer holidays and higher incomes.* John's opponent, the prominent Northwestern University economist Robert Gordon, took Prescott's position: Those long European holidays were depriving them of precious cash.

John opposed the motion, and so did the vast majority of readers who left comments on the site (www.economist.com/debate/overview/160). Most of the Europeans and at least half the Americans writing in were derisive of Gordon's position: Give up my holidays for a few extra euros? Are you nuts, man? John takes pride in having won the debate 79 to 21 percent, but he's just fooling himself. He could have written nonsense in Martian and won. People like vacations. They like time off.

So why did Europeans get this right while Americans didn't? No doubt Prescott is correct that taxes play a role. High burdens at the top mean long work hours don't bring the same monetary rewards they do in the States. But the more important reasons have to do with specific policies mandating time off or ensuring workers a choice between time and money.

The Netherlands Takes the Lead

A few years ago, John met with a University of Amsterdam professor who recounted a conversation with the manager of the Dutch division of an American company. The manager had come to the Netherlands from the United States two years earlier.

PROFESSOR: Do you notice a difference between the approach to work time and free time here compared to the United States?

MANAGER: Yes, it dawned on me my second week on the job. It was a Friday evening, eight o'clock, and we had an important shipment to get out on Monday. I called my assistant at home and told her to call some of the workers to get some things done on the weekend in preparation for the shipment.

PROFESSOR: And what did she say?

MANAGER: She said, "Excuse me, sir, but I don't work on weekends, and I don't expect to be called at home about work when I'm not working."

PROFESSOR: And what did you say?

MANAGER: I said, "Well, excuse me, but I'm the new manager here, and we're a company that competes in the global economy, and we have an important shipment to get out, and we appreciate employees who are team players." Then she said, "OK, I can do what you ask of me, but I have to remind you of a couple of things. First, under Dutch law you have to pay me double time for unscheduled, over-time work performed on the weekend. Now I could use the money and have no other big plans. But if I call these people, they'll just get mad at me for interrupting their family time, their sports, what-ever it is. Don't worry, we'll come in Monday, work hard, and get the job done."

PROFESSOR: So what was your response?

MANAGER: I said, "Oh, forget it, then!" And I hung up the phone in frustration and stewed all weekend.

PROFESSOR: And then what happened?

MANAGER: They came in Monday and got the job done. They work very hard when they're working, so everything was fine. And that's how it's been ever since. I've actually gotten to like it that way be-cause now even I have a life.

Less work, more life. It's a trade-off that many American workers might appreciate.

The Netherlands today, along with Norway and Germany, has the shortest working hours in the world. The average Dutch worker puts in less than 1,400 hours a year, compared with nearly 1,800 for Americans.[12] And yet the Dutch economy has been very productive. Unemployment in recent years has been much lower than in the United States, while the Netherlands boasts a positive trade balance and strong personal savings. Gallup ranks the Dutch fifth in the world in life satisfaction (2010), behind only the Nordic countries (excepting Iceland), and well ahead of Americans.

Dutch emphasis on free time dates to at least 1982, when Dutch employers and unions agreed to a landmark pact called the Wassenaar Agreement. The unions agreed to restrain wage growth to combat inflation in return for reductions in working hours and the expansion of part-time employment. The agreement ended the inflationary pressures of the 1970s, while greatly reducing unemployment. The International Labor Organization called it "a ground breaking agreement, setting the tone for later social pacts in many European countries."[13]

Wassenaar led to an economic turnaround that came to be called *the Dutch miracle*. Unemployment fell from 12 to 5 percent. The number of part-time workers increased sharply. The average workweek was cut by three hours. And the Dutch, while continuing to be the hard workers they'd always been, began to take leisure time just as seriously.

The Working Hours Adjustment Act

Since the Wassenaar Agreement, the Dutch have continued reducing time on the job through work-sharing policies. Ruud Lubbers, the former *conservative* prime minister of the Netherlands, explains why.

> It is true that the Dutch are not trying to maximize gross national product per capita. Rather, we are seeking to attain a high quality of life, a just participatory and sustainable society. While the Dutch economy is very efficient per working hour, the number of working hours per citizen are rather limited. We like it that way. Needless to say there is more room for all those important aspects of our lives that are not part of our jobs, for which we are not paid, and for which there is never enough time.[14]

Amen!

In 2000, the Dutch parliament passed the Working Hours Adjustment Act, perhaps the most important piece of time-balance legislation ever approved anywhere. The law requires that employers allow workers to cut their hours to part-time. Employers can refuse this only if they can demonstrate that such a reduction would cause serious financial hardship for the firm—something that happens in less than 5 percent of cases.[15]

Employees keep their jobs, opportunities for promotion, hourly pay (in any case, European law requires that part-time workers be paid the same hourly rate as full-timers doing the same work), health care, and prorated benefits such as sick leave, pensions, and vacation time. Employees are also allowed to increase working hours, though few choose this option. The law means a lot to working parents, who wish to reduce the combined stresses of working and caring for children.

Marius de Geus, a Leiden University professor, used the law to cut the number of his workdays from five a week to three. His salary was cut by 40 percent, and so were many of his benefits. But his health care, like that of all Dutch workers, is a universal entitlement and remained unchanged, except that his own monetary contribution to it was reduced in accord with his lower income. On top of that, his smaller salary put him in a lower bracket in the Netherlands' steeply progressive income tax system. He estimates that he takes home 70 percent of what he did before for 60 percent of the work. He told John he was delighted with his new situation and thankful for the law that made it possible.

Anmarie Widener, a health researcher and part-time instructor at Georgetown University, bubbles with enthusiasm as she discusses the Dutch devotion to time balance she witnessed while earning her Ph.D. at Leiden University. Her dissertation compares life satisfaction among Dutch and American parents.[16] Not surprisingly, she says, "My polling showed that in almost every area of life, Dutch parents are substantially more satisfied than their American counterparts."

And so are their children. A 2007 UNICEF study ranked children's welfare in the Netherlands as the highest in the world.[17] The United States was twentieth of twenty-one wealthy countries studied. Talking over dinner at her suburban home in McLean, Virginia, Widener says that she and her husband thought hard about staying in Leiden to raise their two children. They came back to the United States only to be closer to other family members.

On the other hand, Annette van der Feltz, who was born in Holland but now lives in New Jersey, says she remains in the United States because she likes the climate, the less formal culture, and the open space. Her Swedish husband has a good managerial job here, with benefits, so she can stay home as a full-time mom.

> However, I do some freelance work on the side, just to stay sane. If we were in Holland, I would work three days a week and my husband would work four days a week (at least all of my friends do). The days off are accepted and respected by co-workers. We would take vacations to other European countries twice a year. It sounds so ideal and we would not mind moving back, but we are very happy here (perhaps because we already have the European work ethic and refuse to work ourselves to death).
>
> But the U.S. work ethic should change. I worked for an airline—a ground staff position which required only a high school degree. I loved the job but had to quit because of the work-life balance; I was "punished" for taking time off to be with my son in the ER. I worked every single weekend and holiday for two years straight—no overtime or weekend compensation. I had three vacation days the first year, which were assigned to me. Meanwhile, my counterparts in the Netherlands scratched their heads and wondered how this was possible and why we accepted this.[18]

The Netherlands provides a clear example that you can have a thriving economy while working reasonable hours. One recent study, the Legatum Prosperity Index, ranked the Netherlands second in the world in "optimism about job availability" (the United States was eighty-sixth) and third in "satisfaction with standard of living" (America ranked twenty-eighth).[19]

Whose Freedom?

The Working Hours Adjustment Act is very popular (and Germany now has a similar law) and has led the Netherlands to the world's highest percentage of part-time workers. (With benefits and security, part-time work is not stigmatized as second-class work, as it is in the United States.) On the other hand, the Dutch have the lowest percentage of people in

Europe who overwork; less than 2 percent of them toil more than forty-eight hours a week, compared to more than 20 percent of Americans and 28 percent of Japanese.[20]

The act isn't perfect. The gender gap is still strong in the Netherlands, and Dutch feminists point out that by far the majority of part-time workers are female. And of course, some employers complain that the law creates scheduling stresses and other problems for their companies. But the law (passed with broad multiparty support) is very popular, and the Dutch economy is one of the most productive and competitive in the world.

In the United States' present ideological climate, such a law would be dead-on-arrival in Congress, though there is some hope of a "Right to Request" law like that in the United Kingdom, which guarantees that workers who ask to have their hours reduced cannot be fired for asking. But a policy like the one in the Netherlands would be seen by practically every legislator as an unwarranted restriction of the free market and the freedom of business owners.

A restriction it might be, but employers are far fewer in number than employees. So consider "the greatest good for the greatest number over the longest run." For hourly and salaried workers, who constitute some 90 percent of the U.S. workforce (the rest are business owners or self-employed), such an act offers an enormous *expansion* of real freedom to choose.

Think of what it would mean to you to be able to decide your own hours of work and shorten those hours if you wanted to, without losing your job, promotion opportunities, health care, and other benefits. Hundreds of thousands of Americans feel forced to stay in jobs they hate so as not to lose their employer-provided health care or other benefits. Many would accept less money in trade for more time, but they do not have the opportunity to make that choice.

In practical terms, there could scarcely be a law that offers more freedom to shape one's life according to personal ideas of happiness, or to determine one's own quality of life, than the Netherlands' Working Hours Adjustment Act. It offers real choice regarding what amounts to more than half the waking hours of average workers—time spent on the job or commuting, the two activities ranked lowest in studies of daily life satisfaction (see chapter 2).

Moreover, if it existed in the United States, such a law would offer that choice to 90 percent of the population, while restricting the freedom of only 10 percent (many of whom might actually find that the law, by making employees happier and healthier, actually boosts their own bottom line as well).

And finally, the law matters for "the longest run." It improves the prospects of each worker for having a longer run—that is, longer life expectancy. But more important, it leads the Dutch to simplify their lives in ways that are essential for long-term environmental quality. (In chapter 9 we'll show how precarious our environmental future actually is, and how American economic policies actually exacerbate impact on the planet.)

Trading Productivity for Time

Working fewer hours also produces tangible environmental benefits.

- Less need for convenience products. Fast food, for example, is in part a response to an increasingly pressured way of life. Highly packaged and processed foods and other products, including throw-away products, also appeal to those who feel time is at a premium.

- More time to reuse and recycle. Separating wastes into paper, plastics, metals, compost, or trash takes time. People often skip this activity if they are feeling rushed or overwhelmed.

- Time to make other behavioral choices, such as drying one's clothes on a clothesline rather than in a dryer. When pressed for time, "convenience" tends to take priority.

- Time to choose slower and more energy-friendly forms of transport, including walking, cycling, or public transit, rather than driving, and trains rather than planes.[21]

Moreover, reductions in work time translate into reductions in energy use, carbon output, and air pollution (as seen in the 2008 recession). A study conducted by the Center for Economic and Policy Research, a prominent Washington, D.C., think tank, concluded that if Americans were to reduce their working hours to European levels, they would almost automatically reduce their energy/carbon impacts by 20–30 percent.[22] Another, conducted by the Swedish researcher Jörgen Larsson at the University of Gothenburg, found that a 1 percent decrease in working hours results in a 0.89 percent drop in energy use and CO_2 output. Longer hours increased those impacts by a similar percentage.[23]

The Great Vacation Squeeze

Europeans have a multiplicity of ways to reduce work time, including such policies as mandated paid sick days and paid family leave, *Kurzarbeit*, offerings of sabbaticals to workers outside academia, phased retirement plans, and other ideas. But perhaps the single benefit that most improves their time balance is the fact that, by law, *every European worker gets at least four weeks of paid vacation time a year.* You can't join the European Union without guaranteeing this benefit to your workers, and even European nations that haven't joined the EU, like Switzerland and Norway, still mandate four weeks or more of paid time off.

In many European countries, the norm is more like five or six weeks, and it's not uncommon for workers in these countries to get two months off every year. France's famous thirty-five-hour workweek doesn't fix that limit for each week of work; what it requires is that a worker's average annual hours cannot exceed thirty-five per week. If they work longer, as John's French cousin, Bertrand Jacquier, does, they cut their overall average to thirty-five hours by taking more vacation time—Bertrand gets ten and a half weeks, all paid.

Back to reality. As John was writing this, he received a call from a woman named Olga who works in a furniture store. She told him that her company had just eliminated paid vacations for employees. "I couldn't believe they could do this, so I went to see what the law said. I found out there is no law. People here in USA have no rights to vacation at all. I came here from Ukraine, and there everyone gets two days paid vacation per month. People would be in the streets if they didn't get that, but here people don't even realize what they don't get. They just take it; they don't complain. Now I wonder why I ever came to America. It's just bullshit, that's all it is."[24]

The United States is one of only a handful of countries (the others are Guyana, Suriname, Nepal, and that paragon of human rights, Myanmar) that mandate no vacation time at all for workers.[25] As a consequence, paid vacation time in the United States has actually been declining in recent years. And since real wages have stagnated, many Americans can't afford to take unpaid time off.

Remember the two-week family vacation—the road trip with the kids fighting in the backseat until they got to Disneyland or a national park? The stuff memories were made of. Gone, the way of the dinosaurs! Only 14 percent of Americans took an actual two-week vacation in 2007. The median annual paid vacation time for Americans has now dropped to little more than one week, according to recent polls.

Twenty-nine percent of Americans got no paid vacation time at all in 2007, and that number has grown, especially during the current economic downturn. In Washington State, for example, 73 percent of businesses offered paid vacations in 2007; by 2008, that number had dropped to 63 percent, and it is still falling. Vacation time is becoming increasingly a privilege of the elite. Low-income workers are least likely to receive any paid time off.[26]

House Resolution 2564, the Paid Vacation Act of 2009 (sponsored in Congress by Democratic representative Alan Grayson of Florida, would mandate at least some paid vacation time for American workers. It's a very modest proposal: one week for workers in companies with over fifty employees; two weeks in companies with more than a hundred employees. It would be laughably inadequate almost anywhere else in the world, but in the United States, conservative bloggers excoriated it as wildly radical, threatening the end of Western civilization as we know it.

Yet modest as it is, the law would be an important first step toward "the greatest good for the greatest number over the longest run." To begin with, vacation time is essential for good health. Arnold Pallay, a cherubic and loquacious family physician from New Jersey, has been an active supporter of Grayson's bill. He always tells his patients just how important vacations are: "They have to get away. They come in and they're stressed out and they're bouncing off the walls and they need help, and I tell them that before they take a pill or get therapy they need to take a vacation. Many of them haven't had one in six years or more. I tell them, 'Take two weeks off and call me in the morning.' Usually it works."[27]

But Pallay's wife, Robin, says many of his poorer patients can't get any time off. "They have no paid vacation time, and they are working two or three jobs. They don't even have weekends off."[28]

Centennial Freedom

The Grayson Bill is history. Grayson was badly defeated in the 2010 election. One hundred years ago, President Taft would have signed a far more ambitious bill into law—though Congress never gave him one. But today's leaders are not yet enlightened (or gutsy) enough to advocate what most American corporate leaders thought reasonable then, much less what a conservative president championed. We have gone steadily backward.

Taft was actually a latecomer to the issue. It was John Muir, the prime advocate of our National Park System, who first advocated mandated vacation time for workers. As recounted in Donald Worster's biography of Muir, *A Passion for Nature*, he did so in 1876, when he called for "a law of rest" that would provide "Centennial Freedom" for all Americans, regardless of race, gender, or station in life.

"Compulsory education may be good," Muir wrote, but "compulsory recreation may be better." "We work too much and rest too little," he declared. "You cannot leave your business? Yes, but you will leave it. Killed by overwork, you will end up in the hearse of the jolly undertaker." Muir's solution was simple: "Set free the many urban slaves who are duty bound," Muir concluded. "Give every person enough leisure to go into nature."[29]

"Climb the mountains and get their good tidings," Muir wrote of his favorite haunt, Yosemite. "Nature's peace will flow into you and your cares will drop off like autumn leaves." He would be appalled if he knew that the average visitor to Yosemite now spends less than five hours there. Those who spend more are as likely to be European as American. Visitors dash through magnificent Yosemite Valley, oohing and aahing for a moment and snapping quick photos of its granite cliffs and shining waterfalls while trying to talk on their cell phones at the same time.

Time's Future

Driven by the insatiable demands of an economy that understands neither happiness nor limits, time in America grows increasingly scarce, leaving simple pleasures lost in the rush. By contrast, a friend of John's (a very conservative Republican legislator, actually) told him of a summer trip her family took to visit relatives in Norway. "Everybody left work at five. They had long dinners, time with family, walks in the woods, bike rides.

And the best part of it all," she recounted with a gleam in her eye, "is that everybody wasn't trying to get filthy rich!"

Some say that if Americans had more time, they'd simply spend it watching even more television. And perhaps they would, but probably only at first. For it's in countries where people work the longest (Japan, South Korea, the United States) that they spend the most time watching the tube. In short-work countries like the Netherlands and Norway, people have enough energy after work to make plans with friends and engage in more active and satisfying leisure. Think about it: When do you feel most like flopping on the couch and flipping between channels, when you're exhausted or when you feel refreshed?

Time for life may be the greatest difference between the social-democratic, softer capitalisms of Europe and the turbocharged market fundamentalist laissez-faire American model. Surely any economy based on the "greatest good" would take seriously the need for leisure, which the philosopher Josef Pieper called *the basis of culture.*

But wouldn't that make us less competitive? Jody Heymann and Alison Earle don't think so. In *Raising the Global Floor,* they use data from the World Economic Forum to demonstrate clearly that countries with generous policies affecting work time are every bit as competitive as the United States and other workaholic nations, and do not have higher average rates of unemployment.[30]

Moreover, Leslie Perlow and Jessica Porter of the Harvard Business School have shown that "Making Time Off Predictable and Required" results in better economic performance. They conducted a study wherein a Boston company provided two control groups. The first worked long hours (fifty or more a week), skipped part of their vacations, and were constantly on call when not at work. The second worked a shorter forty-hour week, took their full vacations, and left their BlackBerries at the office.

At the end of their study, Perlow and Porter found that "people on time-off teams reported higher job satisfaction, greater likelihood that they could imagine a long-term career with the firm and higher satisfaction with work/life balance." No surprise there. But the time-off control group also reported increased learning and development, better communication with their teams—when they could not reach everyone all the time, they learned to communicate more effectively face-to-face—and, most surprising of all, they actually produced more total output than their workaholic colleagues.[31]

The Vancouver-based activist Conrad Schmidt uses humor to warn his fellow Canadians not to fall into the American trap of work without end. He started the Work Less Party, which competes in British Columbian elections under the slogan WORKERS OF THE WORLD, RELAX! They haven't won any elections yet but get lots of press attention for their annual "rat race" through the business district and other antics. Humor can help us see just how destructive of life our time pressure can be. Cecile Andrews, an equally fun-loving American leader of the voluntary simplicity movement, has suggested that America doesn't need the Tea Party, or even the liberal Coffee Party. It needs a Decaf Party, so we all can slow down the pace of life.

There are those who would suggest that work is what the economy is for. They believe the long-working-hours culture in the United States makes Americans stronger and more competitive. We believe it has little, if any, impact on competitiveness, while having a huge impact on Americans' health, social connections, and environmental stewardship. It is clear that, as in many other areas of the economy, the United States can learn from the experience of other countries, particularly those such as the Netherlands that pay great attention to time balance. Americans can begin now to do something about this, and they should, because there's no present like the time.

CHAPTER 7

The Greatest Number

The fact is that income inequality is real—it's been rising for more than 25 years.

—PRESIDENT GEORGE W. BUSH, 2007[1]

So far in this book, we've explored the concept of *the greatest good*. It's time now to consider the second leg of Gifford Pinchot's stool: *the greatest number*. What do you think that means? For political economists like Jeremy Bentham and the Utilitarians as well as for Pinchot, *the greatest number* came from a notion that in a good society, the good things would be broadly distributed so that as many people as possible could enjoy them. This was harder in poor societies, where even necessities were in short supply and comforts or luxuries almost nonexistent. But in wealthy societies like our own, it is materially possible for the great majority of people to have access to a quality of life far beyond subsistence.

The concept of *the greatest number* is really about fairness, the moral sense that everyone has reasonable and similar access to the good things in life. So how do we know if a society is fair, if our own society is fair?

Well, first of all, we can look at the gap between rich and poor in any society. Let's put this one in simple terms: *the gap between rich and poor in America is the widest in any industrial country*; wider even than in poor Latin American nations like Guyana and Nicaragua.[2] And that chasm is getting wider all the time. Despite continued economic growth, poor and middle-income Americans have seen little if any increase in their real purchasing power for the past three decades, while the incomes of the richest Americans have skyrocketed. A rising tide of GDP was supposed to lift all boats; it instead floated the yachts and swamped the rowboats.

In 1915, when Wilford King at the University of Wisconsin estimated that the richest 1 percent of Americans earned 15 percent of national income, the country reacted in shock; now we seem to yawn at a wider gap. Here's how big it has become: In 1980, the richest 1 percent of Americans earned less than 10 percent of the national income. By 2008, they were earning more than 20 percent of the national income; indeed, they earned more income than the bottom 50 percent of Americans all put together.[3]

The top 20 percent of Americans earn fourteen times as much as the bottom 20 percent, up from eight times as much in 1980. Despite productivity gains of 80 percent since 1972, the median American worker in 2008 earned only eighty-three cents for every dollar he or she earned then. During the same period, average CEO pay increased from being thirty-five times that of the average worker to as much as four hundred times as great.[4]

There's a problem here: Traditional free-enterprise economics suggest that the marketplace works well because people vote with their dollars. This so-called *consumer sovereignty* supposedly ensures that the market democratically produces what people actually need and want. But in our schoolrooms, we learned that *democracy* meant "one person, one vote." In the marketplace as it currently stands, those CEOs have 262 votes for every one their workers have. The poor might need apartments or buses or health care, but they don't have the "votes." So we get a run on private jets, yachts, and $5,000 handbags.

Economists use what they call the *Gini coefficient* to determine relative equality among nations. Absolute equality of incomes is represented by a zero, absolute inequality by a 1 (that would mean that a single individual earned all of a country's income). Since 1980, the U.S. Gini coefficient has risen from 0.388 to 0.45. America's Gini rating of 0.45 contrasts sharply with the ratings in much more egalitarian countries: 0.23 in Sweden, for example, very high 0.2s and low 0.3s in most of Europe and Japan. In other words, the distribution of income in the United States is about *twice as unequal* as in Sweden.[5]

Ignoring Louis Brandeis

That's income. The gap in *wealth* owned by Americans is even greater. Back in 1977, John made his first documentary film, *A Common Man's Courage*. It was the story of John Toussaint Bernard, an immigrant from Corsica who came to the United States at the age of twelve in 1905. A tiny man, but tough and sinewy, with magnetic oratorical powers, Bernard had tried to start a union in Minnesota's iron mines. He was fired and blacklisted. Later, he became a New Deal–era congressman, elected as a candidate of the populist Farmer-Labor Party, which later merged with Minnesota's Democrats. In most of Bernard's many speeches throughout his life, he quoted the late Supreme Court justice Louis Brandeis: "We can have democracy in this country or we can have great wealth concentrated in the hands of a few, but we cannot have both."[6]

You are free to decide for yourself whether Brandeis was right, but one thing is certain: the United States *has* concentrated great wealth in the hands of a few, more so than in any other industrial nation and more than at any time since the late 1920s. Consider the following facts.

- The United States has a far greater percentage of people living in poverty than any other industrial nation.
- In 1960, the top 20 percent of the American population owned thirty times as much wealth as the bottom 20 percent. Now they own seventy-five times as much.
- By 2001, the top 1 percent of Americans owned *forty-four hundred* times as much wealth per person as the bottom 40 percent![7]
- By 2005, the top 20 percent of Americans earned 47 percent of our national income and owned 84 percent of its wealth.[8]

Our inequality falls particularly hard on certain groups of Americans. For example, the median white family in America owns eleven times as much wealth as the median black family. At the time of the civil rights movement, black Americans were 1.6 times more likely to die in childhood than whites. Today, a black child is 2.4 times more likely to die.[9] The good news: in 1968 black Americans earned fifty-five cents for every dollar that whites earned; by 2001, they were earning fifty-seven cents for every dollar. Progress?

Share of Total U.S. Income Received by Top 1% of Americans

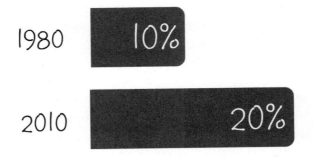

1980   10%

2010   20%

Women are in a similar position: a single twenty-something woman working full-time earns 90 percent of what her male counterpart earns. Sounds good, but when the gender expert Joan Williams of the University of California compared all women's income with men's, she found that they earn only fifty-nine cents for every dollar earned by men.[10]

Americans are not unaware of this inequality in wealth. According to a 2007 Pew poll, 73 percent believe that "today it's really true that the rich just get richer and the poor just get poorer."[11]

Who Won the Class War?

Some would keep it that way. In 2008, at a presidential campaign stop in Toledo, Ohio, Barack Obama was confronted by one Samuel Wurzelbacher, also known as "Joe the Plumber." Joe challenged Obama's advocacy of higher taxes for the richest Americans. Obama replied that in his view we'd all be better off if we "spread the wealth around," by ending income tax cuts for the very rich. In fact, though Obama retreated from his position, the evidence (which we'll get to later in this chapter) shows that he was actually right.

But Joe, and the right-wing radicals for whom he became a hero, screamed loudly that spreading the wealth around was socialism, and Obama was a *socialist*, and we all know what that means. It's a word meant to scare the daylights out of us.

Obama has called for a slight increase in the highest marginal tax rates—the richest would pay 39 percent, as they did under Bill Clinton, rather than the 35 percent they paid under Bush the Second. Some radical conservatives label Obama's call for such a tax increase *class warfare*. But in fact, that has been going on for at least thirty years, during which time the wealthiest Americans gobbled up by far the lion's share of new wealth. Warren Buffett put it simply: "Yes, there is a class war and my class is winning."[12]

Equality Matters

Let's put it plainly: *In our view, growing inequality is not good for America, period*. In more equal societies, *everybody* does better. That's the surprising conclusion, supported by an impressive marshaling of the evidence, that Richard Wilkinson and Kate Pickett reach in *The Spirit Level*. That evidence (also presented on their Web site, www.equalitytrust.org.uk) shows that inequality exacerbates a host of social problems and that the more equal countries perform better on almost every social indicator.

Wilkinson and Pickett consider twenty-nine different areas of life, including longevity, infant mortality, mental health, crime, incarceration, life satisfaction, education, teen pregnancy, and drug abuse. And while there are some exceptions—Singapore, one of the world's most unequal industrial nations, has its lowest infant mortality rate, for example—the general trends are unmistakable.

The United States, the *most* unequal of industrial nations, ranks near the bottom for every indicator except gross domestic product, while the most egalitarian countries, especially the Nordic countries, are on top. What is especially important about these findings is that in the more egalitarian countries, even the rich live longer and are more satisfied with their lives. Equality seems to be a win-win proposition. As Barack Obama told Joe the Plumber, we *all* do better when we spread the wealth around.

In many ways, the evidence from American states mirrors that of countries around the world. The least equal states, primarily in the South, exhibit far worse physical health, mental health, and other social indicators than more egalitarian states; rates of violent crime and homicide are much higher and children fare worse in less equal states.

In August 2010, *Newsweek* magazine ranked the world's one hundred "best countries." The rankings were remarkably similar to Gallup's national happiness surveys. Australia and Canada joined a host of small European countries at the top of the list, while the United States came in a respectable eleventh, buoyed by its score in the category of "economic dynamism." All of the top ten nations (Finland, Switzerland, Sweden, Australia, Luxembourg, Norway, Canada, the Netherlands, Japan, and Denmark) are relatively egalitarian, certainly much more so than the United States. With the exception of debt-stressed Iceland, all of the Nordic countries made the top ten.

The number one nation was Finland, a country which ranks near the top of happiness polls and *at the top* in educational success (as we will see in the next chapter). Finland ranks high in every indicator considered by *Newsweek*. Its economy, led by the cell phone giant Nokia, has consistently been rated one of the planet's most competitive by the World Economic Forum. Poverty is nearly nonexistent, and the gap between rich and poor in Finland is narrow. The Finns are inwardly happy, and they are outwardly prosperous.

Finland's Secrets of Success

The Finnish professor Hilkka Pietilä argues that it was equality that made Finland's prosperity possible: "The common belief is that a country must first become rich, and then it can provide welfare for its people. The history of the Nordic societies tells a different story; here, wealth has been built by building welfare for people."[13]

Pietilä points out that "Finland was not a wealthy country in the 1940s and 1950s." The country was devastated during World War II—"the whole of northern Finland was burned down by the Germans"—and was forced to pay reparations to the Soviet Union after the war. Fearful of offending its powerful Soviet neighbor, Finland rejected Marshall Plan assistance from the United States and remained neutral during the Cold War.

As recently as the 1960s and '70s, the Finns actually had a reputation for unhappiness. One segment on the TV newsmagazine *60 Minutes* described them as the most depressed people on Earth. But while some Finns still do battle seasonal affective disorder and alcoholism due to their dark winters, comparing the old, poor, and morbid Finland of legend (and a fair amount of truth) with the happy, wealthy country it has become is like comparing night and day.

Led by a very active women's movement, and a commitment to being self-reliant and sustainable as a nation, the Finns found a middle way to progress, avoiding the economic extremes of the West, but without the restrictions on freedom of the Soviets. According to Pietilä: "Despite its poverty, Finland began to create one of the world's most generous social welfare systems. The aim was to build the economy while eradicating poverty. The aims supported each other; the growing well-being of people provided a healthy and trained labor force, and the economic growth was redistributed to people as social benefits."

As social benefits. The Finns didn't simply redistribute cash. Well-funded public services (including child support allowances, forty-four weeks of paid parental leave per child, defined benefit pensions, free education through university, free health care, free school meals, subsidized public transportation, free day care, and subsidized elder care, plus a high minimum wage and generous unemployment benefits) helped create the world's largest middle class (as a percentage of the population) and a skilled workforce. Finland is one of only two countries that have outlawed compulsory overtime, and Finns have the world's longest paid vacations. Yet they are remarkably productive. Pietilä continues:

> The welfare system here is a lifelong social insurance, a guarantee that whatever may happen, children will not lose access to education, people will not be left at the mercy of relatives or charity organizations, no one will be abandoned in case of illnesses, accidents, unemployment or bankruptcy, and everyone will have old-age income and care no matter what . . . This success was built on a notion of welfare entirely different from welfare as understood in the United States. In the US "being on welfare" is humiliating, and welfare benefits often depend on the recipient's relationship to something or someone else. What is radically different about the Finnish system is that here welfare benefits and services are rights that everyone living permanently in the country is individually entitled to.

Healthy and well educated, the Finns are highly productive when they work. But they value families and leisure; the sauna is never far away, nor are the tiny cabins where they relax during summer holidays. But being the "world's best country" doesn't come cheap. "Finland has financed its welfare system mainly through highly progressive taxation on salaries and wages," writes Pietilä.

Is Small Size Key to Nordic Success?

Moderate American conservatives do acknowledge Nordic success. But they write it off as simply the result of countries like Finland being small and homogeneous. "Can't work here, not in a big and diverse country like ours," they say. Case closed. Or is it?

It's true that Finland, Sweden, and Denmark are small countries and, until recently, have seen little ethnic or racial diversity. There is some evidence that due to the persistence of racism, homogeneous societies find it easier to cooperate, and harder to scapegoat immigrants or other "others" for economic failures. Yet these nations also lack some of the advantages enjoyed by the United States and other larger countries.

Americans often hear that the United States is a victim of *globalization*, the race-to-the-bottom supposedly *required* by the integrated economy of Thomas Friedman's "flat" world. But countries like Finland are far more susceptible to globalization's threats. The United States has an immense domestic market—86 percent of its products are sold at home. The economist John Schmitt points out that European and Japanese companies open plants here simply to save transportation costs in selling to the American market. But the Nordic countries have small domestic markets, so far more of their production must be sold abroad. They have to be competitive to do that. According to the World Economic Forum, they are. All rank in the top twenty among the world's "most competitive" countries (those whose products compete most effectively on the world market), and Sweden ranks ahead of the United States.[14]

The Nordic nations must import many resources since they have few of their own—Norway's oil is an exception. They are cold and dark much of the year, requiring more energy for heating and lighting. They speak languages no one else speaks, so they must learn English, or perhaps German, to be understood in global commerce. They have smaller populations than even many American states, so they have smaller risk pools to share the uncertainties of insurance.

Instead of racing to the bottom, these countries have raced to the top, creating healthy economies on a base of social welfare—or, as Steven

Hill calls it, *workfare*—that, according to advocates of American-style capitalism, should leave them unable to compete.

The "T" Word

It's tempting to say that greater equality and a stronger social safety net and all of those things folks like the Finns take for granted may sound appealing, but there's no free lunch. Those things cost money, and the United States doesn't have any. It's broke. Its states are broke: California is offering IOUs to its workers. Hawaii is dramatically shortening its school year. Michigan is ripping up its paved roads and turning them into gravel because it can't afford to maintain them. U.S. cities are broke: Colorado Springs, for example, just turned off a third of its streetlights. The federal deficit is frightening. How can Americans possibly pay for this stuff?

First of all, it's probably unnecessary to mention that Germany, Sweden, Finland, Denmark, and other such countries provide these things even though their per capita GDPs are *smaller* than America's. They fund them and create their livable societies in no small part through higher taxes than we pay here and through a different mix of taxes.

It *is* necessary to point out federal tax bills for Americans are now at their lowest level since 1950. Americans pay an average of 9.2 percent of their incomes in federal taxes, only three quarters of the average for the past half century.[15] In the era BR (Before Reagan) many Americans understood that, as the great Supreme Court justice Oliver Wendell Holmes put it, taxes were the price of civilization. Taxes were seen as *investments* in our future. Taxes allowed for social insurance, allowed us to buy that insurance in bulk, provided the services the market did not deliver, and provided them well. (More about this in chapter 10.) Today, we are conditioned to think of taxes as *burdens* and their elimination as *relief.*

As the linguist George Lakoff points out, these are loaded words; from the beginning the concepts of the *tax burden* and *tax relief* create an ideological *frame*—taxes are a bad thing, and the less of them the better. All too often, even progressives fall into this language trap. They announce that they will provide middle-class tax relief. And indeed, though it may sometimes be helpful to reduce taxes, this is far from always the case.

Most Republicans in Congress want more tax cuts for the rich, who, they say, pay all the taxes while lower-income Americans pay none. This is simply nonsense: Lower-income Americans may pay little or no federal income tax, but their share for payroll, property, excise, and state and local sales and other taxes is actually higher as a percentage of income than that of the rich.

The top 1 percent of American income earners pay about 29 percent of their incomes in taxes, while the bottom 50 percent pay 24 percent of theirs. Warren Buffett points out that his secretary actually pays a *higher* percentage of her income in taxes than he does.[16]

Here is the overall breakdown.

- *Federal income tax.* The top 1 percent pay 22 percent of incomes. The bottom 50 percent pay 3 percent.
- *State and local taxes.* The top 1 percent pay 5 percent; the bottom 50 percent pay 10 percent of their incomes.
- *Social Security.* The top 1 percent pay 2 percent of incomes; the bottom 50 percent pay 9 percent.
- *Other taxes.* The top 1 percent pay less than 1 percent; the bottom 50 percent pay 2 percent.[17]

Tax cuts at the top in no way guarantee an increase in jobs. Indeed, American businesses earned their highest quarterly profits in history in 2010, while making almost no effort to reduce unemployment. Businesses invest and produce not simply because they have money to do so, but because there is *effective market demand* for their products. The rich spend far lower percentages of their money to create such demand. Indeed, *it is jobs, including government jobs*—and the wealth they share—*that create jobs*, because workers spend most of their discretionary income and create more effective demand.

In the two years following the economic collapse of 2008, the top five hundred American corporations saw a large increase in profits, and by 2010, were actually sitting on $1.8 trillion of new wealth. But instead of adding jobs, they cut them.

The subject of what kind of taxes work best is huge and complicated, and we cannot do it justice here. Because of frequent changes in parts of the economy, a "diversified portfolio" of taxes is most reliable, as is diversity in stock holdings. There are some lessons to learn from others countries about taxes.

- In many European countries, *corporate income taxes* are lower in principle than in the United States, but they are more consistently collected; here, loopholes allow many companies to escape taxation entirely. For example, the largest U.S. company, General Electric, paid no taxes in 2010 on a profit of $14 billion.[18]

- *Personal income taxes* in Europe generally have higher top marginal rates than in the United States and fewer loopholes for the wealthy.

- *Value-added taxes* (VAT) play a major role in European tax systems. They are similar to sales taxes. Whenever you buy something in a European country, the price already includes the VAT, which has been paid at each level in the production of a product. For example, VAT would be paid on the raw materials and machinery used to make a car, on the car itself when it goes from manufacturer to dealer, and again when it is sold to the final customer. Such taxes are very hard to evade so they produce consistent revenues. They are sometimes kept lower on necessities and higher on luxuries—serving as what the economist Thomas Frank calls a *progressive consumption tax*. Dave and John do not completely agree on the usefulness of VATs. Dave believes that like sales taxes, they are regressive and fall more heavily on the poor. John agrees that this is true, but believes they serve a positive purpose because they ensure that everyone who consumes contributes to social investments. And the poor are the greatest beneficiaries of what the VATs make possible—free health care, higher education, transportation subsidies, housing subsidies, and so forth—because they are least able to pay for these things in the market.

- *Property tax* revenues rise and fall sharply with housing bubbles, but if properly targeted, these taxes can help prevent sprawl and encourage smarter building practices.

- *Payroll taxes* such as Social Security, health insurance, Medicare, unemployment insurance, pensions, and some other benefits come out of your check before you receive it. They ensure that everyone pays in for what they will or may use later and are applied in all industrial countries. In the Netherlands, money is even taken out for vacations; this *vakantiegeld*, or vacation pay, is then returned to workers *in full* right before summer begins so they will have the money to take a vacation. One problem with payroll taxes in the United States is that they are assessed for each worker rather than on total payroll as in most European countries. This encourages American employers to hire fewer employees and work them longer hours so as not to pay another set of benefits. Many part-time workers receive no benefits at all as a result.

- *Excise taxes,* such as gasoline taxes or taxes on alcohol and cigarettes, are also higher in Europe and help direct the market to provide more socially useful, sustainable, and healthy products while discouraging unsustainable consumption. In most other industrial countries, gasoline taxes are at least double what they are in the United States.

- *Estate taxes* help improve economic mobility by reducing the amount of inherited wealth that can be passed from generation to generation. Dubbed *death taxes* by the Republicans, they are actually among the most progressive of taxes because they fall almost entirely on the richest members of the population. While many rich Americans want to repeal them, some, such as Warren Buffett and Bill Gates, see them as essential parts of a fair tax system.

The important thing to understand is Oliver Wendell Holmes's mantra: *Taxes are the price of civilization.* If we want an economy that truly provides the greatest good for the greatest number over the longest run, we must invest in public goods with smarter taxes. Though tax cutting may sometimes be justified and useful, it is no panacea for our economic problems, and it has played a central role in creating many of them.

Who Is Productive?

As a whole, providing the greatest good for the greatest number does require a greater level of public provisions and social insurance, and therefore, something of a transfer of wealth from richer to poorer. Such redistribution challenges deep-set beliefs. There is no doubt that the personal responsibility philosophy extolled by conservatives resonates deeply with many Americans and remains a fundamental ideological barrier to the expansion of our social safety net and greater economic security.

In part, that philosophy has its intellectual roots in the writings of Ayn Rand, an embittered Russian émigré in the United States who argued that a very few creative, productive, and ambitious people (symbolized by John Galt, the entrepreneur hero of her bestselling *Atlas Shrugged*) actually make possible all the good things in life, while most people—especially in Rand's view, paid laborers—survive only because the John Galts and other self-made men of the world provide work for them. John Galt, Rand opines, should be praised, not taxed. If he and other jobs creators stopped working to protest their oppressive taxation, the rabble would starve.

When John read *Atlas Shrugged* in the 1970s, he found it cold and heartless, full of cardboard characters and intellectually vacuous. But many people, obviously, feel differently. At its core, Rand's philosophy was distilled to a few simple words when John was challenged by a conservative student during a speech he gave at Georgia Tech: "So what I hear you saying is that you would take money away from the productive people and give it to the unproductive people?" In other words, the student said, John de Graaf would take cash from John Galt and give it to John Lazy.

Our response to that charge goes something like this.

And what we hear you saying, young man, is that those people who grow your food, harvest it in the fields, and transport it to the stores, those people who clean your streets and take away your garbage so you don't have to live in filth, those people who will teach your children if you have any, and take care of your infants and toddlers while you do your "productive" business, those people who build the cars you drive in and many other products you use, those people whose work benefits you every day of your life—those people who have seen precious little improvement in their real wages during the past generation of policies favoring John Galt—those are the "unproductive" people whose survival only the Galts make possible.

And meanwhile, those other people, the ones who have seen their incomes mushroom and their taxes wither, those "self-made" people with expensive educations whose brainpower and hard work have created such wonders as exploding derivatives and credit default swaps, whose "products" never affect your daily life except when you have to bail out the disasters they create, those people who earn far more in a week than your child care providers will earn in a year, whose year-end bonuses often equal the lifetime earnings of ordinary workers—*they* are the "productive" people.

And you, young man, have a problem with taxing those "productive" people to provide a little more security for the ones you consider "unproductive." Well, we see *no possible moral justification* for labeling the first group unproductive and the latter productive—quite the contrary, in fact—unless you automatically assume that Group B is more productive solely because its activities earn more in the market as it presently exists. Indeed, we believe that in a moral world we would offer greater compensation to those whose labor actually makes life better. In which case, there is absolutely no moral argument at all against greater equalization of incomes. In fact, we find the distribution of earnings in this economy to be morally obscene.

In the heady heights of Randian philosophy, however, what people earn from the market is what they are really *worth*, and is the result of their efforts alone. Taxing them in such a situation is a theft of their property. Their efforts alone make the world better; indeed, Randians suggest that government security measures, not deregulation, are to blame for the current crises. If only we had left it *all* to the market, they proclaim, things would be fine.

The problem with this argument, first of all, is that no one is truly self-made—Warren Buffett points out that he would not be a billionaire if he'd been born in Bangladesh. Moreover, it is impossible to prove or disprove the claim that, if we were true to the market, things would be great, since it is totally theoretical. It is akin to the radicals of the 1960s and '70s who dismissed criticisms of the Soviet Union by saying: "Well, that's not *real* socialism. Under real socialism, you wouldn't have these problems." But their more conservative critics countered correctly that *actual* socialism was all we could truly judge, and it was a failure.

Let's turn that on its head: Americans have now had thirty years of *actual* tax-cutting, deregulating, privatizing government policy. We are demonstrably less fair, less secure, less satisfied, more indebted, more stressed, less healthy in comparison to people in other countries, and less happy than we were when Ronald Reagan first took office.

For most of those thirty years, we limped toward mediocrity and greater insecurity. But finally, in the fall of 2008, after continued deregulation of Wall Street, the "you're on your own" philosophy came crashing down, stealing the rug from under millions of Americans, not to mention the roof and walls.

The Land Opportunity Forgot

You might agree that the Grand Canyon between rich and poor in America is huge and growing, but not think that is as big a deal as we do. "No one in America ever guaranteed anyone equality of results," you might say. "What we offer here is equality of *opportunity*; it's up to everyone to grab the golden ring for herself." There was a time when this might have been true, a time when the claim that America was classless, though not really accurate even then, was at least buttressed by our relative *economic mobility*: how much chance a child born among the poor had to grow into an adulthood of wealth or at least comfort, how often a child from the lowest quintile of the population ended up in the highest. The United States may not have been number one in this area, but it was always close to the top. America truly was a land of opportunity.

It is now a land that opportunity has forgotten. A 2007 Pew Charitable Trust report, *Economic Mobility: Is the American Dream Alive and Well?*, found that "the United States has less relative mobility than many other developed countries." Among the rich countries studied, only in the United Kingdom was economic mobility more restricted (and only a little more than in the United States).[19] In every other country, a person born poor had more chance of becoming comfortable or even wealthy than here. Danes have three times as much chance, for example; Canadians two and a half and Germans one and a half times the chance.

In spite of these damning statistics, or perhaps because they are not well understood, Americans are still twice as likely as Europeans to believe that hard work brings rewards: 69 percent believe that "people are rewarded for intelligence and skill." If that is still true, and America still offers more opportunity than Europe, then there can be only two possible explanations for the fact that Americans are twice as likely as western Europeans to live in poverty or for that fact that fewer than half of Americans are officially middle class (their incomes fall between 60 and 150 percent of the median), while nearly two thirds of Europeans fit that category.

The first is that Americans are genetically different: they have far more stupid people as a percentage of the population than Europeans do. This seems highly unlikely; science finds no such genetic differences in IQ between different countries. The second possibility is that more Americans simply don't work as hard as Europeans; this too seems to counter the evidence. American workers are at least as productive per hour and work much longer than their European counterparts.

Something else, then, is going on here. We would put it this way: The American economy operates in a way that creates a wider gap between rich and poor than in other wealthy countries. It's less fair, period, less well-structured to promote the greatest good. That needs to change. The inequality gap is the most significant difference between the United States and almost all other rich countries. Yet the evidence is clear that our lack of attention to promoting the greatest good for all of us has led to a lower quality of life for almost all of us, except perhaps the very rich.

Gus Speth, former dean of the Yale School of Forestry, points out that even a cursory glance at the annual well-being statistics provided by the Organization for Economic Cooperation and Development reveals that the United States ranks at or near the bottom in nearly every category. No economy provides complete equality, and complete equality would end economic incentives to work hard. But Wilkinson, Pickett, and many other scholars make a powerful case that America's growing income chasm is a recipe for failure. Indeed, as Justice Brandeis made clear long ago, the future of American democracy itself demands that the gap be narrowed.

CHAPTER 8

The Capacity Question

Ill fares the land to hastening ills a prey/Where wealth accumulates and men decay.

—OLIVER GOLDSMITH, *THE DESERTED VILLAGE*

Corrections: In last week's issue, *The Onion* mistakenly said that education is the key to success. Being born into money is actually the key to success. *The Onion* regrets the error.

—FROM THE *ONION*, A SATIRICAL NEWSPAPER, MARCH 17, 2011

There are good reasons for seeing poverty as a deprivation of basic capabilities, rather than merely as low income.

—NOBEL PRIZE–WINNING ECONOMIST AMARTYA SEN

The laissez-faire critique of the "welfare state" and promotion of "personal responsibility" has always contained an important kernel of truth, however poorly conservative policy performs in improving quality of life. That kernel: *people do not want everything done for them by others, either through state-provided welfare or through private charity.*

In his conservative (though again, we would argue that his prescriptions are for radical, not conservative, change) handbook, *The Battle*, Arthur Brooks writes that "people flourish when they earn their own success."[1] He is correct: Our need for self-esteem is satisfied most effectively when we accomplish things of value through our own efforts.

So far, so good.

But Brooks doesn't stop there. He suggests that a system that minimizes the public sector and maximizes the role of the "free market" and "free enterprise," through reduced regulation, low taxes, and privatization of virtually all government services except the military, the police, and the courts (to ensure property rights), is the kind of system most likely to offer its citizens the opportunity for success—however we choose to measure it.

We need to spend a little time with Brooks, both because of his influence as president of the American Enterprise Institute, a powerful think tank, and because his ideas are at the core of the radical conservative defense of inequality. But however commonsensical they may seem, they are profoundly in error.

"More than any other system," Brooks writes, "free enterprise enables people to earn success and thereby achieve happiness. For that reason, it is not just an economic alternative but a *moral imperative*" (italics his).[2]

Because "earned success" is so important, Brooks contends, efforts to reduce inequality are unimportant, even counterproductive. "Earned success means the ability to create value honestly," says Brooks, "not by winning the lottery, not by inheriting a fortune and" [most of all in his mind] "not by picking up a welfare check."[3]

Earned success, Brooks argues, is the "creation of value" in our lives and the lives of others: "It isn't just related to commerce. Earned success is also what parents experience when their children do wonderful things, what social innovators feel when they change lives and what artists feel when they create something of beauty."[4]

We have no quarrel with this. But in each of these cases, "earned success" comes from creating something that benefits others; it is the sense that you *made a difference* in the lives of other people that provides the happiness Brooks sees as a consequence of such activity. Yet for Brooks, the opportunity to earn success in this way must *also* include limitless opportunity to earn more money. Why is this so, if happiness comes from creating something of intrinsic benefit to yourself and others?

Brooks has an answer to this question. The wealthy, he writes, "already have enough money to meet every need they could ever have, but they still crave earned success like the rest of us, so they are driven to create value at greater and greater heights. The money is just a symbol, important not for what it can buy but for what it says about how some people are contributing."[5] In other words, expectations for such gains become addictive cravings that drive the rich to accumulate more and more wealth.

This kind of unsatisfied craving—which finds relief only through continual increases in income—hardly seems a recipe for greater happiness. Indeed, all of our great religions see it as the kind of addiction that leads to misery. Yet somehow Brooks feels that without the opportunity of limitless wealth, productive Americans won't continue to do things that benefit others. To us, this logic is sort of strange.

If the money is just a "symbol," as Brooks declares, why wouldn't satisfaction come from the actual services you provide and the lives thereby improved? In fact, happiness research shows that, indeed, satisfaction isn't about the money. The psychologists Tim Kasser, Rich Ryan, and others have pointed out that those who work with the primary motivation of "making a lot of money" are much less likely to be happy than those who work with the goal of serving others.[6] Why, then, does "earned success" require the *unlimited* opportunity to increase one's material wealth?

A couple of pages later, Brooks makes another leap of logic. "If money without earned success does not bring happiness," he writes, "then redistributing money won't make for a happy America."[7]

Sounds plausible, doesn't it? But isn't it possible, even probable, that redistribution can *broaden* the opportunities to earn success and, therefore, contribute to the greatest good *for the greatest number?* Redistributing wealth doesn't mean merely giving a handout to the poor.

Improving Capacities

The bulk of income redistribution in western Europe, for example, doesn't go for welfare; it goes for what Steven Hill terms *workfare*, contributing to programs that make for a more capable labor force and provide greater opportunities and security for ordinary workers to earn success in various ways.[8] It includes, for example, helping workers' children learn and grow, and giving those workers the time to express their artistic creativity. It is an *investment* in the workforce of the future.

In fact, the *primary purpose* of sensible wealth redistribution is to create opportunity for all people by improving what Amartya Sen calls their *capacities* to make the most of their innate gifts. For example, good, low-cost child care doesn't just give children a "head start"; it allows mothers to contribute to the world of work outside the home.

As we've mentioned before, the opportunity to develop these capacities starts at birth. More equal societies get an immediate jump: Infant and children's mortality is lower in such countries; they have fewer low-birth-weight babies; they offer mothers more opportunity to breast-feed during work. Most important, they allow parents sufficient paid leave to bond with their children, improving those children's health, and their capacities to learn, while also improving opportunities for parents to combine work with raising children.

We must concede that, in the short run, the shift of a portion of society's resources to provide paid parental leave results in either a reduction of business profits or higher tax rates, even for people who do not have children. In both cases, then, it is a redistribution of wealth. According to Arthur Brooks, it should not make anyone happier. But in fact it improves the opportunities for our children to "earn" success in the future.

Those who receive such benefits—all who have children—are not receiving them for doing nothing, but rather, for helping (through their parenting) to improve the capacities of the next generation of citizens. The security offered by such paid leave improves the immediate happiness of the parents and the long-term prospects for happiness of the children. Yet the United States is the only industrial country that does not provide paid childbirth and parental leave by law. Brooks and his allies would keep it that way.

After infancy, policies intended to improve capacities involve redistributing wealth to provide broader educational opportunities for all. Most Americans, including conservatives, believe in this, sort of.

Missed Opportunities

Children's capacities for earning are powerfully influenced by the quality of the education they receive. In most other industrial countries, professional and high-quality child care or "preschool" is provided between the time parental leave benefits expire and official schooling begins. Such care either is free for parents or comes at very affordable rates. In many of these countries, preschool teachers are highly trained and often have required master's degrees. They earn excellent salaries.

By contrast, there are few child care subsidies for American parents, and high-quality child care is very expensive. In *The Motherhood Manifesto*, Joan Blades and Kristin Rowe-Finkbeiner point out that decent child care and preschool can cost well over $1,000 a month, making it more expensive than a typical public university.

Much of the affordable child care is catch-as-catch-can. Child care providers generally earn little more than the minimum wage—an average of around $17,000 a year.[9] Their centers are crowded, and often there are long waiting lists for the few spaces. Tax credits are not provided to allow parents to stay home and care for their own children. Even single mothers are required to spend thirty hours working in low-paying jobs or looking for work to qualify for income supplements, while affordable child care is not available for them.

Further, unlike the situation in many other nations, where all schools receive roughly the same funding and are able to attract uniformly competent teachers, there is an enormous difference between the schools in wealthy American suburbs and those in the inner city. Broken windows, graffiti, guns, drugs, old books, and poor equipment compete with the finest modernity has to offer. In a futile effort to keep up, the less-endowed schools organize cookie sales and car washes and, in some states, even sell their wall space to corporate advertisers.

When John was producing the film *Affluenza* in 1996, he visited a Colorado high school where large advertisements for candy bars and soda pop adorned the walls: M & MS ARE BETTER THAN STRAIGHT A'S! He was shown California math texts that asked students to count and multiply Oreos and corporate "educational" freebies for schools that taught the "history of the Tootsie Roll"! It made John want to scream. We're not making this up, and it would be appalling to people in almost any other country.

The world's richest nation ranks below average for industrial countries in all international tests of educational achievement.[10] To correct this deficiency, political leaders demand longer school hours and more testing. Blamed for a failure that is a direct result of *inequality*, teachers must adhere to rigid curricula demands and teach for tests. Many leave the profession, unable to cope with constantly greater demands and less opportunity to control their own syllabi.

In many of the poorest school districts, the idea holds sway that the answer is simply to keep the kids at their desks longer. One by one, they have even eliminated such "nonproductive" times of day as elementary school recess. In Tacoma, Washington, a school administrator defended the elimination of recess by saying, "We must increase instruction time to prepare the children to compete in the global economy." We're talking second graders here. Put kindly, this is lunacy, especially in the middle of an epidemic of childhood obesity.

Finland Gets an A in Education

Interestingly, *Newsweek*'s "best country," Finland, also ranks highest in the world in its children's performance on international tests of science and reading and second only to South Korea in math performance. We say *interestingly* because Finnish students have among the *shortest* class hours in the world, receive very little homework, and spend more time on *art and music* (just the subjects our schools are slashing) than students in other countries. What they have going for them is small class sizes and teachers who are well paid, honored, and not overworked, teachers with the energy to inspire and the chance to teach students how to think instead of how to take tests. School quality is uniform throughout the country because tax revenues are fully shared.

Finland does this, not because it is richer than the United States, but because the Finns understand what is obviously beyond Arthur Brooks: Inequality affects our ability to "earn success," and right from the start.

Universities in Decline

We Americans, with good reason, do take pride in our colleges and universities. Our postsecondary educational institutions are second to none in the world. But for many lower-income Americans, access to them is getting harder and harder. Through the 1970s, the United States ranked at the top in terms of the percentage of its population with postsecondary degrees. We recognized that a well-educated workforce was a boon for our entire society. Our heavily subsidized public institutions were affordable for nearly everyone.

In 1964, John entered the nation's then-most-prestigious public university, the University of California at Berkeley. He paid no tuition and barely over $100 in fees each semester. Three years later, at the University of Wisconsin, he could afford tuition and room and board on a ten-hour-a-week work-study job. In her enlightening look at American higher education, *DIY U*, Anya Kamenetz points out that "since 1980, tuition at both private and public colleges has soared relative to both inflation and family income. College tuition and fees leaped 439 percent from 1982 to 2007, after inflation."[11]

A *New York Times* headline recently announced, HIGHER EDUCATION MAY SOON BE UNAFFORDABLE FOR MOST AMERICANS. According to the story, tuition at even a public university now costs 55 percent of the income of the poorest fifth of Americans. Increasingly, seats in top American universities are filled with students from other countries. An estimated 168,000 qualified American students don't enroll at all in college each year because they cannot afford it.[12]

Today, among citizens of developed countries between the ages of twenty-five and thirty-four, the United States ranks twelfth in the percentage of postsecondary degrees and its ranking is dropping steadily. Forty-one percent of Americans in that age group hold at least an associate's degree. Not surprisingly, the percentages are higher in states that are more willing to tax themselves to pay for education and other social services. Massachusetts, the leading state, has more than twice as many graduates per capita as Arkansas, the lowest-ranked state.[13]

With notable exceptions such as New York, these state rankings run closely parallel to the gap between rich and poor in various states, with more egalitarian states having higher percentages of graduates. When we see that Americans with college degrees earn 67 percent more than those

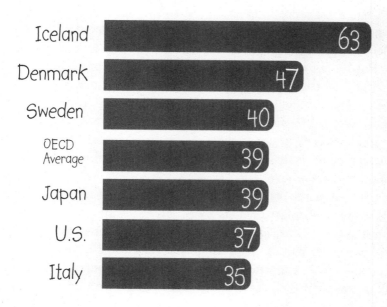

College Graduation Rates
2007

Iceland	63
Denmark	47
Sweden	40
OECD Average	39
Japan	39
U.S.	37
Italy	35

without them, the impact of inequality on "earned success" becomes even clearer.

Sadly, our university system, once the world's best, is not just less afford-able; it's in decline. *DIY U* author Anya Kamenetz writes of a recent visit to the University of Tennessee, where she found tuition climbing and budgets shrinking, while key academic programs, including foreign languages, religious studies, and geology, were facing elimination. At the same time, the university was building a new $200-million football stadium.[14]

Historical comparisons are often overused and shallow, but somehow the fall of the Roman Empire does not seem so far removed from our condition: the glorification of circuses and entertainment spectacles; the denigration of intellect; the pugnacious patriotism, flag-waving hubris, and bullying of critics; the far-flung phalanxes in foreign lands; the conspicuous consump-tion and unfettered demands ("drill, baby, drill!"); the slavish devotion to the rich and powerful; the pitiless disdain for the poor and weak.

Surely all of these phenomena had their defenders and rationalizers, then as now. One cannot help but imagine that the modern Vandals and Visigoths are hiding nearby or that Alaric lurks near the White House gates. At least the Roman climate wasn't changing . . . But let's not get ahead of ourselves. We can still change.

Radical Monopoly

For now, let's just change *lanes*. In the previous chapter, we presented evidence that economic mobility in America is no longer what it once was. But it's not only our economic mobility that's in decline. Consider actual *physical mobility*, the opportunity or capacity to move easily from place to place. We're on a downward slide there too. And in this area of life, our vaunted freedom of choice may come up the shortest of all. The United States is car country; there is just about one car or truck for every American adult. It's said that we just *love* our cars. But could it be we've got nothing else to love?

Decades ago, the brilliant social critic Ivan Illich (in *Tools for Convivi-ality*) wrote of what he called *radical monopoly*, the idea that monopoly was not just about AT&T controlling all the phone lines (a reality then) but about particular modes of meeting needs (such as the automobile) mo-nopolizing all the opportunities to do so and crowding out others.

Our love affair with cars left many Americans with no other methods of mobility, undercut transit systems, crowded out the trains, and left no room for bicyclists and few opportunities to walk from place to place without fear for one's life. Those with no money for a car, no driver's license, or other limitations were, in many places, without mobility options at all. Mass transit in most American cities is better now than it was then (but for how long in this era of budget slashing?), yet the radical monopoly of autos still exerts its power.

All Aboard . . . None Aboard

Our train system, for example, would be an embarrassment in nearly any other industrial country. A few years ago, John traveled around Europe by train. It was an altogether pleasant experience. Virtually every train was on time and comfortable. They glided on smooth tracks through the countryside with only short intervals between them, offering lovely vistas and good wine.

In Austria, John arrived in Salzburg near the end of the day without hotel reservations. Bad idea. It happened to be the celebration of Mozart's two hundredth birthday, in his hometown. There was not a single hotel room to be found, and night was closing in. So John hopped aboard a bright red train bound south into the Alps. He asked the Austrians on board where he should get off the train to find an inexpensive hotel for the night. They buzzed in German, called on their cell phones to friends, and finally said, "Get off in two stops at St. Johann (a village about an hour south of Salzburg), go left out of the station, then right down the block to a bridge. Cross it, and there will be some good hotels right there!"

The first hotel was both lovely and inexpensive, and the town of St. Johann was exquisite, a hamlet right out of a fairy tale, and with great Chinese food and cheap pilsner besides! John spent a wonderful night and returned to the train station in the morning. In minutes, a local train, bound for Innsbruck and towns in between, pulled up, and John began a ride through some of the loveliest countryside on Earth.

Later in his trip, John rode the really fast trains, the astonishing Trains à Grande Vitesse, or TGVs, of France, which roar through the land at nearly two hundred miles per hour. By contrast, you might have had the experience of lurching and bouncing along on Amtrak, as John has, stopped frequently because the freight lines had priority on the track (on land given to them free by the people more than a century ago!), six hours *late* on a twenty-hour trip from Seattle to San Francisco (a route French or Japanese trains would cover in five hours), with the bathrooms all stopped up and the bistro out of everything.

Free Wheeling

Besides trains, many other industrial countries also offer slower, more sustainable ways to get around easily. The cities of Europe are replete with pedestrian-only streets and malls. John remembers a visit to Freiburg, near Germany's Black Forest, in 1997. The entire center of the city was off limits to private cars, thanks to rules installed by the Green Party when it controlled Freiburg's city council. When the council was debating these rules, local businesses were much opposed, suggesting that their customer base would dry up. But it didn't.

Instead, people flocked to Freiburg's pedestrian-friendly downtown, and local businesses are thriving. Yet in John's own city of Seattle, the city fathers couldn't even keep a single downtown block, called Westlake Plaza, free from autos. Large retailers, like Nordstrom's, threatened to close up shop if the street was not reopened to cars. The city capitulated.

Bicycles provide another simple and sustainable mode of mobility. Some American cities and towns are becoming friendlier to them; in all honesty, progress *is* being made. But in most American cities, you take your life in hand when you ride a nonmotorized two-wheeler on the streets. By contrast, consider the Netherlands or Denmark, those notoriously happy lands where everyone young and old believes in pedal power. Their towns and countryside offer endless kilometers of safe and pleasant bicycle paths completely removed from automobile traffic. Even in the big cities, everyone rides; parking garages boast level after level of bike spaces; visiting Amsterdam, John wondered how, in the immense jumble of bikes, anyone finds theirs again. Do the Dutch have a special sense of smell?

It's common in the Netherlands' open-air markets to see men and women in their seventies or eighties on their bikes, groceries hanging from panniers or handlebars, smiling as they pedal. This activity keeps them in shape and living longer. John's cousin Letty and her husband, Bert, both retired, live in the remote northern Dutch village of Westerbork and would never think of driving somewhere they could bike to in half an hour. But isolated as they are, every couple of hours a fast train stops near their village ready to whisk them to Amsterdam if they desire.

So What's This Got to Do with Economics?

Answer: plenty.

America's radical monopoly of autos was in no small part imposed by corporate economic power. Prior to the 1930s and '40s, the suburbs of U.S. cities were connected to downtown by trolley or rail systems. Commercial centers grew up around the trolley stops, and people lived close enough to the trolleys and trains to walk to the stations or stops. Jim Klein's popular film, *Taken for a Ride*, documents how General Motors and other auto companies muscled out the trains and trolleys to create a radical automobile and bus monopoly (GM built buses then too) with payoffs to city officials and other corruption.

And while the Europeans and Japanese were subsidizing the development of fast rail systems, the United States required that gasoline tax dollars support road building only. It kept gasoline taxes low to encourage driving and discourage other forms of transport, with more than a little lobbying help from Big Oil.

But even if there were no conspiracies such as the demolition of urban transit systems, Americans' economic priorities (as the labor advocate and lawyer Thomas Geoghegan shows in his lively part-travelogue, part-political broadside, *Were You Born on the Wrong Continent?*)[15] drive a geography of urban sprawl and auto dependence.

Geoghegan points out that thirty years of increasing inequality and wage stagnation, as described in the previous chapter, have led American families to work more. Tax cutting has decimated urban schools. A growing underclass has increased fear of crime. Parents flee the cities for the suburbs, where they expect the schools, funded by higher-income taxpayers, will be better and they will be safer (though a study by the Sightline Institute in Seattle shows that you're more likely to die from a traffic accident in the suburbs than from any cause, including a bullet, in the city).

Geoghegan shows how land costs make homes in the suburbs cheaper than in the city and homes in the exurbs cheaper than those in the suburbs, so people move farther out, unable to buy homes closer to where they work, or worried that urban schools will mishandle their kids. Now they have long commutes on top of long working hours. Exhausted when they get home, they have little interest in or energy for going out, as Europeans do. So they are more likely to stay at home and amuse themselves with plasma TVs and home entertainment centers (how big is yours?).

They seldom know their neighbors and do not share appliances, so they must each buy their own lawn mower, leaf blower (don't you just hate those things?), or whatever. All of this consumption requires bigger homes and more garage space. When John was making the film *Affluenza*, he spoke with a man who had four garages. His several cars and boats were all outside. "It's for storage," he told John. "You never have enough storage so you can never have enough garages." The biggest homes are built farther out, where land is still cheaper. People follow the homes. Their commutes get even longer, and they need to work longer to pay for all the stuff their isolated suburban lives require. Driving everywhere, they spend more on exercise machines for their homes—these might need their own rooms . . .

They drive because their public transit options are limited and because they are too far out to bike or walk (and it's unsafe anyway). They pay through the teeth for nannies or child care or the exploding costs of health care or colleges, because such social supports are not adequately funded as in Europe. All hands on deck must work to make money, but they work in different places so each must have a car. It's a vicious cycle. Their decisions are not so much the result of greed as of growing inequality and lack of options.

It's quite different in Europe, as Tom Geoghegan explains. European economies are more egalitarian despite some increases in inequality in recent years. Life is safer, and schools are more likely to be excellent. No need to go so far out for a house—and in many countries, no room to do it either. Europeans don't pay through the nose for health care or college or child care, so they don't have to work as hard. Shorter working hours leave everyone with more energy, while greater attention to public amenities, paid for in part through higher taxes, means more options for fun outside the home: cafés, cultural offerings, pedestrian streets, parks, concerts. There's less need for so many individual home entertainment centers. It's a *virtuous* cycle.

Geoghegan points out that Europeans' greater equality depends in large part on distributive taxes, but that much of the taxes they pay comes right back to them in the form of services. As with health insurance, buying these services through taxes instead of purchasing them individually in the market has the effect of *buying in bulk*: You get more for less. *The greatest good for the greatest number.*

Who Governs?

In one sense, the capacity to "earn success" isn't just about ability or opportunity; it's about power to make and influence decisions. We Americans have always prided ourselves on how democratic our country is. For decades, from the 1910s to the 1970s, from the direct election of senators and the establishment of the process of initiative and referendum to the Voting Rights Act, our country *was* getting more democratic. So democratic, in fact, that some highly placed observers conjured visions of the rabble at the gates, a messy mob storming the Bastille (Wall Street), perilously close to guillotining the establishment. The late Harvard political scientist Samuel Huntington warned of a "democratic distemper" loose in the land, an "excess of democracy," threatening Western civilization or, at least, the Hamptons.

No such luck these days.

Part of the reason so little concern is paid to *the greatest good for the greatest number over the longest run* in our economy is that money talks louder here than in other places. The dollars of the rich flow in a ceaseless stream to the politicians to finance their campaigns, and the politicians do their bidding. We won't dwell on this because you are probably already saying, "You think I'm dumb or what? Everybody knows this." Indeed everyone does, and the realization makes all of us increasingly cynical about government and less likely to be politically engaged. It should, instead, make us determined to stop this *dictatorial* distemper and take the money out of politics.

But things only get worse. In 2010, the Republican Meg Whitman of eBay spent more than $130 million of her own money in an unsuccessful effort to buy the governorship of California. A few years earlier, the Democrat Jon Corzine spent almost as much to buy the governorship of New Jersey. But most of the money comes from corporations. Money in politics is a bipartisan thing. Over the years, the Republicans have gotten more corporate donations, but Democrats are certainly not immune to this bribery.

In what must rank as one of the rankest legal decisions of all time, the

United States Supreme Court, in the *Citizens United* case, ruled that limitations on direct corporate financing of elections were a violation of free speech. With such a legal framework, and with corporations granted the legal rights of individuals, is it any accident that candidates who would restrict greed or mandate social-democratic safety nets are so easily defeated? Americans are aware of this problem; 64 percent say they favor an amendment that would, at least, overturn the *Citizens United* decision.[16]

Improving the Work Environment

But even if we could get a bit more control over the wholesale auctioning of our political decisions, democracy is more than politics. Many of the decisions that most affect us daily are made in the workplace, the venue where we spend about one third of our lives, if not more. The Gallup organization conducts daily happiness polling in the United States. In April 2011, its national averages were as follows:

Overall Well-Being Index	66.1
Percent Thriving	50.6
Basic Access to Goods	82.4
Emotional Health	79.1
Physical Health	76.2
Healthy Behaviors	63.1
Work Environment	45.4[17]

In other words, Americans rate their work environment lowest among the well-being domains measured by Gallup. Satisfaction with the work environment in the United States is at its lowest levels since Gallup began measuring work satisfaction several decades ago. This finding is worrisome, both for the health of our economy and for our happiness. According to happiness experts, work satisfaction is enhanced by the degree to which work allows people to use their skills, contribute to the common good, and find social connections with others, and *by the degree of control people have over their working conditions*. But American workplaces are decidedly *un*democratic.

The destruction of organized labor, which began in the Reagan era (more on this in chapter 11) and continues with the wholesale elimination of public employee bargaining rights in some states, has meant less de-

mocracy on the shop floor, while the globalization of commerce and deregulation of finance have given corporate power brokers greater license
to move whole industries and squeeze absolute obedience from workers
still lucky enough to have a job after outsourcing and downsizing.

There are alternatives. Perhaps the most intriguing and democratic is a
policy called *codetermination*. In German companies with more than two
thousand employees, workers codetermine policy. The law requires that
half of the companies' boards of directors be elected directly by the workers. We're sure this comes as a shock, so let us say it again: *In Germany,
half the boards of directors of large companies must be elected by the workers.*[18]

Believe it or not, this extreme measure was not the idea of Germany's
huge and powerful union, IG Metall. It was imposed on Germany by the
Allies, particularly the Americans, after Germany lost World War II.
The victors wanted to punish the Krupps and other German captains of
industry for supporting Hitler during the war. But some were also New
Deal believers who saw the new German economy as a possible experiment in social democracy far exceeding what was politically feasible in
the United States. At first the rule applied to only a few industries, but in
1974, it was extended to all large companies. As a British historian once
explained to John, the real winners of World War II were the German
workers. Life is stranger than fiction.

What has codetermination meant for the Germans? Among the highest wage and benefit compensation packages in the world, for one thing.
Job security, for another. When American bosses were blissfully transfer-
ring their plants to Kathmandu or Timbuktu (actually Juárez or Beijing,
but we like the ring of the other place-names), German bosses naturally
wanted to follow suit. But guess what? The workers on the boards of
directors weren't ready to ship their jobs abroad. They said *Nein* to such
suggestions, and almost all the plants stayed right there in Germany.

Western economists were appalled. No way could the Germans compete. Not in Thomas Friedman's flat world where their leading competitors, the Americans, were shipping jobs to China and the Chinese were
paying peanuts on the dollar to their workers. Predictions of German
economic demise were rife. Surely the Germans would have to slash their
obese salaries in order to compete.

But Tom Geoghegan shows how the Germans confounded the odds.
They improved the skills of their workers and the capacities of their plants
and gained a reputation for quality products and diversification. They

kept selling big-time. And they did this while giving everybody six weeks of vacation a year! With one hand tied behind their backs, as Geoghegan puts it.

Indeed, not until 2009 did China exceed Germany for total sales of exports, despite having fifteen times its population. Before that, the Germans sold more abroad than the Chinese, even while the rapidly rising euro made their exports more expensive. In contrast to America's dismally negative balance of trade, German numbers are highly in the black. Knowing this, American investors, no dummies even if they are a bit greedy, have invested highly in German industry. Codetermination, far from destroying German industry, has helped preserve most of it. The Great Recession that began in 2008 hit Germany hard, precisely because it's an exporting country. But another enlightened policy, *Kurzarbeit*, explained in chapter 5, allowed Germany to keep its workers employed while America's were shown the exits. And now, with the euro dropping in value, German exports are hopping again.

In addition to their power on corporate boards, German workers have power over such issues as scheduling through elected *works councils*, and major clout in determining salaries and benefits though industry-wide bargaining by their big unions. Geoghegan writes that, paradoxically, Germany is the most "socialist" country in the world when it comes to the power of workers to shape policy, but it is also the most successful big capitalist country. Something for Glenn Beck and other screamers about "European socialism" to consider, though they are unlikely to have their minds confused by facts that don't fit their frames.

Codetermination as a model is most advanced in Germany, though a form of it exists in other European countries including Sweden, where smaller percentages of seats on the boards of directors must be allotted to workers. In these countries, workers don't participate in major investment decisions. But they do exercise important power in the day-to-day activities of the plant—such as the speed of the assembly line—through their works councils.

Codetermination and works councils represent real, practical democracy in the workplace, where we all spend so much of our time. Any economy concerned with the greatest good for the greatest number would do well to consider their potential. The idea that such policies make countries uncompetitive is not supported by the facts. According to the World Economic Forum's 2010 Global Competitiveness Index, Sweden ranks second and Germany fifth. The United States ranks fourth, but of the top twenty countries, eleven are European nations with strong public sectors and high taxes. Four are Nordic countries. Here is the list.

1.	Switzerland	5.63
2.	Sweden	5.56
3.	Singapore	5.48
4.	United States	5.43
5.	Germany	5.39
6.	Japan	5.37
7.	Finland	5.37
8.	Netherlands	5.33
9.	Denmark	5.32
10.	Canada	5.30
11.	Hong Kong	5.27
12.	United Kingdom	5.25
13.	Taiwan	5.21
14.	Norway	5.14
15.	France	5.13
16.	Australia	5.11
17.	Qatar	5.10
18.	Austria	5.09
19.	Belgium	5.07
20.	Luxembourg	5.05[19]

Among the criteria are taxation rates and flexible work rules (where the United States ranks high), but also physical infrastructure, the comparative capacities of its workers, health and educational levels, and the quality of its governance (all areas where America ranks low). Our system sacrifices workers' quality of life to be competitive. The evidence shows that you *can* do things the American way and be successful in the world market, but you don't have to. Europeans generally understand that if they do it our way, the capacities of their citizens to "earn success" will be more limited.

The Message of Mondragon

Another model for workplace democracy is the cooperative, in which workers actually own a company through shares of stock or other means.

There are thousands of such cooperatives in the United States, and as Gar Alperovitz points out in his book *America Beyond Capitalism*, they are generally quite successful. Salary differences between top and bottom are much smaller. Greater participation in workplace decisions character- izes such firms, and they are generally more stable than traditional small businesses.

In the Basque region of Spain, a federation of giant industrial co-ops called the Mondragon Corporation was established in 1956 and is now the seventh largest corporation in the country. Founded by Jose Arizmen- diarrieta, a Basque priest, Mondragon employs eighty-five thousand people working in 256 companies in four areas of activity: finance, indus- try, retail, and knowledge. The cooperatives are owned by their worker- members, and power is based on the principle of one person, one vote. Mondragon companies also run a college for workers.[20]

The difference in pay between managers and minimum-wage workers ranges from 3:1 to about 9:1 at Mondragon, with the average being about 5:1 or less. The workers themselves, as co-owners of the cooperative, set these wage levels. Workers earn about 13 percent more and managers about 30 percent less than in similar noncooperative businessess in Spain, and also earn a share of profits. The cooperatives provide extensive continued train- ing for their employees to regularly update their skills and improve their capacities, not just as workers but as citizens. The success of Mondragon shows again that companies need not operate on a model of squeezing workers and fattening owners to compete in the global economy.

The Capacity for Wonder

In a world running out of resources and increasingly poisoned by indus- trial waste (as we describe in chapter 9), there is a forgotten capacity that may be most important of all in preparing for the future. It is the capac- ity to use leisure time well. We live in a society of constant entertainment and the continual introduction of new products, advertised as needs and presented as exciting escapes from the everyday boredom of life.

During the last great era when Americans worshipped wealth, our busi- ness leaders suggested that we become exactly what we have indeed be- come. "The American citizen's first importance to his country is no longer that of citizen but that of consumer," the pro-business *Flint* (Michigan) *Journal* editorialized in 1924. "Consumption is the new necessity."[21]

In what might be called the "Age of Affluenza," we all have constantly growing expectations of new products, but each seems to satisfy less than the one before—a phenomenon economists describe as *diminishing marginal utility*. Yet this pattern of disappointment does not lead most of us to question the promises of materialism, but only to demand the next "high" even more quickly. We have become addicted to consumerism. If we did not want all these things, we could have more time, as we pointed out in chapter 6. We could *be* more instead of simply *having* more.

To understand *earned success* as the development of our gifts, rather than the right to endless novelty produced by others and hyped by marketers, requires the capacity for using leisure well. In the 1960s, we Americans assumed that we would soon have enough stuff, and since we could make it faster and faster, we would have a lot of time on our hands. We worried that unless people were prepared for the leisure society, they might simply spend all their time soaking in passive entertainment. All around the country, leisure studies and recreation departments were established at colleges and universities to teach people how to use leisure appropriately.

Sadly, over the past few years, many of our leisure and recreation studies programs have been closing down. They should be *expanding*. They are needed now more than ever.

Our levels of consumerism are not sustainable. As Dean Fortin, the mayor of Victoria, British Columbia, put it: "Our children are not going to be the consumers that we are. The world cannot stand that level of overconsumption."[22] We must begin trading productivity for time instead of stuff if we are to have a habitable planet for future generations. We need to be able to use this expanding leisure in ways that enhance well-being.

We need to train the teachers who can restore a sense of natural wonder in children jaded by ever-more-addictive and violent electronic media. We need to expose children to the natural world and to the literary and artistic treasures of human history, to the values of meditation and contemplation and focus, instead of more and more multitasking and distraction. They need to take joy in identifying trees and flowers as they now identify corporate logos.

We need to help children become friends and listeners and conversationalists, knowing that human connection is essential to happiness and to health. We need to teach them to grow their gardens and delight in the miracle of awakening life. We need to encourage them to become engaged as citizens and makers of culture rather than mere consumers, puppets on the strings of commerce. We need *investments* that will prepare them to live in a sustainable society with a sense of joy instead of deprivation.

Lyle Grant of Canada's Athabasca University, drawing on the ideas of the economist Tibor Scitovsky, author of *The Joyless Economy*, suggests that "the problem of over-consumption is rooted in the lack of *skilled consumption*" (italics his). "For Scitovsky, this skilled consumption [means] valuing . . . literature, music and conversation as worthy and superior alternatives to resource-intensive material consumption . . . Without acquisition of consumption skills, people generally fall into a pattern of engaging in resource-intensive work to consume resource-intensive material goods."[23]

If a nation seeks the greatest good for the greatest number over the longest run, it will *invest* no small proportion of its resources toward enhancing such capacities in all its citizens. It will understand that we are not truly poor in scientists and engineers and makers of *things* but poor in those who practice and teach what the nineteenth-century economist John Stuart Mill called "the Arts of Living." It will not devote all its resources to training technical specialists whose claim to such resources is that they can keep producing more stuff faster and faster.

For those who measure success wholly by the growth of the GDP, such suggestions probably seem frivolous. Yet if we do not invest in preparing our children for a new society richer in connections and capacities but not in things, the results will be catastrophic, as the next chapter warns.

CHAPTER 9

The Longest Run: Sustainability

In this chapter, we explore the third leg of Gifford Pinchot's economic stool: *the longest run*. It's pretty clear from Pinchot's background what he meant by that term. Pinchot was the first chief of the United States Forest Service. He was concerned about preserving our natural resources so they would be there for generations to come. Academics call that idea *sustainability*. It's a wonkish word, but an important one without easy synonyms.

Natural Capital

Sustainability is what gets Dave going in the morning. You see, he is an ecological economist who studies the impacts of the economy on our planet. The picture he sees isn't pretty. What is obvious from his studies is the way we humans, especially in the United States, are rapidly *wasting* our *natural capital*, all the things we get from nature to provide for our needs. Earlier in this book, we talked about different types of capital, including *built capital* (our factories, the roads we drive on, the machines that harvest our food, and so forth); *human capital* (our education and capacities); and *social capital* (our connections with family, friends, and community). But *natural capital* may be the most essential capital of all.

Understanding the value of natural capital was a by-product of Dave's childhood. He grew up in suburban Tacoma, Washington, with a half-acre "little woods" next door, a sixty-acre "big woods" public park close by, and Mount Rainier National Park only an hour away. That's a lot of beautiful nature. Fishing, clam digging, birding, hiking, and camping with a loving, environmentally aware family made for a wonderful childhood. It was time well spent. Later, Dave did graduate work in ecological economics at Louisiana State University, with the professor many consider to be the founder of the discipline, Herman E. Daly. Daly emphasized that natural capital is essential to every economy.

Economics is about preferences and choices. If you haven't thought much about the value of natural capital, try Dave's test: Would you rather have all Bill Gates's wealth (some $50 billion) or just one of nature's services, say, photosynthesis, and the good it produces—oxygen (which has no market value at all, no GDP value)? If you think you'd choose Bill's money, try holding your breath for five minutes. Of thousands in audiences that Dave has spoken to, all but two people chose oxygen. Dave quickly challenged each one to come up front and hold their breath. A college student on the swim team lasted almost two minutes.

The Sustainability Paradox

Humanity faces a paradox. Never in human history have we been more successful and powerful. The human population has never been larger; we have never been wealthier, and our technological prowess has never been greater. Yet this success and the sheer size of the human enterprise now threaten to unravel the planetary systems upon which we all depend. Our successes are endangering the sustainability of our successes! You could call it *the Sustainability Paradox*.

Consider the following facts, all flowing from the Sustainability Paradox. They indicate that we cannot keep increasing our production, consumption, resource use, and waste disposal impacts on the planet.

- There are nearly 7 billion people in the world,[1] who all need resources.
- The Earth's atmospheric, oceanic, and land temperatures are rising, threatening to increase the size of deserts, flood seacoasts, spread tropical diseases, and more.[2]
- Agriculture and grazing systems already occupy 24 percent of the Earth's land area.[3]
- Global fish catches peaked in the late 1980s; today one quarter of fisheries are overfished.[4]
- Freshwater shortages are rapidly escalating, threatening drinking water, irrigation, and industry.[5]

- World oil production has been flat since 2005 and is expected to decline.[6]
- Twenty-five countries are now completely deforested.[7]
- Human consumption runs rivers dry, including the Nile, Yellow, and Colorado.[8]
- Industrial chemicals damage the ozone layer, causing higher skin cancer rates.[9]
- Human-driven species extinction is occurring at a rate seldom known in geologic history and one thousand times the natural rate.[10]
- Hurricanes and typhoons are larger and more frequent.[11]
- Harmful industrial chemicals are found in every human being's body.[12]
- World food prices are rising, while one billion people remain malnourished.[13]

Whew!

We Have Seen Bigfoot . . . and He Is Us

How far from sustainability are we?

More than a decade ago, two scientists at the University of British Columbia, Mathis Wackernagel and Bill Rees, developed a gross measure of sustainability called *the ecological footprint*. In short, it is a measure of the resources, energy, and space needed to provide your stuff and absorb your waste. Wackernagel and Rees developed this measure to provide a way for people to assess and reduce their negative impact on the planet. It is also a broad estimate of whether our economy is sustainable or in *overshoot*, that is, unsustainable, implying an eventual and undesirable ecological reckoning. The ecological footprint measures the share of the Earth's productive land and water necessary to provide for the lifestyle of an individual or a country. And we Americans fill the biggest shoes on the planet. (Check out your ecological footprint size by taking a simple test at: www.myfootprint.org.)

Both authors of this book took the global footprint measure and both use roughly fifteen acres of land and resources. We are like the average European, who uses about twelve acres. If we were average Americans, we would use over twenty acres.[14] There is a problem with that. The

Global Footprint Network (www.footprintnetwork.org), which now promotes the concept of the ecological footprint around the world, calculates that there are less than five acres of productive land and water available for every person on Earth. So if everyone were to adopt the current American lifestyle, we would need five planets to meet the demand. That leaves us about four planets short.

The figure below tracks the hectares per person consumed by the United States and other countries. Our big feet take eight hectares per person. The Global Footprint Network estimates that we are already using 1.5 Earth's worth of biocapacity each year to meet humanity's demands.[15] In other words, we are already in overshoot, depleting and degrading critical natural systems. And we are still growing by leaps and bounds.

Now for some good news: Fortunately, we know how to reduce our footprint. Taking individual action is important. How you invest your time, energy, expenditures, and space really does count.

Importantly, we understand these problems better than people understood past problems. Consider, for example, the Black Plague in the four-

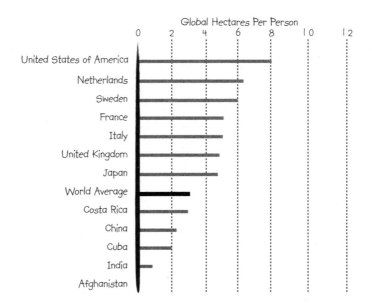

Ecological Footprint

teenth century. Back then, nearly one third of humanity died without anyone knowing that bacteria were the cause. Explanations for the plague included bad smells, maggots, the wrath of God, Jews, heretics, excessive merriment, excessive sadness, and the "evil eye." "Cures" applied included smelling sweet fragrances, avoiding maggots, flailing yourself to appease a wrathful God, killing Jews and heretics, cultivating sadness or euphoria, hiding, or heading for the hills (which also spread the plague). Desperate guesses, self-interested ideology, and ignorance left humanity without effective solutions, leading people down a horrific trail of tears, sickness, suffering, and death.

Bacteria are not to blame for the Sustainability Paradox; rather, as the comic strip character Pogo put it, "We have met the enemy . . . and he is us."

We need to unhitch the rail cars of ecological catastrophe from the economic engine, not just in the United States but worldwide. The National Academy of Sciences summed up the situation in 2009: "The world is entering a new geologic epoch, sometimes called the Anthropocene, in which human activities will largely control the evolution of the Earth's environment."[16]

The Right Picture

On January 10, 1610, Galileo saw the moons of Jupiter with the recently invented telescope. He assumed they were stars. But on the next few nights, he saw them move with Jupiter across the night sky. Incredibly, they changed position in relation to each other, unlike any star. Then it dawned on him. He was watching moons orbit Jupiter.

He published his findings in March 1610, making the case that the Earth and planets orbit the sun. That was earthshaking news. Religious teaching had it that *all* heavenly bodies orbit the Earth. Galileo's view was strongly resisted. Though forced to recant, he eventually won the argument. The older worldview was proven false. Today, it is considered absurd.

There is no substitute for getting the big picture right. In the economic cosmology of twentieth-century economics, the economy is the big thing, a container with no physical limit to expansion and one that contains everything else. The environment is seen as but a subsector within the economy, providing resources (as shown on the following page).

Incorrect World View

Correct World View

The actual physical relationship between the environment and the economy is quite the opposite of that implied by our current economic paradigm. The economy is actually a physical subset of the environment, the source of all that comprises the economy (as shown above).

Solving the Sustainability Paradox requires understanding the true relationship between the economy and the environment. For too long, we have considered the environment to be part of the economy—the source of our resources. We need to begin to think instead of the economy as a wholly owned subsidiary of the environment. As the famous environmentalist David Brower once put it, "There will be no corporations on a dead planet."[17]

Economies Need Nature

Natural systems provide foundational economic goods (things you can drop on your toe) and services (benefits that you can't drop on your toe). *Nature's goods*, including oxygen, water, land, food, timber and fiber, minerals, and energy, are required by all economies. In fact, every atom of the economy came originally from nature. Nature's goods can be measured by weight, volume, and space.

Nature's (or "ecosystem") services are far more difficult to measure. Ecosystem services include storm protection, a stable climate, flood protection, waste assimilation, nutrient cycling, and natural processes that cleanse the air, water, and land. If these services are lost, we suffer damage and pay for lots of costly built capital replacements, like dikes or levees. Nature's services also include educational, spiritual, cultural, recreational, and aesthetic benefits that contribute to the economy and our quality of life. *All* economies and the habitability of the planet require nature's goods and services.

We can categorize the goods and services *that we know of.* Each of these categories holds many subcategories. For example, recreation includes hiking and biking. These goods and services are shown in the table on page 160.[18]

A Junk Tree Saves Lives

Nature holds far more value than meets the economic eye. Consider just one item in one category of the accompanying table. Northwest loggers using two-man crosscut saws left some "valueless" trees standing in the 1920s. Thus a scruffy 250-year-old Pacific yew (*Taxus brevifolia*) tree still flourishes in Dave's yard. More recently armed with chain saws, loggers slashed and burned yew trees without replanting them across millions of acres of Northwest timberlands. Then, unexpectedly, extract from the bark of a Pacific yew tree found twenty-five miles from Dave's house was tested and discovered to have cancer-fighting properties. That extract, called Taxol, is now the world's most widely used and most successful

Ecosystem Goods, Services and Benefits

	Good/Service	Economic Benefit to People
Provisioning	Fresh Water	Water for human consumption, irrigation and industrial use.
	Food	Food for human consumption.
	Fiber and Fuel	Biological materials used for clothes, fuel, art and building. Geological materials used for energy, construction or other purposes.
	Medicinal Resources	Biological materials used for medicines.
	Companion Resources	Ornamental and companion uses (flowers, plants, pets, and other).
Regulating	Gas Regulation	Generation of atmospheric oxygen, regulation of sulfur dioxide, nitrogen carbon dioxide and other gaseous atmospheric components.
	Climate Regulation	Regulation of global and local temperature, climate, and weather, including evapotranspiration, cloud formation, and rainfall.
	Flood Protection	Protection from floods, storms, and drought.
	Soil Erosion Control	Erosion protection provided by plant roots and tree cover.
	Water Regulation	Water absorption during rains and release in dry times, temperature and flow regulation for people, plants and animals.
	Biological Control	Natural control of diseases and pest species.
	Water Quality and Waste Processing	Absorption of organic waste, natural water filtration, pollution reduction.
Supporting	Soil Formation	Formation of sand and soil from decaying vegetation and erosion.
	Nutrient Cycling	Transfer of nutrients from one place to another; transformation of critical nutrients from unusable to usable forms.
	Biodiversity and Habitat	Providing habitat for plants and animals and their full diversity.
	Primary Productivity	Growth by plants provides basis for all terrestrial and most marine food chains.
	Pollination	Fertilization of plants and crops through natural systems.
Cultural	Aesthetic Value	The role which natural beauty plays in attracting people to live, work and recreate in an area.
	Recreation and Tourism	The contribution of ecosystems and environments in attracting people to engage in recreational activities.
	Scientific Knowledge	The value of natural systems for scientific research.
	Educational Value	The value of natural systems for education.
	Spiritual and Religious Value	The use of nature for religious and spiritual purposes.
	Cultural Value	The value of nature for cultural purposes.

treatment for breast cancer. Yew trees suddenly rose from junk tree status to medicinal wonder, becoming the most valuable trees in the forest!

Taxol is a wildly complicated molecule. Without nature having created it, humanity would never have synthesized it. It is not a perfect cure. Eliminating industrial carcinogens would do more to reduce cancer fatalities. But Taxol has made a great difference for many women. Without the yew tree's cure, many more would have died. Many more children would have been without mothers. How much value would have been lost? And how many Taxols still await discovery? Ecosystems are valuable. Biodiversity is valuable even if we don't know its full value yet.[19]

Vital Concepts of Ecological Economics

Nature is the original economic engine. Ecosystems can be self-maintaining, solar-fueled, self-governed (a libertarian's dream!), and provide benefits in perpetuity (if we don't destroy them). For example:

1. *Natural systems produce whole suites of goods and services.* Forests prevent flooding; provide timber, water, water filtration, habitat, shade, oxygen, recreation, beauty, and more.

2. *Natural systems require less maintenance than built capital.* Though restoration and other investments are often required, healthy ecosystems can be largely self-maintaining. Built capital requires maintenance and still falls apart. Restoring the Mississippi Delta wetlands provides self-maintaining hurricane protection indefinitely. Levees fall apart every fifty years or less.

3. *All "built capital" is built out of natural capital.* The metal, glass, rubber, and plastic comprising cars and the rest of our "stuff" comes right out of the planet. In addition, water delivered to your house requires nature's good, water, and built capital, the pipes. Natural and built capital are complements. Pipes don't substitute for water.

4. *Matter and energy are conserved, and useful energy is disbursed.* This is basic science. Matter does not magically appear or disappear, and energy is dissipated (the first and second laws of thermodynamics). Economies do abide by the laws of science, yet much of economic theory was developed without attention to physical balances. Thus toxic waste and greenhouse gases and their costs didn't exist in economic models.

5. *There are limits to the physical size of the economy.* As the physical dimensions of the economy expand, natural systems and the

essential values they provide are damaged or lost. Eventually, the lost benefits and increased costs of degraded natural and social systems outweigh the marginal benefits of a physically bigger economy. Herman E. Daly calls this *uneconomic growth*. Attempting unlimited physical growth of the economy is neither possible nor desirable.[20]

In the 1930s, when the discipline of macroeconomics was born, natural capital was abundant and thus less valuable. Indoor plumbing and built capital were scarce and more valuable. No wonder our economic measures focused on the stuff we made. Today, clothes, plastic toys, asphalt, and other material goods are wildly abundant and relatively less valuable. Water, flood protection, climate stability, oil, fish, and all the other goods and services of natural capital are increasingly scarce and more valuable. Solving the Sustainability Paradox requires that our economic actions reflect these scarcity and value changes.

The situation facing North America's largest river delta highlights the confluence of the economy and nature, the concepts of ecological economics, and the Sustainability Paradox.

Lessons from Louisiana

Louisiana and the Mississippi River Delta are laboratories for sustainability lessons. The delta is the sportsman's paradise and houses more than 2 million people, 40 percent of the nation's coastal wetlands, abundant fisheries, wildlife, shellfish, agriculture, timber, trade, beaches, endangered species, water, shipping, oil, gas, chemicals, Cajun culture, jazz, and Tabasco Sauce. It is also home to the aptly named *cancer alley*, but we won't go there, at least not yet.

As a graduate student, Dave worked a summer for the Louisiana Geological Survey examining the ecosystem services provided by the wetlands of the Mississippi Delta, including the hurricane reduction value of the wetlands, and the trade-offs between oil production and renewable natural resources.

There are facts that no one disputes. Since 1930, the Mississippi Delta has lost 1.2 million acres of wetlands, converted to open water. Levees channel billions of tons of sediment and trillions of gallons of freshwater from the Mississippi Rive off the continental shelf into the Gulf of

Mexico. That lost water and sediment could rebuild and sustain the delta. Mississippi Basin dams catch sand, once destined to build barrier islands. Canals for oil drilling cut up the wetlands, wiping out huge tracts. The waters of the Gulf of Mexico are heating up. That warmer water powers hurricanes, which have become larger and more frequent since 1970. The sea level is rising. Atmospheric temperatures are rising. The delta is sinking. If the landscape falls apart, so do the economies it contains.

Hurricanes gain power over open water and lose power over wetlands. But the Louisiana coastline has retreated more than thirty linear miles in some areas. Dave returned to Louisiana after Hurricanes Katrina and Rita had done their damage. Standing on the shoulder of a remnant levee overlooking the gaping breach where Hurricane Katrina's storm surge swept away houses and the lives of men, women, and children, he experienced a cold sweat of horror. Katrina alone caused $200 billion in damage. It disrupted the nation's oil supply, drove 2 million people from their homes, and killed another fourteen hundred.

Tragedies require good detectives, but hurricanes leave sizable fingerprints, clues to the source of the damages. Louisiana State University professors Paul Kemp and Hassan Mashriqui marshaled their students and recorded the debris lines along the coast. They revealed a stunning pattern. Where there was open water, the debris line was high, showing a big storm surge. Levees were demolished. Where there were barrier islands, wetlands, scrub oak, cypress swamps, and other natural barriers, the debris line was low, and levees were intact. For generations, many had said that wetland features dramatically reduce hurricane storm surge. Now there was hard proof.

Wetlands reduce the storm surge by more than one foot for about every 2.5 miles of wetlands. With twenty-five miles of wetlands, a hurricane's storm surge could be reduced by ten feet. That saves levees, property, and lives. As little as one mile of wetland in front of a levee reduces the pounding wave action to a bathtub-style rise, substantially protecting levee integrity. The hurricanes of 2005 demolished or severely damaged over fifty levee sections, while wetlands protected most other levees.

Wetlands provided another advantage: Fifteen Gulf cities treated waste using wetlands. These systems were up and running again within months, while traditional sewage treatment plants were destroyed. New Orleans and other cities have switched to wetlands waste treatment because it also builds cypress swamps, providing added hurricane protection.

The choice for people in the area is clear: relocate or restore. Abandon the coast or invest in restoring the phenomenally productive Mississippi River Delta. Fortunately, there's an able ally: *The Mississippi River itself has the energy, sediment, and water to restore the delta.* Dave is now on a scientific panel to identify projects to restore this delta, which will provide greater hurricane protection, increased fisheries production, recreation, "dead zone" reduction in the Gulf of Mexico, carbon sequestration, and reduced upstream and downstream flooding.

The wetlands expert John Day, professor emeritus at Louisiana State University, suggests that "as the great Mississippi River Delta disappears, so do the ecosystems, economies and people that it holds. The Mississippi River is the solution. It has the water, sediment and energy to rebuild land, defend against hurricanes and again provide habitat, safety, livelihood, and prosperity. We must look to the natural functioning of the delta to guide us in restoration."[21]

It will cost about $15 billion to restore the Mississippi River Delta. Is the investment worth it? Is sustainability worth the cost? The 2010 study *Gaining Ground*, conducted by Dave and six others, partially valued eleven of twenty-three categories of economic services that the Mississippi Delta provides, showing $12–47 billion in benefits *every year.* Products and services, such as drinking water, fisheries production, hurricane protection, recreation, carbon sequestration, and flood protection were included in the calculation.[22]

Treated like a capital asset, the delta's minimum asset value would be between $330 billion and $1.3 trillion.[23] Aggressive restoration would provide at least $62 billion in avoided costs and additional benefits. Large-scale restoration is a good investment. In addition, reconnected wetlands do not degrade in fifty years like a levee. If the wetlands are maintained, these economic benefits could flow indefinitely. Levees, cities, economies, and people require healthy natural systems.

If Hurricanes Katrina and Rita weren't enough, the Gulf of Mexico got hit again on April 20, 2010, when an explosion and billowing fire broke out on BP's Deepwater Horizon off-shore oil rig in five thousand feet of water, drilling thirteen thousand feet below the seabed. The U.S. government guessed that 4.9 million barrels (254 million gallons) of crude oil belched into the biologically rich Gulf waters. At $100/barrel, that oil would have sold for $490 million on the global market. Disturbingly, the GDP recorded the spill as a vast economic gain, far greater than if the oil had actually been refined and sold. Cleanup costs, legal costs, ships rented, and compensation paid out all added to the GDP, between $5 billion and $8 billion by June 2010 and still rising.[24] BP is selling assets and setting aside $15 billion over three years for the compensation fund.[25] Losses related to the spill, such as lost fisheries production, are not counted as losses in the GDP; they just don't appear at all. Louisiana typifies the confluence of challenges forcing economic transformation: peak oil and climate change.

Trouble Peaking on the Horizon

Through the eyes of an economist and geologist, the oil spill marked even deeper trouble. The United States is drilling in deep water because *it is running out of oil*. In 2005, Chevron bought a two-page *New York Times* advertisement stating, "It took us 125 years to use the first trillion barrels of oil. We'll use the next trillion in 30." It continues, "One thing is clear: the age of easy oil is over." The ad was both a warning about peak oil and a pitch to "drill, baby, drill."

It takes tremendous amounts of energy to obtain oil from deep water. Why is the United States investing the last of its cheap and easily recovered oil to pursue expensive, hazardous, hard-to-get oil? It pays off for oil companies, which receive between $6 billion and $36 billion in federal subsidies annually to go get it. However, it would be far more sensible to burn less gas commuting (an unhappy activity anyway) and invest to get off oil. U.S. and world oil reserves are shrinking. Climate and water are also economic game changers. The Sustainability Paradox really means that our current economy is less viable every year that water and oil scarcity rise and the climate heats up. Fortunately, we can burn less oil. We can use water more efficiently. We can build a climate-friendly economy that is better than what we have now. Economic achievement and ecological disaster need not be coupled. We've got solutions.

The Solutions Are Here

Solving the Sustainability Paradox is not about finding more solutions. As the Mississippi Delta demonstrates, we actually have potential solutions identified and largely worked out. This goes for virtually all of our ecological problems. More investment is needed, but know-how and

Solutions

lems		
efficient ildings	**Solution/New Fields:** Green architecture LEEDs and other green building standards	
	Individual Actions	Actions Together
	• Living in smaller homes • Implementing energy efficiency improvements	• Including green building benefits and costs • Instituting impact fees that reflect true costs
erfishing	**Solution/New Fields:** Marine Protected Reserves Ecosystem based fisheries management	
	Individual Actions	Actions Together
	• Buying only sustainable seafood (Follow Monterey Bay Aquarium s seafood recommendations) • Helping restore local marine areas	• Enforcing science-based fisheries regulation • Developing community based fisheries management
mployment	**Solution/New Fields:** Ecological economics Green (sustainable) job growth	
	Individual Actions	Actions Together
	• Buying local sustainable goods and services • Investing in green economic industries	• Replacing payroll taxes with resource and a more steeply graduated income taxes • Enacting a Civilian Conservation Corps (CCC)
ate nge scale d)	**Solution/New Fields:** Climate trust Climate economics — Low carbon intensity technology	
	Individual Actions	Actions Together
	• Reducing household green house gases (GHG) emissions • Shifting to non-fossil fuel alternatives, reducing carbon intensity	• Providing tax incentives for carbon reduction, and tax disincentives for carbon emissions • Investing in conversion to low carbon infrastructure and

ogy are not significant barriers to adopting successful solutions. er solutions we've got in hand, solutions that work today. The de- ould take books to describe, and in fact, books with the details . The table above shows a cursory overview of problems, identified s/new fields (dealing with these problems), and actions that we can

Endangered Species	Solution/New Fields: Conservation biology Ecosystem services	
	Individual Actions	**Actions Together**
	• Supporting local conservation • Restoring specific endangered species habitat	• Implementing the Endangered Species Act • Identifying and securing sufficient habitat to retain national biodiversity
Hydrologic Impacts	Solution/New Fields: Ecological Economics Environmental hydrology Ecosystem service modeling and mapping	
	Individual Actions	**Actions Together**
	• Restoring local watersheds and building home rain gardens • Conserving water	• Establishing a watershed investment district • Changing accounting rules to include values for potable water, flood protection and stormwater conveyance
Toxic Materials	Solution/New Fields: Clean production Industrial ecology ecology Greenchemistry Non-toxic material science	
	Individual Actions	**Actions Together**
	• Purchasing green products • Removing household toxic substances	• Mandating phase out of toxics • Enacting cradle to cradle producer responsibility
Sustainable Agriculture	Solution/New Fields: Permaculture Agroecology	
	Individual Actions	**Actions Together**
	• Gardening • Purchasing local food	• Shifting subsidies and taxes • Compensating Ecosystem service compensation

take as individuals and collectively to help solve these problems. Is it more complicated than this? Yes. Can existing solutions be implemented? Yes.

These are just a few of thousands of solutions available. What we need to secure prosperity over the longest run is to *implement* the solutions we have in hand. That would resolve the Sustainability Paradox. So why aren't our solutions being applied at the scale required to solve our problems? What is the problem with solving our problems? Besides politics, the answer is simple: We are not investing in solutions.

Investment: The Key to Securing the Longest Run

All these solutions require investment sufficient to the scale of the problems. Solving the Sustainability Paradox requires enough investment to transform the economy and our behavior so we live well and within our ecological and planetary means.

Let us be clear about our assumptions regarding positive change.

- The economy's future requires securing environmental sustainability.
- Fixing the environment requires fixing the economy.
- Fixing the economy requires shifting investments from problem promotion to solution implementation.

It's actually easier to change the economy than to reengineer human biology to safely absorb carcinogens. It is easier to reduce carbon dioxide emissions than defend ourselves against ever-larger hurricanes, floods, and droughts. It is less costly to manage better what we best understand and control: the economy.

In the largest sense, economies are easy to change. Transformation is what economies do. Every thirty years we rip up the roads, gut the buildings, replace stocks of clothing, appliances, lights, cars, trains, planes, and electronics, save for a few antiques. At a slightly slower pace, all private ownership, all leadership, all management turns over, as one generation passes onto another. We redo practically the whole economy every few decades (without the present urgencies). This habit is wasteful and needs to change. We need to ditch the "throwaway" in our throwaway society. In a generation, we have used more resources than all the people who ever lived before the mid-twentieth century.

Durability is valuable and sustainable. But the point is that economies are constantly remade, even within ten years. And changing the way we design our economy is imperative and not just possible; it is well within our reach.

Between 1934 and 1944, the U.S. economy was transformed (see chapter 10). Ten years after World War II devastated European countries and Japan, their economies were rebuilt, not into prewar economies, but into new systems. China galvanized investment from the United States, Europe, and Japan since the early 1990s on a scale never known in human history. Much of global manufacturing moved to China in a single decade. In 2010, China became the world's second-largest economy.

The universal excuse for not investing in solutions to shift our economy to prosperous sustainability is: "It costs too much." Truly effective investments are frowned upon as unsupportable costs, while real costs are *externalized* (dumped on someone else). Every day, this kind of thinking slows the adoption of less expensive, better, fairer, more efficient and productive sustainability investments.

As built capital is more abundant and relatively *less valuable*, while nature's goods and services are scarce and *more valuable*, investing in more built capital may actually increase the scarcity of what is most valuable to us, undermining both ecological and economic sustainability.

Investing in Sustainability

If saving the environment and saving the economy both require shifting investment, what does it take to do that? Six improvements in economic analysis (accurate accounting, cost/benefit analysis, pricing and green taxes, private investment tools, banning bads, and moving big money) could move trillions of investment dollars from the unsustainable side of the balance sheet to the sustainable side.

Accurate Accounting. Seattle's population quadrupled between 1880 and 1889. The city had no sewer system. Four unregulated private water companies drew water from local lakes, into which sewage was often dumped. After epidemics of cholera and typhoid, Seattle became known as one of the unhealthiest cities in the United States.[26] Finally, in 1889, citizens had had enough.

That year, Seattleites voted (93 percent "yes") to establish Seattle Public Utilities (SPU) to provide water to the city. SPU purchased much of the upper Cedar River Watershed in 1899 to secure a safe water supply on a scale dwarfing the city's needs. Had the Seattle City Council required a quick return on the investment, the purchase would likely have been rejected. However, the goal was not to maximize "net present value," but to provide a safe, reliable, and sufficient drinking water supply for the people of Seattle *in perpetuity*. By 1901, clean water was flowing, banishing cholera and typhoid.[27] By 1909, Seattle was considered one of the healthiest cities in the United States.

It was a sound investment by any measure. Today, SPU would have to pay $200 million to build a filtration plant to do what the Cedar River Watershed does for free. Filtration plants, like all built capital, depreciate and fall apart. The forest in the watershed did not depreciate or fall apart. It appreciated and grew. Relative to the size of the asset, a forest also requires light maintenance. The watershed now provides far more water and far more dollar value than ever imagined by most citizens in 1899. Today, Seattle's tap water is also among the cleanest in the world. Better than bottled water, it has no endocrine disruptors or pharmaceuticals, because no one is flushing anything into the watershed above the supply source.

Contemporaries of Gifford Pinchot in Seattle, San Francisco, Tacoma, Portland, Vancouver (British Columbia), New York, and other cities put his goal of *the longest run* into durable practice, accessing forested watersheds to provide clean water *in perpetuity*. Impressively, the management and staff of these utilities have held true to that mission.

In November 2010, these six watershed public utilities, which provide water for over 16 million Americans, met in Seattle to discuss a problem with their bottom lines.[28] These utilities' current balance sheets list their watersheds as assets only for their bare land and timber values. There's not a penny of value on their books for providing and filtering water. Yet these watersheds require investment: fencing cows back and improving septic systems in New York; funding restoration on private lands in San Francisco; reducing siltation by removing roads in Seattle and Portland; acquiring additional watershed lands for Tacoma and Vancouver. That takes financial investments.

Watershed operations and maintenance are chronically underfinanced. If SPU needs a new fleet of vehicles, it can borrow money, buy the vehicles (counted as assets), and pay back the loans with income from water sales. But there is no dedicated capital budget to restore the watershed. It's hard to invest in a valueless asset. If the value of the watershed for providing water counted as an asset on SPU's books, the utility could sell bonds and invest to restore the watershed, improve water quality and production, and bill ratepayers for the capital improvement. That is far less costly to ratepayers than building a filtration plant. A watershed with an asset value for producing water also justifies a sufficient budget for maintaining the watershed.

In addition, the utilities realized their watersheds are providing a lot of other valuable goods and services, including flood protection, biodiversity, carbon sequestration, habitat, and more, all of which don't show up on the books.

Facilities, pipes, vehicles, buildings, roads, computers, and copy machines count. This is not utilities' choice, nor is it their fault. The accounting rules for governmental entities are set by the Governmental Accounting Standards Board (GASB). Six major U.S. utilities are moving to request an accounting change from GASB so they can actually count watersheds as assets that provide and purify drinking water. That would enable increased financing for productive investments to conserve and restore these watersheds.

Water is the tip of the iceberg. The deeper issue is that legal accounting rules require governments and private industry to account for *built capital* assets, but not *natural capital* assets, though both may produce the same product. But the economy has changed. Natural capital is now scarce and more valuable. Enabling adequate investment in natural capital requires improved accounting rules. We need accounting that appropriately values the benefits of aquifers, deltas, climate, forests, farms, snow pack, rivers, lakes, wetlands, and other natural systems that affect every American community.

Cost/Benefit Analysis. What counts as cost and benefits in the economic analysis that guides investment is important as well. All federal and state agencies, cities, counties, and many private firms utilize cost/benefit analysis to make infrastructure investment decisions.

For about a decade, the United Kingdom has required that ecosystem services be valued and factored into all flood protection cost/benefit analysis. This has resulted in the more long-term and cost-effective approach of buying out some properties, setting levees back, and providing more robust flood protection, adding habitat, improving water quality, increasing recreation, lowering flood insurance rates, and reducing property damage.

Nature's goods and services are a bargain and a good investment opportunity. Washington's Puget Sound Basin houses more than 4 million people. Its natural systems provide "work" and benefits worth at least $9 billion, and up to $83 billion in value every year.[29] Treated like an economic asset, the natural capital of the Puget Sound basin would be valued between $300 billion and $12.6 trillion.[30] That's big value. And it can now be included in economic analysis. How can we better include ecosystem services in economic analysis?

The next generation of tools is being developed to do just that and help guide public and private investment. Ecosystems and economies are dynamic, living systems that interact across the landscape and in people's daily lives. From every drop of water you drink, bite you eat, toilet you flush, or breath you take, something is provisioned. Watersheds and aquifers provision water. On the other hand, airborne mercury from burning coal contaminates lakes, then fish, then people. These stocks, flows, and processes can be mapped and modeled. Dave and his colleagues, led by Ferdinando Villa, received a National Science Foundation grant to develop cutting-edge ecosystem service modeling. Their software program utilizes geographic information systems (GIS) combined with modeling software, enabling the mapping and modeling of natural systems and economies as never before.

Here's the simplified description. Picture each ecosystem service in a watershed, like flood protection, drinking water, or recreation, mapped for an area with three overlays.

1. A map of the provisioning area for that service.
2. A map of the people and industries that benefit from that service.
3. A map of the impairments to that service.

Flood protection, for example, is provided by both natural and built capital assets, and these can be mapped. These assets include forests and rivers, snow pack, permeable soils, dams, and levees. Rainfall levels and how water moves through the landscape can also be modeled. That's the first mapping/modeling process. The beneficiaries of flood protection usually live in the lower reaches where flooding most often occurs. They can also be mapped. Impairments to flood protection, such as a bridge or natural constriction narrowing the floodway, denuded hills, floodplain fill, impermeable surfaces, or other features, can also be mapped and modeled. Drinking water is provisioned differently by natural assets that overlap with flood control and a built capital distribution system. The beneficiaries include well-sourced households and people served by public utilities. Impairments might include a plume of polluted water threatening the aquifer. Recreation has another map. The water supply for San Francisco, for example, is sourced from public lands, in this case, Yosemite National Park, a critical conservation and recreation area.

Now consider combining the three maps for each of the ecosystem services in a single watershed. Suddenly, a new view of value emerges. Overlap on the landscape between the provisioning of drinking water, flood protection, recreation, salmon restoration, storm water conveyance, biodiversity, carbon sequestration, and other services can be revealed. That mapping, when used to influence public policy, design restoration, or build infrastructure, can provide better services and save a lot of money. This analysis is stronger than traditional cost/benefit analysis because it is spatially specific. It shows the beneficiaries and how investment value is distributed in time and space.

Prices and Green Taxes. In the U.S. market economy, the citizen consumer is king. Personal consumption is the largest portion of our GDP, accounting for 70 percent of the total. But central to the concept of consumer sovereignty is the idea that consumers understand the full costs of their purchases—to themselves and to others.

Markets can only function efficiently if all costs are included in the price of the product. Otherwise, market values are distorted. The costs of such *negative externalities* as the pollution caused by burning gasoline are often not included in the price of the product and are borne by someone outside the transaction—taxpayers or asthma victims, for example. Negative externalities are unjust, uneconomic, and undesirable. Most economists agree on that. Thus, if prices don't reflect true costs, markets may be doing more damage than good.

Citizens can't be good sovereigns if prices don't reflect true costs. If you don't adjust the price, the costs will be there anyway. It's just that they come later in the form of cancer, a financial crisis, extinction of species, flood damage, or other problems. Cigarettes are a good example. Once barely taxed, they produced incalculable damage and billions of dollars of losses in lawsuits and medical expenses. Today, the price of cigarettes is closer to the real cost, people smoke much less, and the tax money is in part used to pay for treatment of people who get lung cancer. It is better for everyone to get these true costs right initially, and that can shift investment on a grand scale.

Private Investment Tools. Getting the prices right and improving private investment tools are closely related. Green building provides an example: Were the full benefits of conserving water or using nontoxic materials included in the price of homes and buildings, investment would quickly shift to green building, industry-wide. If a sufficient portion of the savings generated by a green building could be returned to the builder, owner, and renter, that would adjust the cost, asset, and income variables in the real estate investment models that large and small developers utilize. It would quickly shift billions in real estate investment.

Markets do not naturally include the cost of pollution in the price of the product. As the example of cigarettes has taught us, government taxes and charges can be used to correct for externalized costs. These green taxes make markets and economies more efficient. In the twenty-first century, paying attention to what guides investment is really the key to saving the environment and the economy.

Every firm and industry has financial tools to direct internal investment. Industrial indicators are planning tools that integrate environmental, social, and financial goals to assist companies in performing better. Better indicators can help answer the most common request from industry middle management: "Help me make the financial case to justify green investment."

These tools help businesses measure negative and positive environmental impacts, to the firm and society. Some businesses don't care (that's the topic of the next section). This section is about innovators, not greenwashers.

Five paper mills in Washington State (Simpson Tacoma Kraft, Port Angeles Nippon Paper Industries, Port Townsend Paper Corporation, Boise Wallula, and Grays Harbor Paper) were willing to surpass environmental compliance standards by developing and applying new indicators. Saving energy and improving processes also helped the bottom line. The paper mills contributed staff time and data.

The indicators were developed not to compare paper mills (which have fundamentally different products and processes), but to assist mill managers in combining improved performance, energy efficiency, better environmental outcomes, wood chip sourcing, and improved bottom lines. They include forty-two environmental indicators, fourteen economic indicators, and sixteen social indicators, ranging from emissions and energy consumption to jobs, customer satisfaction, worker conditions, and value added.

Potential investments identified were extensive, including fixing compressor leaks, surveying wildlife, and sourcing wood chips from state-certified timberlands. These changes enable paper mills to better implement green investment improvements within their regular maintenance and capital improvement schedules, reducing costs and improving environmental performance. Adopting indicators specific to every industry would shift trillions of investment dollars toward sustainability.

This requires a lot of "nitty-gritty" in every industry, in every single plant. That's a lot of good that do-gooders can achieve, but what about bad actors?

Banning Bads. Full-cost pricing would go a long way toward shifting investment and improving products. But in many cases, economic efficiency is best served by banning toxic chemicals and other dangerous products entirely. Had asbestos been banned earlier, lives and bankrupt corporations could have been saved. Some trade should also be banned, for example, the trades in ozone depleting substances, toxic waste, or endangered species. These trades are not trades in "goods," nor are they fair and just commerce. No price adjustment can make them so. There is no replacement for just law, well enforced. When a United Nations agreement, the Basel Convention, banned the export of hazardous waste from rich to poor countries, such exports became rare. As Jim Puckett, the executive director of the Basel Action Network (BAN), puts it: "If you don't allow toxic waste to be cheaply dumped or exported, it's like plugging the exhaust pipe. Costs rise, industry suddenly decides that investing in cleaner technology and not producing toxic waste is affordable. That's the real solution. As enforcement has risen the trade in raw hazardous waste has withered. We see few cases these days. Now it has shifted to hidden wastes in 'recyclable' products." Puckett is now working to reduce the toxics in recycling electronic waste, car batteries, and ships. If these products were designed to be nontoxic and to be easily recycled, we would have a more efficient and sustainable economy.[31] (See www.ban .org for more information.)

Moving Big Money. Changing accounting rules, improving economic analysis to reveal costs and benefits, strengthening financial regulation, and changing taxes and pricing are critical to changing incentives and investment at the scales of the household, firm, nation, and world. Here are three additional ideas that would move large amounts of money to shift our economy to sustainability.

An *Atmospheric Trust* is the suggestion of Working Assets founder Peter Barnes and Robert Costanza.[32] The trust would be a new institution, administered by trustees with the mission to "protect the assets of the climate system and atmosphere) for the benefit of current and future generations." Since greenhouse gases are a current threat to the climate, it would regulate greenhouse gas emissions. The trust would create a global cap on carbon based on precautionary science. The price of carbon would be set to meet this cap either through a carbon tax or through a cap and trade system. Caps set quantity and allow price to vary; taxes set price and allow quantity to vary. For that reason, Barnes and Costanza prefer a cap and trade system.

The Atmospheric Trust would auction carbon permits under the cap and trade system. If the auction price were ten to eighty dollars per ton, a global trust would bring in between about $1 trillion to $3.6 trillion. Because all of humanity and future generations are the "shareholders" in the atmosphere, the revenues would be spent in three ways.

First, every person would get a portion refunded (this would redistribute wealth from carbon emitters to carbon conservers and raise incomes in poor countries). Second, a portion of the funding would go for replacing coal and other carbon-intensive technologies with renewable energy and compensate for ecosystem services and carbon sequestration. Third, a portion would be spent to run the Atmospheric Trust. Interestingly, the fund would not give money to governments. Trustees would be appointed for their commitment to the mission of protecting climate and the atmosphere, not based on any political, geographic, or other criteria. All expenditures would be posted on the Internet.

No system is perfect, but the Atmospheric Trust is a refreshing proposal because it is an institution set at the scale of the problem with a mission to solve it and a funding mechanism to do so.[33]

Another suggestion is a small currency and financial transactions tax of less than about .25 percent further described in (chapter 12). This tax would shift a significant part of $4 trillion in daily speculative currency and stock trading out into more constructive investment. This would likely crowd about $3 trillion into actual investments rather than speculation. Real investors would pay little and gain from greater market stability. The tax would also raise substantial funds from remaining speculators, on the order of tens of billions. This could be dedicated to investments in our energy/climate transition.

Shifting off a declining fossil fuel economy and onto a sustainable path requires investment on a large scale, both private and public. That implies changing the incentives that guide trillions of dollars in private investment, ensuring that sustainability investments outperform ecological crash-and-burn investments. That takes active government policy. In addition, American corporations and citizens will have to pay higher taxes to accomplish this infrastructure shift and keep the deficit under control. Raising the marginal income tax rates more in line with those of Europe would generate the funds to create jobs and build an economy that will be more sustainable and prosperous than the unsustainable and currently declining American economy.

Regarding peak oil, as Republican representative Rosco Bartlett stated before Congress, "What we need is a program that has a total commitment of World War II, the technology focus of putting a man on the moon, and the urgency of the Manhattan Project."[34]

Solving the Sustainability Paradox

Humanity faces a paradox. The economy that produced affluence is now degrading the very ecological systems that support it. Shifting our economy off oil and fossil fuels to renewable sources, conserving water, and biodiversity will entail tremendous investments.

How can we afford it? Finance has never been cheaper. First, move trillions from speculation to investment with the right accounting and incentives. Second, create institutions at the scale of the problem with funding mechanisms to solve the problem. Third, shift taxes to move public finance, generate green jobs, and implement transition.

Solving the Sustainability Paradox is not a case of figuring out what is causing our problems. It is a problem of committing ourselves to implement well-known cures, a sacrifice at first, but one that will pay off soon, and handsomely, in better lives for all. Largely the only argument against pursuing a sustainable economic path is "it costs too much," and that rebuttal is based on faulty accounting and erroneous calculations of overall costs.

Threats at the personal and planetary scale make the transition to a new and better economy even more imperative. More of the same "economic growth" is not the solution. We Americans can build a new and better economy quickly. As the next two chapters make clear, we've done it before. Understanding how we got here, the economic ideas that built our economy, and how to make the needed transition to sustainability and happiness requires a bit of a trip through American economic history.

CHAPTER 10

Ancient History

So, as far as we can see, whether it's about quality of life, social justice, or sustainability, our economic performance looks a little blue around the gills. Has it always been this way? Hardly. The United States was truly the envy of the world in the 1950s and '60s, outperforming nearly every nation in virtually every category we've been looking at, while building the largest middle class in world history.

It was no accident. Americans transformed the economy in the first half of the twentieth century: the progressive movement, breakneck industrialization, conservation, booming agricultural production, an unparalleled educational system, the paradigm shift from laissez-faire to macroeconomics, the far-reaching government policies of the New Deal, World War II production, and the focus on a rising middle class. In a short half century our economy improved dramatically, as we shall see in this chapter. The changes were enormously beneficial. American economic history is impressive and laden with vital lessons for today.

Cowboy Politics

To the horrified shock of those enriched by the status quo, the youngest president in United States history, Republican Theodore Roosevelt, landed in the White House at age forty-two with seemingly limitless transformative energy after President William McKinley was assassinated. "I told William McKinley it was a mistake to nominate that wild man at Philadelphia. I asked him if he realized what would happen if he should die. Now look, that damn cowboy is President of the United States," exclaimed the powerful and reactionary senator Mark Hanna, a member of Roosevelt's Republican Party.[1] Indeed, New York–born Teddy Roosevelt (TR) had spent three years as a cowboy on a ranch in Dakota Territory.

Great leadership crafts progress. But the tsunami of economic and political transformation about to hit the United States in 1901 was driven by far more than a lone cowboy. For the next twenty years, millions of Americans organized together for progress, taking seriously the words President Abraham Lincoln had uttered less than forty years before, "that government of the people, by the people, and for the people, shall not perish from the earth."

The threats to freedom and democracy in America were not from belligerent foreign powers or a civil war, but from an economy and political system governed by very few people. Americans took it into their own powerful hands to remake the nation's democratic institutions, change the national and state constitutions, reign in tyrannical corporations, and reshape the economy.

Ending slavery had required a brutal civil war and two constitutional amendments, yet in 1901, child labor—slavery by any other name—was rampant in America. An estimated 18 percent of children, between the ages of ten and fifteen, worked in 1900, often putting in sixty-hour weeks with no schooling.[2] Children as young as five were wielding razor-sharp knives filleting fish all day, tending textile machinery, or sorting coal in mines.[3]

The average American adult worked ten hours a day, six days a week. Some laborers worked twelve- or fourteen-hour days, six days a week, in mines and factories.[4] For many workers, job conditions were terrible and pay near subsistence level, while owners raked in enormous profits. Sharecroppers and factory workers in company towns were economic hostages to debts held by plantations and companies. Women lacked voting rights. Americans of Native American, African, Asian, and Latino descent faced pervasive discrimination. City, county, state, and federal governments were riddled with corruption. Party bosses selected most candidates.

There were no primary elections. American senators were not directly elected by the people. Farmers and workers paid escalating property and excise taxes, while the wealthy paid little or nothing. There was no income tax. Alcoholism was rampant. Using vicious tactics, monopolists secured strangleholds on essential industries and manipulated prices. Banks and the stock market were mostly unregulated. Banking collapses were routine. Financial scams were endemic. Natural resources were being plundered. Drinking water was contaminated nationwide. Diseases were widespread, and the medicines were nearly as bad as the diseases.

The Volunteer Poison Squad

For example, Bonnore's Electro Magnetic Bathing Fluid claimed to "cure cholera, neuralgia, epilepsy, scarlet fever, necrosis, mercurial eruptions, paralysis, hip diseases, chronic abscesses, and 'female complaints.'"[5] Medicines had no standards, testing, or regulations. Who could differentiate between deadly drugs and authentic cures? Various "patent medicines" contained addictive drugs, such as heroin, morphine, opium, and cocaine (good customer retention), or formaldehyde, even radioactive ingredients. "Medicines" laced with neurotoxins demonstrated instant potency. One dose jolted patients into convulsive writhing until it wore off. Shock kills pain. So it seemed to work on all pains. Most people seemed to recover from neurotoxic medicines, though some were left permanently paralyzed.

The government chemist and drug safety activist Harvey Wiley formed the "Volunteer Poison Squad" in 1902, as part of a campaign for regulation. Young men voluntarily ate food preservatives to have their effects scientifically recorded.[6] Muckrakers such as Upton Sinclair[7] exposed the injustices of child labor, low wages, and filthy food, urging the populace to action. An outraged American public had had enough of laissez-faire economics and demanded government oversight of markets and business. In 1906, over the ferocious opposition of powerful companies, President Roosevelt pushed through the nation's first food and drug regulations: the Meat Inspection Act and Pure Food and Drug Act.[8]

BUYER BEWARE was replaced with SELLER BE HONEST. That's good economics. No market is "free" when filled with liars and thieves. Increased transparency and truthful consumer information improved markets. Outlawing deadly ingredients and requiring testing with the burden of proof on those bringing the product to market solved problems. Regulations secured better public health and delivered greater profits to companies that produced medicines that actually cured illnesses. Regulation was the ruin of ruinous medicine-makers. Quacks went bust. Or, as in the case of Coca-Cola, dropped the false medicinal claims, replaced cocaine with caffeine, and marketed a successful "soft drink."

Progressives Build a Movement

The regulation of drugs was not an isolated case. The Progressive Era (1900–1920) saw a broad swath of Americans join forces to reject laissez-faire economics, fundamentally transforming the nation.

Three presidents, Theodore Roosevelt, William Taft, and Woodrow Wilson, though often at odds, supported greater federal regulation and progressive agendas. A loose amalgam of farmers, laborers, women, prohibitionists, children's advocates, government reformers, environmentalists, birth control advocates, churches, doctors and nurses, students, banking reformers, and antitrust advocates chose to *work together* to solve many problems all at once. Progressives of both the Republican and Democratic parties had to work together because they were up against an unbridled economic ideology and the most sophisticated, powerful array of moneyed special interests in the nation's history. The Supreme Court long upheld both of these enemies of progress.

In 1905, Supreme Court justice Oliver Wendell Holmes aired his disgust in a dissenting opinion when the majority ruled unconstitutional a New York law limiting bakery working hours to sixty hours a week: "The case is decided upon an economic theory which a large part of the country does not entertain . . . But a constitution is not intended to embody a particular economic theory, whether paternalism and the organic relation of the citizen to the state or of *laissez faire*."[9]

Most powerful were the "trusts," enormous corporate conglomerates, run by ruthless, unregulated monopolists. They controlled scores of critical industries including steel, banking, meatpacking, flour milling, cast-iron, railroads, and oil. John D. Rockefeller had secured a stranglehold on the nation's oil industry, owning or otherwise controlling nearly all oil exploration, oil rigs, refineries, petroleum products, transportation, and retail outlets. Rockefeller manipulated the market with secret shipping agreements with railroads that gave him a discounted rate and raised rates for his competitors. In 1911, in a landmark case the Supreme Court broke up Rockefeller's Standard Oil into thirty-nine separate companies, ensuring healthy competition in a growing oil-based economy until the 1980s.[10]

With banking, steel, and railroad trusts threatened, the banker J. P. Morgan went to the White House to meet with President Roosevelt. Morgan reportedly told the president, "Send your man to my man and they can fix it up." But Morgan left empty-handed. Roosevelt wasn't bending. This was not a business deal, he told Morgan. The government was neither in collusion nor in competition with the corporations. Companies were not the government's peers. The president wasn't out to ruin anyone, proposing "to proceed by evolution and not revolution."[11] Monopoly power was against the law, and Roosevelt intended to enforce the law.

> We do not wish to destroy corporations, but we do wish to make them subserve the public good . . . The biggest corporation, like the humblest private citizen, must be held to strict compliance with the will of the people as expressed in the fundamental law. The rich man who does not see that this is in his interest is indeed short-sighted. When we make him obey the law we ensure for him the absolute protection of the law.[12]

The government would set rules for the public, markets, and corporations, and by enforcing fair rules would provide the framework for efficient markets, fair competition, consumer protection, and a prosperous economy. Roosevelt's rejection of laissez-faire economics in favor of more productive and fair, regulated, markets set the stage for a successful twentieth-century American economy. Presidents Taft and Wilson both aggressively prosecuted monopolies, and Wilson strengthened antitrust legislation.

To overcome entrenched opposition, progressives built majorities and successes at the city, county, and state levels, working together across issues. Wyoming was the first state to recognize women's right to vote. Massachusetts passed the first child labor laws. Oregon created the initiative, referendum, and recall processes. Wisconsin approved the first permanent income tax. All were expanded to other states. With reformed state legislatures representing the population rather than political machines, the progressive movement gained the momentum to pass constitutional amendments.

Four amendments to the Constitution were ratified in the first twenty years of the twentieth century. In February 1913, the Sixteenth Amendment, allowing the federal government to collect income tax, was enacted. In April 1913, the Seventeenth Amendment, for the direct election of the U.S. Senate, followed. In January 1919, alcohol was banned under the Eighteenth Amendment (repealed in December 1933). And in August 1920, the Nineteenth Amendment, giving women the vote in all elections in the United States, was enacted. "I voted in the first national election that women could vote in," Dave's grandmother once declared. "I was thrilled. I was proud. And I never missed an election since."

At the federal level, the National Park Service and the National Forest Service were established, to protect natural resources; the Food and Drug Administration, to protect health; and the Commerce Department, to strengthen interstate commerce regulation, break up monopolies, and promote economic expansion.

About nine hundred amendments to state constitutions were also passed. Oregon passed forty-five state constitutional amendments in two decades. In that same time, thousands of city and county charters were changed to clean up government, give people rights, and regulate markets and businesses. Public utilities multiplied to solve the practical problems of growing cities. Initiative, referendum, and recall processes as well as primary elections were created, undermining corrupt party bosses with more direct democracy. States approved worker's compensation, public health, sanitation, prison reform, state highways, civil service, child labor, worker safety, fire safety, and consumer protection laws. Progressives also focused on education, building public school and university systems and increasing enrollment in existing institutions. Ninety-four percent of the population was literate.[13]

Unions and workers fought for higher and minimum wages, shorter working hours, workplace safety, and an end to child labor. Their victories improved pay and labor conditions for other workers. These changes built a stronger economy and a budding middle class. Industrialists fought them, but some, like Henry Ford, believed that their employees should receive rising real wages, sufficient incomes to purchase the products they made. Ford paid autoworkers high wages and shortened work to an eight-hour day, while increasing production.[14]

The odd structure of the Federal Reserve Bank reflected U.S. politics. A banking panic in 1907 convinced most in Congress that the United States needed a central bank. Creating the Federal Reserve System in 1913 was wildly divisive. Many progressives opposed it. Banking conservatives proposed a privately owned and run central bank. Farmers demanded a bank wholly owned and run by the government. Western and southern states wanted the bank nowhere near Wall Street. In the end, the Federal Reserve System would be owned by private banks, but controlled by the U.S. government, with twelve branches.[15]

Every victory required a political struggle, and a battle with archaic ideology. For example, consider three arguments used against women's suffrage.

1. The founding fathers intentionally excluded women from voting.
2. Women didn't pay taxes, so they didn't deserve representation.
3. Women, by nature "excitable and emotional," would vote without proper thinking and wreck the country.[16]

The period was not all positive. African Americans were effectively excluded from equal opportunity, education, and voting. Native American lands were taken. Racist immigration laws blocked many. Americans adopted racist policies most likely because the majority of Americans at that time were racist. But the foundation for better confronting racism was also laid. Overall, the hard work of a generation of politically active American citizens brought improvements all across the country. Progressive voters generally supported the greatest good for the greatest number over the longest run, and their success built a better economy and quality of life for future generations.

The Roaring Twenties

America's entry into World War I in 1917 shifted resources from domestic progress to building a fighting machine. The war increased demand for food and manufacturing. Incomes in rural and urban America rose. Elected president in 1920, the Republican Warren G. Harding was no friend of labor, yet he still signed legislation regulating agricultural markets to defend farmers against commodity traders. But his administration was most famous for corruption. Scandals included oil giveaways, stolen medical supplies, kickbacks of government money, purchased paroles, and more. Harding said, "I have no trouble with my enemies . . . but my friends, they're the ones that keep me up all night."[17] He died in office, and the staunchly conservative vice president, Calvin Coolidge, took over.

Coolidge defended his hands-off, pro-corporate policies, proclaiming that "after all, the chief business of the American people is business . . . If the federal government should go out of existence, the common run of people would not detect the difference in the affairs of their daily life for a considerable length of time."[18] Coolidge argued that if the wealthy paid fewer taxes, they'd invest and increase employment. Yet at the same time, he increased the budget for national parks, forests, and highways, regulated the radio airwaves, and initiated federal flood control projects.

In 1928, Commerce Secretary Herbert Hoover was elected president. Urban incomes rose in the 1920s, while farm revenues declined and the income gap in America widened dramatically. Unemployment in rural America rose to an estimated 10 percent. The fortunes of the wealthy rose with the booming stock market. Wall Street and the banking system had successfully dodged progressive reforms. Banks were poorly supervised, while the stock market remained virtually unregulated.

During the 1920s, an unregulated financial bubble expanded, as it would eighty years later. "Buying on margin," a stock purchaser could pay as little as 10 percent of the stock value, borrowing the rest with a *call loan* provided by a stockbroker on commission, who borrowed money from a bank. The stock was the collateral for the loan. If the price dipped, the stock would be sold to cover the loan. Stock purchasers expected rising value and the opportunity to sell at a higher price, paying off their loans and pocketing a profit.

When borrowed money is used to purchase stock, foreign currency, real estate, or companies, it is called *leveraging*. The less you pay of your own cash, and the more you pay in borrowed money, the more *leveraged* the deal. Purchasing on margin became the rage on Wall Street. Stock prices soared as increasingly leveraged, and more numerous, investors bid them up. As prices skyrocketed, returns skyrocketed, too, pulling more investment into the market. But rising stock values were not based on goods and services produced and sold at profit. Easy lending, borrowed money, little cash down, high expectations, big profits, and rising prices set the stage for the crisis to come (as in 2007).

Standard Oil of New Jersey, John D. Rockefeller's remaining company after the antitrust breakup, provides a good example of what happens when markets shift corporate finance from productive investment into speculative bubbles. Rather than investing the company's money in real production, like oil drilling, shipping, or refining, Rockefeller lent $65 million a day, at interest, to brokers for loaning to speculators. Why invest in a well when short-term loans have a higher rate of return? Investment in productive assets declined as capital shifted to high-return, but unproductive, speculation.

Investment provides the capital to expand production, including hiring employees to produce real economic goods and services. *Speculation* is the allocation of capital, not to produce any goods or services, but simply to re-distribute wealth from those that produce goods and services to the specu-lators. Currency trading (*arbitrage*) is a good example. Arbitrage speculators bet on the rise or fall of currencies. This activity does not produce any real goods or services. However, by predicting or manipulating currency prices, speculators can skim a bit of value from currency holders. Everyone in the productive economy loses a small bit of value as the currency they hold loses value, and the few speculators who make the right bets gain.

Speculation is possible with any market asset, but well-designed rules can eliminate many of its incentives and excesses. For example, a small charge on currency transactions would eliminate the profitability of arbi-trage, and that capital would move elsewhere, possibly into the produc-tive economy. Speculative bets gone wrong can have catastrophic effects on the real economy. Real companies go bust. Real people are thrown out of productive work and lose their incomes. That's not the speculator's intent, but at times the resulting economic collapse is so great, it sinks all boats, speculators included. In 1929, the speculators went under fast.

The Great Depression

By 1929, recognizing that stock prices were wildly overvalued, some stockholders began selling. In a few days in October 1929, the stock mar-ket crashed, losing a third of its value by mid-November. WALL STREET LAYS AN EGG, read a headline in *Variety* magazine. But while the stock market crash has been considered the catalyst for the ensuing Great Depression, it was not the actual cause of the calamity. The causes were falling consumer demand, goods sales, and incomes, coupled with rising defaults, bank failures, foreclosures, and unemployment.

As purchasing declined, factory orders fell, prices fell, and manufac-turers laid people off, lowering incomes, so purchasing declined further. Federal, state, and local tax revenues declined, spurring layoffs. Banks held little cash. Depositors "ran" to withdraw their money. As bank depos-its disappeared, loans were called in, straining borrowers. Banks failed, and slow-footed depositors lost their savings. The Federal Reserve had fueled the bubble with easy money, but then it tightened the money sup-ply when banks needed it most, making things worse. As the crisis began to affect other countries, wild currency rate fluctuations made international trade difficult. The United States raised tariffs to support domestic producers, kicking off a global tariff war. International trade declined dramatically.

At the helm of a sinking economy, President Hoover felt that volunteerism, aid from churches, and voluntary groups could solve the problem. Church food kitchens fed many, but the program was hopelessly insufficient. The bitter suffering that fell upon millions of Americans is hard to imagine today. There was no unemployment insurance, welfare, or food stamps. People without regular income had no money when their savings dried up. Homeless millions built shantytowns called "Hoovervilles" in every American city. Desperate poverty engulfed millions of Americans. By 1933, unemployment rose to an estimated 25 percent nationally and as high as 80 percent in the hardest-hit cities. Farm prices fell by 60 percent.[19]

A drought caused by climate change and unsustainable farming practices brought biblical dust storms across the Midwest, blackening the sky with airborne soil and choking people. Dave's mother, Nell Batker, grew up on a thirty-acre California farm and vividly remembers the Depression. "We never had it as hard on the farm as many city people did. We always had enough to eat. But we only got one pair of shoes each year when school started. In the summer we all ran barefoot."

While Americans worked hard to keep family and farm afloat, economists were trying to figure out what was happening. There were two basic economic philosophies for approaching the Depression: do nothing, or do something. Indeed, the predominant economic policy prescription of the time was to *do nothing*, believing that the business cycle and market adjustments would eventually fix the economy, delivering another boom cycle. The prescription of nineteenth-century laissez-faire economics to do nothing was the problem. Shrinking incomes reduced spending and demand in a downward spiral, which combined with tight monetary policy to drive the country deeper into the crisis.

The New Deal

Elected president in 1932 by a populace growing hopeless, the Democrat Franklin Delano Roosevelt was a consummate politician and coalition builder. Perhaps more important, he was a free thinker, unencumbered by economic ideology. Roosevelt was pragmatic, experimenting with policy, keeping the good and culling the bad. His New Deal was designed to build a new economy, not to bring back the economy of the 1920s. It was a plan to bring about an economy of greater fairness, stability, and prosperity. FDR confronted a stunning array of problems. As he took office, thousands of banks were on the verge of collapse. The day after his inauguration, Sunday, March 5, 1933, FDR called Congress into special session and declared a "banking holiday," temporarily closing all the banks in the United States. He ordered Hoover's appointees and his own appointees to cooperate and write banking legislation in four days. They did. It was approved by Congress the next Thursday. FDR completed his first week in office with his first fireside chat that Sunday, and America's banks reopened on Monday.

Regulating Wall Street, preventing bank runs, strengthening regulations, and building the middle class were all central pillars of the New Deal. The Federal Deposit Insurance Corporation (FDIC), for example, guaranteed people's savings to $5,000 in member banks. Coupled with banking regulation, the FDIC helped end the chronic banking instability that had plagued the nation since its birth. Some had advocated for the nationalization of banks. Roosevelt's solution was pragmatic and dramatically effective. His actions brought clear goals (stabilize the banking sector), new measures (bank reserves), new policies (reserve requirements), and well-governed, new institutions (FDIC), with the necessary authority at the scale required to deal with the whole problem. Institutions like the FDIC and the Securities Exchange Commission were found to be sound and inspired countries worldwide to implement their own version of banking reform with similar institutions.

Roosevelt set a high mark for future presidents with his record of accomplishments during his first hundred days in office. These were not just Roosevelt's victories. He was a pragmatist and adopted good ideas from both political parties. In addition, many Republicans considered themselves New Dealers. There was no lockstep party line to be held. The New Deal was far more pragmatic, experimental, and internally contradictory than policy based on any single economic theory would have allowed. New Deal legislation included an alphabet soup of programs and laws. Here are a few.

1. The *Works Progress Administration*, which put people to work building parks, schools, and bridges in virtually every commu-

nity in the nation and distributed food, clothing, and other necessities.

2. The *Public Works Administration*, which constructed power plants, hospitals, and water and sewer systems.

3. The *Federal Deposit Insurance Corporation*, which established the foundation for what was for a long time the most stable banking system in the world.

4. The *Civilian Conservation Corps*, which employed 3 million Americans improving national parks, planting over 3 billion trees, and improving devastated farmlands with soil conservation. Politicians credited the CCC for reducing the crime rate as the unemployed went to work.

5. The *Emergency Banking Act*, which gave the government the power to close and reorganize insolvent banks. This legislation proved critical in 2008 and 2009, when the government seized control of failing banks, preventing a cascade of banking failures.

6. The *Farm Credit Act*, which provided emergency funds to farms for refinancing mortgages and prevented further foreclosures.

7. The *Wagner Act* and the *Fair Labor Standards Act*, which gave labor unions collective bargaining rights, banned industrial child labor, limited working hours, established minimum wages, and created production and pricing regulations.

8. The *Federal Emergency Relief Act*, which continued an initiative under President Hoover providing grants to states and local governments to hire people.

In five years between 1933 and 1938, legislation was passed that transformed virtually every sector of the American economy. This change was delivered despite the stiff resistance of about one third of the nation's population, most of the economics profession, conservative Democrats, a hostile Supreme Court (until 1936), and powerful corporate interests.

Though the Depression dragged on, millions of Americans were put back to work. President Roosevelt achieved unprecedented popularity. World War II demanded an even greater increase in the government's role in the economy. The Japanese attack on Pearl Harbor united a country torn between isolationism and joining the fight against fascism. The war brought cooperation between private industry, labor, and government, deficit spending, price and wage controls, rationing to keep prices down, and full employment. The United States unleashed unimaginable manufacturing capacity. A deficit-driven "stimulus" put Americans and industry back to work as the government spent unprecedented amounts of money on war production. Japanese and German commanders were consistently stunned, finding more American equipment and men on the battlefield than their planners deemed possible. By 1944, the economy had been remade, the private sector had fully recovered, and a new rising middle class was emerging in America.

After World War II

By war's end, the United States was the last major industrialized nation standing. European and Asian economies lay in ruin. There was no competition for U.S. products. The U.S. dollar became the global currency. The productivity of the U.S. economy and generosity of the Marshall Plan assisted in the rapid reconstruction of Europe and Asia.

After World War II, New Deal ideas were expanded. The GI Bill provided education and low-interest housing loans to returning veterans. After their unprecedented wartime cooperation, business and labor in America built a social contract: Productivity gains were shared, providing steadily increasing middle-class wages and benefits for laborers, with little social unrest and good profits returned to business owners. Life for most Americans became far more secure. Jobs were more secure. That allowed Americans to purchase their homes. Incomes, education, and retirement were equally secure. Health and life span improved. Leisure time was increasing. Perhaps the most powerful product and driver rising out of the Depression and New Deal was macroeconomics.

A New Economic Paradigm

Hoover and Roosevelt (and their predecessors) had one thing in common. None entered office with a model or theory of how a national economy works. By Roosevelt's second term, a revolution in economics was under way. Hands-off laissez-faire economics neither required nor generated any understanding of how prices, employment, consumption, government, and other economic phenomena are bound into a national economy and contribute to growth or collapse. The Great Depression revealed laissez-faire economics as incomplete, incorrect, and incapable of solving modern problems.

John Maynard Keynes, indisputably the twentieth century's most influential economist, created modern macroeconomics, providing a framework for how a national economy works, and swept other theories aside for decades.[20]

Creating a national-scale theory of economics had profound implications. *New goals* included growth in domestic production, full employment, and stable prices. *New economic measures* included the gross national product, employment, and inflation. *New policies* included deficit-financed stimulus spending. *New national institutions* included the Social Security Administration and a host of other agencies forming the superstructure of a twentieth-century federal government.

Economic theory is a powerful lever for moving policy. Child labor had proven impossible to regulate federally. The employment economist Joan Robinson utilized Keynes's new macroeconomics in 1937 to argue for keeping children in school while the otherwise unemployed could work the jobs children had held. Thus "a year of unemployment is exchanged for a year of education."[21] The next year, federal regulation of child labor was passed and subsequently upheld by the Supreme Court. Millions of American children were freed from work to attend school, and millions of adults were hired. Macroeconomics helped reverse the laissez-faire policies that had dominated child labor law.

After World War II, Keynesian macroeconomics, particularly the concept of *economic growth* (measured by the GNP), became the economic doctrine for both political parties, for liberals, conservatives, and libertarians. Macroeconomic theory is now utilized by virtually every nation in the world today (including communist China). Macroeconomics and King GDP have ruled ever since.

Macroeconomics Rules

President Harry Truman advocated for a national health care program and almost achieved it before the Europeans and Canadians did. The wartime income tax rate hit 94 percent on marginal income of more than

$1 million per year. The Republican president Dwight Eisenhower maintained that high income tax. With the revenue, he paid off huge chunks of the World War II and Korean War debts, built the interstate highway system, and kept New Deal programs (such as Social Security, the FDIC, and more) well funded.

Eisenhower's successor, John F. Kennedy, poured federal money into science, math, and engineering, to keep pace with the Russians in the Cold War, while states invested heavily in universities to improve education. A college education became cheaper, more accessible, and of higher quality in the United States than in any other nation.

The progressives, New Dealers, and even conservative leaders advanced regulations and programs to improve the economy and environment and to achieve a fairer society. Their efforts produced the biggest middle class of all time and prosperity never before known in human history. Economists of the 1960s thought that macroeconomics had solved all economic problems. Letting the unregulated market rule, or laissez-faire economics, seemed moribund. Macroeconomics attained a near religious status based on a central measurement, the Gross National Product, and on a central idea: economies must grow or die.

But as the 1960s unfolded, a generation of young people, raised in the prosperity that macroeconomics had wrought, began to question the very lifestyle that had become the envy of the world. Material prosperity struck them as hollow; they felt, as the Berkeley Free Speech leader, Mario Savio, put it in 1964, like meaningless cogs in a well-oiled machine, children in a chrome-plated consumers' playground. They looked for a new *quality* of life, and they found a surprising ally, a president himself.

Expanding Opportunity—the Great Society

President Lyndon Johnson described the goals of his "Great Society" in a speech at the University of Michigan on May 22, 1964. It was a speech whose clarity and values have yet to be matched by an American president.

> The purpose of protecting the life of our nation and preserving the liberty of our citizens is to pursue the happiness of our people. Our success in that pursuit is the test of our success as a nation.
>
> For a century we labored to settle and to subdue a continent. For half a century we called upon unbounded invention and

untiring industry to create an order of plenty for all of our people. The challenge of the next half century is whether we have the wisdom to use that wealth to enrich and elevate our national life, and to advance the quality of our American civilization.

Your imagination, your initiative, and your indignation will determine whether we build a society where progress is the servant of our needs, or a society where old values and new visions are buried under unbridled growth. For in your time we have the opportunity to move not only toward the rich society and the powerful society, but upward to the Great Society. The Great Society rests on abundance and liberty for all. It demands an end to poverty and racial injustice, to which we are totally committed in our time. But that is just the beginning.

The Great Society is a place where every child can find knowledge to enrich his mind and to enlarge his talents. It is a place where leisure is a welcome chance to build and reflect, not a feared cause of boredom and restlessness. It is a place where the city of man serves not only the needs of the body and the demands of commerce but the desire for beauty and the hunger for community.

It is a place where man can renew contact with nature. It is a place which honors creation for its own sake and for what it adds to the understanding of the race. It is a place where men are more concerned with the quality of their goals than the quantity of their goods.[22]

In the early 1960s, a lot of Americans remained left out of the prosperity that was stifling some. Minorities still faced discrimination at every turn. While schools in the South had been integrated, private businesses had not. Even the admission of a black man, James Meredith, to the University of Mississippi in 1962 produced riots and the deployment of the National Guard to protect Meredith. The civil rights movement grew, and thousands of Americans were inspired to action by Martin Luther King's dramatic "I Have a Dream" speech at the Lincoln Memorial on August 28, 1963.

The next summer, thousands of activists, including many white college students from the North, traveled to Mississippi to register voters and help protect the civil rights of African Americans there. For their trouble, three activists ended up murdered by Klansmen and sheriff's deputies, their bodies buried in an earthen dam in Mississippi. As a horrified country watched these developments on television, support for a comprehensive civil rights act grew, and President Johnson signed it into law on July 2, 1964. He famously acknowledged that he was consigning the Democratic Party to defeat in the South for at least a generation.

Thousands of youths responded to President Kennedy's Peace Corps initiative and to the "War on Poverty" proposed by Johnson. In the early 1960s, poverty in America was still widespread among minorities, and one fifth of all senior citizens fell below the poverty line. Johnson's ambitious "Great Society" tackled poverty with government initiatives, including the VISTA (Volunteers in Service to America) program, a domestic Peace Corps that sent young volunteers to work in poor communities from urban ghettos to Appalachia and the rural South.

John was an early VISTA volunteer. From 1965 through 1967, he worked as a community organizer on the Bad River Chippewa Indian Reservation in northern Wisconsin. As a native of suburban California, he had never encountered poverty before. Living in a tarpaper house without running water in temperatures dropping to thirty degrees below zero in winter, he saw firsthand how the poor in America lived, the racism experienced by Native American children, and how the American Dream had not been extended to all. These experiences still shape his view of the economy today.

Though often maligned by some, the War on Poverty actually worked. In the late 1960s and early '70s, millions of Americans were lifted from poverty and the middle class continued to expand. The War on Poverty's programs were not perfect, and in some cases they helped perpetuate what critics called a "cycle of poverty," but they were certainly not the failure that revisionist history has painted them to be. For many, they were a godsend.

Americans began the twentieth century with the progressive movement rejecting laissez-faire economics. The New Deal, World War II, and the following two decades created macroeconomics, the problem-solving alternative to laissez-faire, and built the superstructure of a modern economy and the unparalleled expansion of the middle class. However, laissez-faire was far from dead.

CHAPTER 11

When (or How) Good Went Bad

In the next ten years we shall increase our wealth by 50 percent. The profound question is: Does this mean we will be 50 percent richer in a real sense, 50 percent better off, 50 percent happier?

—PRESIDENT RICHARD NIXON,
STATE OF THE UNION ADDRESS, 1970

In the language of popular economics, *Chapter Eleven* is a synonym for *bankruptcy*. And in a real sense, that's what this chapter is about: bankrupt Americans and the bankrupt ideas that bankrupted them. The Era of Bankruptcy followed the Era of Middle-Class Expansion, and it started with one of the most tumultuous years in American history.

More than forty years of hindsight suggest that 1968 may well have been the United States' pivotal year, the year two roads diverged and we Americans took the wrong one. For another twelve years, the wrong road ran close to the road we'd been on since the 1930s, crossing it back and forth until, after the election of 1980, it veered sharply to the Right.

John remembers well that turning-point year of 1968 with its wild ups and downs of hope and despair. He was a college student in Wisconsin, and very liberal, though as a freshman, he'd been a bedrock conservative. The 1960s did that to many of us.

The year began with a surprise: In Vietnam, the National Liberation Front, or "Vietcong" as Americans called it, launched its Tet Offensive, overwhelming American and South Vietnamese troops in many cities across South Vietnam. The "light at the end of the tunnel" that President Lyndon Johnson had seen for the war in Vietnam suddenly looked like the headlight of an oncoming train. Though the Americans pushed back, casualties were heavy, and public opinion began to turn more strongly against the war. On many campuses, the words of Phil Ochs's ringing anthem, "I Ain't Marching Anymore," echoed the thoughts of thousands.

> It's always the old who lead us to the war, always the young who fall.
> Now look at all we've won with a saber and a gun and tell me, was it worth it all?

Already, Senator Eugene McCarthy of Minnesota had entered the Democratic presidential race against Johnson, his party's incumbent president. McCarthy's opposition to the war, and his sympathies with many of the quality-of-life changes sought by the youthful American counterculture, attracted throngs of student supporters. They cut their hair and went "clean for Gene," trying to win votes among adult Americans. Those under twenty-one could not yet vote themselves. On March 12, McCarthy surprised the political handicappers by coming within seven points of Johnson in the New Hampshire primary, the first of the election season.

On March 16, as McCarthy gained in the polls, another opponent of the war, New York senator Robert Kennedy, joined the race. Where McCarthy was cool and cerebral, Kennedy was passionate and engaging. Where McCarthy appealed to middle-class students, Kennedy connected with minorities and the urban working class. He shared not only McCarthy's antiwar sentiments but also his broader critique of other weaknesses in American society. Two days after announcing his candidacy, Kennedy gave the momentous speech at the University of Kansas challenging the Gross National Product (see chapter 1 in this book) as a measure of the health of our nation.

For those Americans hoping to see even more progressive change and the immediate end of the Vietnam War, Kennedy's entry into the race was electrifying. Now there were two antiwar candidates, and one of them was a member of the political establishment, the brother of a beloved late president. President Johnson's polling numbers dropped again.

Exit Lyndon Johnson

On March 31, on national television, a tired Lyndon Johnson announced, "I will not seek nor will I accept the nomination of my party for a second term as President of the United States." Had the speech come a day later, it might have been taken for an April Fool's joke. But Johnson was serious. In the antiwar town of Madison, Wisconsin, where John watched the speech that night, revelers filled the streets. In hindsight, Lyndon Johnson was the victim in a Greek tragedy. But for his hubris in expanding the Vietnam War, Johnson might well have been remembered as one of the greatest of American presidents. Instead, he was a lonely and defeated man.

On April 2, McCarthy won a landslide in the Wisconsin Democratic primary. For John and his friends, it seemed almost too good to be true: the war would be stopped, and the drive for greater justice in America would end in victory.

Of course, it *was* too good to be true.

Two days later, in Memphis, Tennessee, Martin Luther King Jr. was slain by an assassin's bullet. In the streets of many cities, angry mobs burned and looted. In spite of fears for his own life amid an Indianapolis crowd enraged by the King shooting, Robert Kennedy mourned the assassination with an eloquent plea for justice and understanding.

But only two months later, Kennedy himself was dead, gunned down after winning the California primary, which all but assured him the Democratic nomination for president. Across the country, millions gathered to watch his funeral train. They listened as his brother Edward eulogized him.

> Beneath it all, he has tried to engender a social conscience. There were wrongs which needed attention. There were people who were poor and who needed help. And we have a responsibility to them and to this country. Through no virtues and accomplishments of our own, we have been fortunate enough to be born in the United States under the most comfortable conditions. We, therefore, have a responsibility to others who are less well off . . . This is the way he lived. My brother need not be idealized, or enlarged in death beyond what he was in life, to be remembered simply as a good and decent man, who saw wrong and tried to

right it, saw suffering, and tried to heal it, saw war and tried to stop it.[1]

Bobby Kennedy understood what the economy is for.

Worldwide Expectations

Despite the tragedies of King's and Kennedy's deaths, there was a glimmer of hope as summer approached. These inspiring leaders had been killed, probably, by lone, crazed gunmen. The vast majority of Americans deeply mourned their passing. More Americans seemed to care about the goals King and Kennedy had lived for; for many, their short but committed lives were inspirations to work even harder for justice.

Moreover, the new desire for a better world was not confined to the United States. In France and elsewhere in Europe, rebelling youth called for economies more committed to quality of life, social justice, and care for planet Earth. In eastern Europe, the signs were even brighter. Nineteen sixty-eight had brought a "Prague Spring" in Czechoslovakia, as the Alexander Dubček government loosened restrictions on both political and economic freedom and promised "socialism with a human face." There was a sense that capitalist and socialist nations alike could become more like "middle way" social democracies, where the quality of life had improved dramatically since the Second World War.

This potential was highlighted on July 22, when the *New York Times* published an inspiring call for just such a change. "Reflections on Progress, Peaceful Coexistence and Intellectual Freedom" was written by the physicist Andrei Sakharov, father of the Russian H-Bomb.[2] Passed originally through the Soviet Union as samizdat, it suggested a new interest in freedom and democracy among the Soviets and called for a future that combined the best aspects of socialism and capitalism. John devoured Sakharov's hopeful manuscript. Perhaps there was still a chance . . .

But hope peaked in midsummer and soon began to fade.

On August 5, the Republican National Convention opened in Miami and nominated Richard Nixon for president and Spiro Agnew for vice president. Nixon suggested that a "silent majority" would prefer to silence students, antiwar critics, and other "nattering nabobs of negativity," as Agnew referred to opponents of the Nixon agenda.

It also became increasingly clear that Vice President Hubert Humphrey would be the Democratic nominee, as a majority of delegates were chosen by party insiders, not primary voters. Because Humphrey had supported Johnson on Vietnam, the prospect of a Humphrey candidacy angered antiwar protestors. They made plans for massive demonstrations in Chicago during the Democratic National Convention, scheduled for August 26–29.

The Beginning of the End

On August 21, shortly before the convention began, Soviet tanks rolled into Prague, crushing the Czech experiment in freedom. For many Americans, fear of socialist totalitarianism was restored. Prospects for Sakharov's convergence were shattered.

The Democratic convention went as predicted, with Humphrey nominated. But less expected were the massive demonstrations outside the convention and the response of Chicago mayor Richard Daley, who urged his police to crush the protests. On August 28, a "police riot" sent hundreds to the hospital. The massive exercise of state power brought a sense of hopelessness to former Kennedy and McCarthy supporters.

But most Americans supported Daley's use of extreme force. They recoiled at the appearance and language of many of the protestors. Their fear would benefit Richard Nixon, who barely edged out Humphrey in the November election. It wasn't yet obvious, but the New Deal consensus, which had created a middle-class America, narrowed class differences, and brought great improvements to the lives of the disadvantaged, was slipping away.

But certainly not all at once.

Richard Nixon, Environmental Champion

Though elected as a conservative, Nixon governed as a moderate. Tough on crime—the bane of 1960s urban life—he doubled federal funding for police. But his vision for America, expressed in his 1970 State of the Union address, was, if anything, more progressive than conservative.

> I see a new America as we celebrate our 200th anniversary six years
> from now. I see an America in which we have abolished hunger,

provided the means for every family in the nation to obtain a minimum income, made enormous progress in providing better housing, faster transportation, improved health and superior education.[3]

Nixon used the speech to promote new rules that were good for the longest run. He warned of "metropolitan areas choked by traffic, suffocated by smog, poisoned by water, deafened by noise."

The great question of the seventies is, shall we surrender to our surroundings, or shall we make our peace with nature and begin to make reparations for the damage we have done to our air, to our land, and to our water? Restoring nature to its natural state is a cause beyond party and beyond factions. It has become a common cause of all the people in this country. It is a cause of particular concern to young Americans because they more than we will reap the grim consequences of our failure to act on programs which are needed now if we are to prevent disaster later.

Imagine a Republican leader saying this today, when the party will not even support the weakest bills to turn back climate change.

Nixon's words grew even more urgent as the speech unfolded.

Clean air, clear water, open spaces—these should once again be the birthright of every American. If we act now, they can be. We still think of air as free. But clean air is not free, and neither is clean water. The price tag on pollution control is high. Through our years of past carelessness we incurred a debt to nature and now that debt is being called. The program I shall propose to Congress will be the most comprehensive and costly program in this field in America's history.

Nixon was talking serious tax dollars here. Imagine even a Democrat doing that today. Then he summed his environmental message up in a grand finale.

We can no longer afford to consider air and water common property, free to be abused by anyone without regard to the consequences. Instead, we should begin now to treat them as scarce resources, which we are no more free to contaminate than we are free to throw garbage into our neighbor's yard. This requires comprehensive new *regulations*. It also requires that, to the extent possible, the price of goods should be made to include the costs of producing and disposing them without damage to the environment.

Richard Nixon, ecological economist. Advocate of a guaranteed income and full-cost pricing. A dangerous leftist by today's standards.

Concern for the environment, fueled by television footage of beaches black from the Santa Barbara oil spill and fires burning in the middle of the Cuyahoga River in Cleveland, culminated in massive demonstrations on the first Earth Day, April 22, 1970. Though the Far Right attacked the event as a sneaky way to celebrate Lenin's birthday (we're not making this up), 20 million Americans joined the Earth Day activities, pushing the government to act.

In his first term, Richard Nixon signed the most significant environmental legislation in American history: the Clean Air Act, the Clean Water Act, the Endangered Species Act, and the Environmental Policy Act, creating the EPA. In the years that followed, Nixon's actions improved our environment in countless ways. The famed environmentalist David Brower, who led the fight for many of these policies, later lamented to John that the environmental movement never thanked Nixon for what he had done.

But Nixon, too, was the victim in a Greek tragedy. The good he did was more than matched by his escalation of the Vietnam War into Cambodia and the horror of the killings of students at Kent State, only two weeks after Earth Day. His response to antiwar and civil rights protestors was COINTELPRO, a program of FBI infiltration, harassment, agents provocateurs, and even cold-blooded assassination of movement leaders, in the case of Black Panther Fred Hampton.

His drive for power led to secrecy and "dirty tricks," including the Watergate break-in. His landslide victory in 1972 emboldened conservatives as Lyndon Johnson's 1964 landslide had emboldened liberals. But the exposure of the illegal actions that helped achieve his reelection led to his resignation two years later, leaving Nixon, like Johnson, isolated, reviled, and defeated.

Business Week *Spells It Out*

For the Right, Nixon's demise was a temporary setback. Corporate America and its highest-income benefactors had seen their profits shrink during thirty years of New Deal reforms. They hoped to turn back the clock by promoting tax reduction, deregulation, and privatization of government functions. They were determined to stop the New Deal consensus in its tracks. A chilling editorial in *Business Week* in October 1974, two months after Nixon's resignation, made clear their goals—and the difficulties involved in achieving them: "It will be a hard pill for many Americans to swallow; the idea of doing with less so that big business can have more. Nothing that this nation or any other nation has ever done compares with the selling job that will be needed to get the people to accept the new reality."[4]

Business Week was talking about the greatest good. But for the smallest number. In fact, this switch is exactly what happened, but the "selling job" was easier than expected.

Elected president in 1976, Jimmy Carter only bought half of the *Business Week* equation. He believed we *all* needed to do with less, including big business. During Carter's term, the nation faced a growing energy crisis and double-digit inflation, in part a result of the rising price of energy, in part because of growing consumer demands, and in part because of galloping federal debt from the costs of the Vietnam War.

Inflation assuredly did *not* give big business more. Credit began to dry up as legal limits on *usury*, the interest charged on loans, ran smack into fast-rising prices. Credit card companies sued states that had caps (about 9 percent) on interest rates. They would lose money, they argued, if inflation was higher than the allowed rates.

In 1978, the Supreme Court *ruled unanimously* to exempt national banks from state-based usury laws. Banks began issuing credit cards that often carried interest rates of 18 percent and above, starting a trend that encouraged very high levels of consumer debt, and a major shift of monetary resources from the manufacturing sector to finance. According to Tom Geoghegan, who has dealt with many usury cases as a labor lawyer:

> [The Supreme Court decision] sealed what had been a trend throughout the country, which is lifting these interest rate caps for banks and giving consumers easy credit on the premise that they

would just pay tons and tons of interest so that the banks were protected if the loans weren't repaid. In fact, the banks had incentive to hand out credit cards and hope that the loans would *not* be repaid, because the interest rates on these credit cards were so high.

You know, if you are Mr. Potter in *It's a Wonderful Life* and can only get six percent, seven percent on your loan, you want the loan to be repaid. Moral character is important. You want to scrutinize everybody very carefully. But if you're able to charge 30 percent or, in a payday lender case, 200 or 300 percent, you don't care so much—in fact, you actually want the loan not to be repaid. You want people to go into debt. You want to accumulate this interest. And this addicted the financial sector to very high rates of return compared to what investors were used to getting in the real economy, the manufacturing sector.[5]

That decision contributed enormously toward big business having more while the rest of us made do with less. The decision, on the surface, was understandable: Clearly, banks need to earn more in interest than the rate of inflation, or they will not loan. But the Court might have set a usury limit at so many percentage points above the inflation rate; it did not have to eliminate usury rules entirely.

At the time of the 1978 decision, the financial sector was earning less than 15 percent of total annual profits in America. By 2008, that percentage had risen to 42. It dropped to 29 percent with the financial crisis but has now been rising again.[6]

Carter's Call for Sacrifice

On July 15, 1979, President Carter delivered his most famous address. Commonly termed the "malaise" speech, though Carter did not use that word, it was a call for sacrifice.[7] Carter suggested turning away from the unbridled consumerism that many saw as the American Dream, and toward energy independence and sustainability. He acknowledged a nation in crisis, where inequality was already beginning to grow and people doubted that the future would be better. He quoted the black mayor of a small Mississippi town: "The big shots are not the only ones who are important. Remember, you can't sell anything on Wall Street unless someone digs it up somewhere else first."

This seems to have been forgotten by many of us.

"Too many of us now tend to worship self-indulgence and consumption." Carter told the American people. "Human identity is no longer defined by what one does, but by what one owns. But we've discovered that owning things and consuming things does not satisfy our longing for meaning. We've learned that piling up material goods cannot fill the emptiness of lives which have no confidence or purpose."

Carter, who installed solar panels on the White House, called for a "solar bank" to provide funds leading to "the crucial goal of 20 percent of our energy coming from solar power by the year 2000." He urged a windfall profits tax on oil companies to fund the bank. And he urged Americans to save energy.

> I ask Congress to give me authority for mandatory conservation and for standby gasoline rationing. To further conserve energy, I'm proposing tonight an extra $10 billion over the next decade to strengthen our public transportation systems. And I'm asking you for your good and for your nation's security to take no unnecessary trips, to use carpools or public transportation whenever you can, to park your car one extra day per week, to obey the speed limit, and to set your thermostats to save fuel. Every act of energy conservation like this is more than just common sense—I tell you it is an act of patriotism . . .
>
> I do not promise you that this struggle for freedom will be easy. I do not promise a quick way out of our nation's problems, when the truth is that the only way out is an all-out effort. What I do promise you is that I will lead our fight, and I will enforce fairness in our struggle, and I will ensure honesty. And above all, I will act. We can manage the short-term shortages more effectively and we will, but there are no short-term solutions to our long-range problems. There is simply no way to avoid sacrifice.

And finally, Carter suggested that America was at a crossroads: "There are two paths to choose. One is a path I've warned about tonight, the path that leads to fragmentation and self-interest. Down that road lies a mistaken idea of freedom, the right to grasp for ourselves some advantage over others. That path would be one of constant conflict between narrow interests ending in chaos and immobility. It is a certain route to failure."

It was, however, the route that Americans chose. As the historian David Shi explained, Carter failed to understand "how deeply seated the high, wide and handsome notion of economic growth and capital development had become in the modern American psyche."[8]

The Problem, Not the Solution

Jimmy Carter's opponent in the 1980 election, the actor and onetime Borax spokesman Ronald Reagan, accused Carter of suggesting that America's best days were behind it. He promised to unleash new growth and remove any need for sacrifice, by cutting back government, slashing taxes and regulations, and privatizing state functions. "Government cannot be the solution to our problems," Reagan said, "because government is the problem." His vision, Reagan made clear, was an America where it was still possible for someone to "get rich."[9]

Smooth-talking and affable, Reagan overwhelmed the nay-saying Carter. He stripped Carter's solar panels from the White House. He appointed an antienvironment crusader, James Watt, as interior secretary, and another, Anne Gorsuch, to run the EPA. Reagan worked quickly to dismantle the structures of economic security that had been in place since the New Deal. He crushed striking members of PATCO, the air traffic controllers' union (which had actually endorsed him), bringing in scabs to take their jobs.

His laissez-faire-leaning administration was fiercely antilabor and exacerbated a decline in unionism from nearly 30 percent of workers when he took office to around 12 percent today. He deregulated the phone companies, the airlines, and other sectors of the economy. He massively increased military spending in an effort to make the Russians say uncle. (They did.) And he cut taxes sharply on the rich, from a marginal rate of 50 percent to only 28 percent.

He called his program *supply-side economics*. The idea was that with lower taxes, businesses would invest more and the economy would grow rapidly. With higher profits for business, wealth would "trickle down" to those below like a golden waterfall. Some of his economists suggested that the low tax rates would actually increase tax revenues, and for a time, they did. But the federal debt and deficit mushroomed dramatically. The new taxes did not make up for the increase in military spending. For some of Reagan's advisers this was a good thing: Lack of government revenue would "starve the beast" (government), making it impossible to fund social programs and requiring cutbacks in domestic spending.

The Reagan era had its successes. Economic growth quickened, and inflation was greatly reduced. But the new wealth did not trickle down. It gushed up, lifting the yachts and swamping the rowboats.[10] Inequality rose dramatically, with conspicuous consumption for the rich, and a "greed is good" ethic on Wall Street, contrasted with long lines at the food banks and homeless shelters. Forty years of policies expanding the American middle class were suddenly history. For Reagan's winners, it was "morning in America." For the losers, it was the beginning of a long, dark night that still shows little sign of dawn.

Under Reagan, America swallowed *Business Week*'s bitter pill. Moreover, "starving the beast" meant the government was less able to provide important services. Hobbled by cuts, government became less effective in meeting needs, less a solution and more a problem, making Reagan's attack a self-fulfilling prophecy and weakening public confidence in the state to a degree from which it may never recover.

For the Right, Reagan was the white knight in shining armor, the hero who remade America for the better. In our view, no one did more to set it on a course toward catastrophe. During Reagan's term in office, while Gordon Gekko raked in the cash, corporations closed hundreds of American manufacturing plants, either shipping them to low-wages countries like China or investing the money that would have been used to maintain them in high-stakes financial speculation, as they did in the period leading up to the financial crash of 2008. Auto companies began to make more on their financing than on their cars.

In gritty working-class towns that had once thrived on industry, workers, hung out to dry, took service jobs paying half what their manufacturing jobs did, and began to survive until the next paycheck with high-interest payday loans. Some inner-city areas were all but abandoned to muggers, crack cocaine dealers, and pimps.

Slick Willie to the Rescue

Had the Soviet Union not collapsed between 1989 and 1991, the years of the first George Bush presidency might have been quickly forgotten. Of course, there was the catastrophic 1989 Exxon Valdez oil spill, and the quick defeat of Saddam Hussein in 1991, but the Bush administration was marked most notably by a recession that brought back the Democrats after a twelve-year hiatus. Unable to quickly turn the recession around, the Clinton/Gore administration tasted defeat in 1994's dramatic loss of Congress to the Republicans, who rapidly slashed government again, cutting the entire welfare program.

But Clinton was a charismatic leader, like Reagan. People sensed that he "felt their pain," and reelected him in 1996. Clinton made an effort to increase equality in America, raising taxes on the rich to a marginal rate of 39 percent. As a result, the gap between productivity and worker's real wages, which had been rising since Reagan's election, did not widen further. Moreover, Clinton's second term was a time of unequaled prosperity, fueled by the computer revolution. For the first and only time between the mid-1970s and the present day, compensation for all workers, even the poorest, increased. Higher taxes and greater prosperity helped Clinton turn the massive Reagan-era deficit into an annual surplus.

America grew giddy with success. Time-poor (from the longest working hours since the 1950s) but cash-rich, higher-income Americans began spending as if there was no tomorrow. They bought new and bigger houses, SUVs, hot tubs, and leaf blowers. They took short but expensive vacations and flew twenty-five times as often as their grandparents did in the 1950s.[11] With cash to spare, many of the rich invested heavily in the stock market, sending the Dow Jones average soaring. But for most Americans, personal savings rates dropped steadily.

Though the dotcom craze that made millionaires of many collapsed late in Clinton's second term, a new bubble took its place. Housing prices exploded, and low interest rates led to a surge in new mortgages, often by first-time buyers, and backed up by very little collateral. Banks sold lots of these mortgages to investors, who packaged them into new financial instruments called *derivatives*. Because these derivatives combined risky loans with more secure ones, they were seen as a hedge against any mortgage failures and as particularly good investments. They received AAA ratings from bond agencies, and their numbers expanded rapidly, as did housing loans.

Many banks grew increasingly leveraged.[12] Where they once had outstanding loans averaging only seven times their assets, now they lent out twenty or thirty times as much. Wall Street loved the derivatives game because each time one of them changed hands, the brokers received a fee.

Bankers traded most derivatives privately, rather than on the open market where they could be regulated.

We Should Have Listened to Brooksley Born

There were some signs that this kind of speculation on ever-increasing housing values was risky—the collapse of an investment firm here or a local government there, millions lost by Procter & Gamble on derivatives that exploded. The dangers worried Brooksley Born, Clinton's appointee as director of the Commodity Futures Trading Commission, whose job it was to oversee financial transactions.

"We didn't truly know the dangers in the market because it was a dark market," Born later explained. "There was no transparency." Born believed that if something big enough went wrong, the derivatives market could destroy the entire financial system.[13]

A brilliant lawyer who graduated first in her class at Stanford Law School and was the first female editor of the *Stanford Law Review*, Born announced plans to regulate derivatives, first and foremost, by requiring transparency in their trading. This was not good news on Wall Street, well represented, as always, in the highest ranks of the government. Federal Reserve chairman Alan Greenspan asked Born to lay off. He told her he would not even regulate *fraud*; it would be exposed, and the market would correct everything. In Greenspan's view, regulating derivatives would cause banks to reduce housing loans, the goose that was laying the golden eggs for a soaring stock market and superheated economy.

Clinton's treasury secretary, Larry Summers (later a top adviser to Barack Obama), also called Born, telling her in no uncertain terms to leave derivatives alone. "They were totally opposed to it," Born said of her efforts to make derivatives transparent. "That puzzled me. You know, what was in this market that had to be hidden? Why did it have to be a completely dark market? So it made me very suspicious and troubled."

Called "irascible, difficult, stubborn, unreasonable" by Securities and Exchange Commission chairman Arthur Levitt, Born decided to ignore Greenspan and Summers. Only Congress could stop her, so Greenspan, Summers, Levitt, and Summer's predecessor, Robert Rubin, went to Congress. "I think it's very important for us not to introduce regulation for regulation's sake," Greenspan, a devotee of the libertarian Ayn Rand, told Congress, which responded by declaring a regulatory freeze, shutting down Born. At the end of 1998, Born resigned, never suspecting what a prophet she would turn out to be.

The following year, bullish over growth in the derivatives market, Congress passed a bill, sponsored by the Texas Republican Phil Graham, repealing the Glass-Steagall Act, a 1933 law that required separation of savings and investment banks. The law had been enacted because under Roosevelt's FDIC, personal savings in banks were backed by government insurance. Consequently, the government wanted to be sure that these savings were not gambled away in speculation on the part of bankers. With Glass-Steagall eliminated, savings banks were free to jump into the derivatives market. In 2000, Congress passed the Commodity Futures Modernization Act, which banned regulation of derivatives. Together, these two actions by Congress created a time bomb.

The You're-on-Your-Ownership Society

Later that year, with a little help from the Supreme Court, George W. Bush was elected president. Bush governed so far to the right that he might have made Reagan blush. He cut taxes again and wanted to privatize practically everything. He called his vision the *Ownership Society*. Americans, Bush said, should be fully responsible for their own health care, retirement, and other needs. As a first step, he sought to privatize Social Security. The ownership society meant that Americans would essentially be on their own.[14]

Bush sold government to the highest bidders (the most generous contributors to his campaigns). He expanded Medicare prescription funding in a gift to the pharmaceutical industry. He expanded military funding to pay for wars in Afghanistan and Iraq. Coupled with his tax cuts, these moves quickly turned Clinton-era government surpluses into some of the worst deficits in American history.

At the same time, with no regulation of derivatives, and the view of most experts that these *financial instruments*—complex mathematical formulas developed by the brightest minds on Wall Street—had taken the risk out of lending, the housing market went wild. Banks lent to nearly everyone, whether applicants had good credit or not. Blamed by conservatives for causing the housing bubble, the quasi-government agencies Freddie Mac and Fannie Mae got into the game themselves *after* seeing the money that everyone else was making in derivatives.

Around the midpoint of the Bush II presidency, a few folks became more aware of how risky the derivative packages of home mortgages were. These people realized that a few defaults could torpedo the derivatives, so they bought insurance against failure of the derivatives. These insurance plans, called *credit default swaps*, began selling like hotcakes. By 2007, the derivative/credit default market totaled about $600 *trillion*.

Of course, since the credit default swaps were actually insurance policies, making money on them beyond the fees charged to exchange them depended on the *failure* of the derivatives. Some firms even began betting against their own financial instruments; they were arsonists hiding in the housing market. With banks then leveraged as high as thirty to one or more, a small number of defaulting mortgages would mean disaster. And that's what happened.

Endgame

As home prices rose, and people took on high-interest mortgages with hardly any money down, the housing market ran into another reality of the Bush years: Except for a modest uptick during Clinton's second term, wages for American workers had not kept pace with inflation or productivity. Indeed, men between the ages of thirty and forty were earning *less* in real dollars than they did in 1975.[15] Under Bush, though the highest 1 percent of earners raked in a bonanza of new wealth, even the modest gains that workers made in the late 1990s evaporated. With a Bush administration that refused to prosecute labor violations by businesses and weakened unions even further, wages actually went *down*.

Between 2001 and 2007, while labor productivity rose by at least 10 percent (and some estimates put the rise at twice that), the median wage for workers fell by 3 percent.[16] "Effective demand" for goods began to dry up, unemployment rose, and the housing market shuddered. America's inequality gap, which widened far more under Bush II than under any president before him, came back to bite us like a starving *Tyrannosaurus rex*.

Unable to keep up with their mortgages, many poorer borrowers defaulted. The housing market collapsed, many derivatives collapsed with it, and so did companies like the American International Group (AIG), which had sold enormous numbers of credit default swaps. The stock market went into a nosedive.

"It was my worst nightmare coming true," Brooksley Born told the PBS television program *Frontline*. "Nobody really knew what was going on in the market. The toxic assets of many of our biggest banks are over-the-counter derivatives, and caused the economic downturn that made us lose our savings, lose our jobs, lose our homes. It was very frightening."

In 2008, the whole House of Trickle-Down crumbled overnight. Around the world, the entire capitalist economy went into a tailspin, especially in countries most heavily tied to American banks. It looked like curtains for the economics of greed. But remember the Golden Rule? Yep, those with the gold make the rules. So all of us were forced to write a $700-billion bailout check to the failing banks. Main Street saved Wall Street, which had already ruined Main Street. The poor saved the rich.

One might have assumed that this would have been the end of the supply-siders, trickle-downers, tax-cutting, anti-egalitarian, privatizing deregulators. Their answer instead was a demand to privatize, deregulate, and cut taxes some more. Keep doing what we'd been doing and hope for a miracle. Which of course, as everyone knows, is the working definition of *insanity*.

CHAPTER 12

The Housing, Banking, Finance, Debt, Bankruptcy, Foreclosure, Unemployment, Currency . . . Hell-of-a-Mess Crisis

I'm tempted to say that the crisis is like nothing we've ever seen before. But it might be more accurate to say that it's like everything we've seen before, all at once.

—ECONOMIST PAUL KRUGMAN[1]

Real estate bubbles, bank runs, currency crises, millions laid off, foreclosures, lost retirement—Americans had seen that before. But some things they hadn't: shadow bank hedge funds (outside banking regulation) wielding trillions, derivatives markets worth trillions, balloon mortgages, financial instrument experiments injected like drugs directly into the economy's arteries. And everything was insured to the eyeballs against the collapse, which occurred, but without private insurance resources sufficient to actually cover the losses realized. Enter the taxpayer.

As the U.S. economy fell down, the world economy came tumbling after. "HELP!" cried the banks. Bailouts, stimulus packages, skyrocketing debt, taxpayers owning hunks of American International Group, General Motors, and dozens of banks, a national mortgage fiasco, all made their debuts.

For some, the bailout worked: The GDP rose. Banks fattened up. Corporations enjoyed their highest profits of all time. Wall Street sold trillions more in derivatives of unknowable risk. But for most of us, the fix didn't work: Unemployment persists, foreclosures mount, real incomes for most Americans shrink, and debt looms large.

What happened? Was (is) the economy a house of cards? Before this mess, economists thought finely tuned macroeconomic policy tools had eliminated any possibility of an economic collapse in the United States. Yet, as with anything else, if our assumptions about the way the world works are wrong, our actions may not deliver the expected results.

What Are Finanical Crises, Financial Capital, and Financial Institutions, Anyway?

A *financial crisis* results when the value of financial capital shrinks, crashes, or disappears on a grand scale. Stocks, bonds, futures, currency, debt (such as mortgages), and complicated financial instruments are *financial capital*—basically paper, plastic, or electronic assets. Creating, caretaking, and profiting from all this financial capital are *financial institutions*. These include the U.S. Treasury Department, mortgage companies, commercial and investment banks, savings and loans, unregulated hedge funds, and the Federal Reserve System (privately owned and publicly governed).

Trade or barter is nearly as old as humanity, but the business of business really took off with money, one of our most practical, seductive, and malleable creations. The evolution from barter to the modern economy has followed the evolution of money, useful energy, production, and technology. Money is the bean used to count the value of capital assets. Modern money has evolved beyond the physical tethers of mass and volume, which prevent beans or gold from being instantaneously transferred from New York to Tokyo.

This is one reason financial assets are loosely, and sometimes not at all, bound by the economic laws of supply and demand. Unlike all other goods and services, there is no physical constraint on money supply. Without bothering to print a dollar, Treasury Secretary Tim Geithner released $600 billion into the American banking sector by buying U.S. bonds held by banks with electronic money created by the Treasury Department.

Independence from physical laws enables financial assets to perform impressive and sometimes dangerous gymnastics. As Herman E. Daly noted, while it is impossible due to physical constraints for real pigs to multiply without limit, the debt incurred by borrowed money to buy pigs, or "negative pigs," can multiply indefinitely. Positive pigs live and die by the laws of physics and biology. Debts, negative pigs, are a function of accounting calculations, free from physical reality.[2]

A house is a house, with walls and a roof. Its mere value, rising or falling, does not mean physical improvements in the building. The mortgage on that house is an associated financial "paper" asset with a calculated, expected stream of payments. The value of that mortgage can rise or fall dramatically with the expectations of financial returns.

Totally unlike built, social, human, or natural capital, money and financial capital require market exchanges to deliver value to people. Your house provides value as shelter regardless of its market value. But a dollar is worth nothing until you exchange it for something you value. Thus the value of a bundle of house mortgages can collapse completely, while the value of shelter associated with those mortgages remains constant, as long as people live in those houses.

Financial bubbles develop when "overly exuberant" (as Alan Greenspan called them) bidders inflate the market value of financial assets. When speculators, investors, or consumers lose trust and change their expectations and purchasing, the bubbles burst—just like stocks in 1929 or mortgage values in 2008.

As the Tufts economist Neva Goodwin points out, "Of all the kinds of capital, the adjective 'productive' is most often questionable when applied to financial capital."[3]

The Finanical Shell Game in a Nutshell

During the Great Depression, legal firewalls were built for the U.S. financial sector, government guarantees protected the bank accounts of average Americans, and the United States had the world's most regulated, robust, competitive, and stable banking sector, supporting the growing middle class.

Until the 1990s, community-based banks and savings and loans provided most mortgage lending. Your local bankers looked you in the eye, checked your finances, and knew your boss. They gave you a loan and filed the house title in the bank vault until you paid it off. That was the American way, and it worked. But hundreds of savings and loans went bust in the 1980s. A deregulation binge spurred corruption and a savings and loan collapse, costing taxpayers $87.9 billion. But loaded with bipartisan contributions from the banking sector, Congress further deregulated the banking industry after the scandal. These days, your mortgage could be owned by a Saudi king, a plumbers' union, or doughnut chain.

This expands the universe of lenders but severs the connection between local lenders and borrowers, eliminating community due diligence and increasing the peril of reckless lending and borrowing.

Thousands of U.S. banks did not participate in predatory lending. Many institutions did not buy the "toxic assets" of subprime loans. Thank God! Yet their participation wasn't required to ignite the financial forest fire that burned everyone. We'll tell the story using the case of the largest commercial bank failure in American history, that of Washington Mutual (WaMu) Bank.

After banking deregulation and the 2000 dotcom bust, Fed chairman Alan Greenspan lowered interest rates to boost economic growth, making borrowing money less expensive. People bought houses. Housing prices rose. As almost all people with sufficient desire, income, and credit had already purchased houses, banks expanded the market and lent to people whose credit or income records were weak, people more likely to default on loans. WaMu was the sixth-largest deposit bank in the nation with forty-three thousand employees. WaMu CEO Kerry Killinger saw an opportunity. Push high-interest-rate subprime mortgages, expand market share, and use new financial instruments that investment banks such as Lehman Brothers had created to bundle these mortgages into investment packages.[4] These mortgage bundles, once appraised, valued, rated, and insurable, could be sold to any investor anywhere. It seemed like a great idea.

Here's how it worked. WaMu (and many banks then *and now*) gave strong financial incentives to mortgage brokers for riskier, higher-interest, higher-profit loans, such as adjustable rate mortgages (ARMs), balloon and zero-down mortgages, lending to people less likely to repay. Many banks, including now defunct Countrywide and Wachovia, did the same. With the help of investment banks such as Goldman Sachs and Lehman Brothers, loans were bundled in a variety of pretty packages and then priced, rated, and sold. These mortgage bundles were assets, providing a stream of income from the mortgage payments, and like other assets, could be insured against performance failure or loss. That meant more business for American International Group (AIG), which insured trillions of dollars of these mortgage bundles. The loans generally originated with commercial banks and were packaged by investment banks, or by the quasi-public financial institutions, Fannie Mae or Freddie Mac, sold to investors, and insured by AIG and others.

For most of the 119 years that WaMu existed, the bank held the loans it made and practiced due diligence. But due diligence became unimportant in the early twenty-first century. Because the loans were to be packaged and sold off, whether the borrower could repay the loan was someone else's problem. Between 2003 and 2007, Killinger and top WaMu management gave standing orders: If someone wants a loan, approve it. The *New York Times* interviewed one WaMu broker who took a photo of a loan applicant mariachi singer with his guitar as evidence that the singer had a six-figure income as a substitute for pay stubs. "The photo went into a WaMu file. Approved."[5]

A congressional investigation noted: "WaMu's compensation system rewarded loan officers and loan processors for originating large volumes of high risk loans, paid extra to loan officers who overcharged borrowers or added stiff prepayment penalties, and gave executives millions of dollars even when its high risk lending strategy placed the bank in financial jeopardy."[6]

Additionally, WaMu "used shoddy lending practices riddled with credit, compliance and operational deficiencies to make tens of thousands of high risk home loans that too often contained excessive risk, fraudulent information or errors."[7]

WaMu was also steering borrowers into higher interest, larger loans.[8]

Lehman Brothers pioneered these financial instruments in the 1980s. The subprime mortgage bundles paid higher returns because subprime borrowers were paying higher interest rates. Pricing was based on mathematical statistics and number theory, with a few assumptions. Expected default rates were based on history and the belief that real estate values would continue to rise. These assumptions also underpinned actuarial calculations for insuring these highly complex bundled mortgages. National and global investors hungrily snapped up the high-interest bundled mortgages.

Remember: even though labor productivity had increased dramatically between 2000 and 2007, real wages actually declined during the same period.[9] Inflation-adjusted median household income in the United States fell 9 percent from 2000 ($52,301) to 2009 ($47,777).[10] While the rich were getting richer, everyone else was either treading water or getting poorer. Many borrowers, especially subprime borrowers, could not make their mortgage payments. As they defaulted on their loans, income from the purchased bundled mortgages declined.

By 2007, the default rate on early subprime loans shot up. Subprime mortgage bundles were labeled *toxic*. Investors suddenly stopped buying. But WaMu and other banks continued subprime lending. They couldn't sell the bundled mortgages. By January 2008, banks like WaMu were suffering losses from holding on to their own subprime loans. Facing huge losses by summer, WaMu sold a chunk of its ownership to a hedge fund for an $8-billion cash infusion. In September, WaMu was downgraded by credit rating agencies. In eight days almost $17 billion was electronically withdrawn by large depositors (not FDIC insured), causing a 1930s bank run on WaMu.[11]

The total Federal Deposit Insurance Fund held about $45 billion. The failure of $300-billion WaMu could have wiped out the fund with hundreds of other U.S. banks yet expected to close. Alarmed federal regulators acted fast. During that week, without the knowledge of WaMu management, board, staff, or investors, federal regulators secretly put WaMu up for sale to a few select competitors, while preparing to seize the bank. On September 25, 2008, the Office of Thrift Supervision seized WaMu and the next day sold most of the bank to the highest bidder, JPMorgan Chase. Valued at over $300 billion in January 2008, WaMu was sold for $1.9 billion in September.[12] Don't you hate it when $298 billion evaporates?

The government had other options. Placing seized banks under temporary government trusteeship, chopping them up and auctioning the parts off, and allowing any bank or institution to bid on them would have raised far more capital and rewarded healthy smaller banks that had stayed out of the rush to folly.

Being sold on the cheap to JPMorgan Chase could have been the end of WaMu. But in America, no financial collapse ends without lawsuits. Among those left holding parts of the $47.3 billion in "toxic" mortgage-backed securities that WaMu sold were the Chicago Policemen's Annuity Fund, Boilermakers National Annuity Trust Fund, and Doral Bank of Puerto Rico, which all filed suit hoping to pick over the bank's meager leftovers.[13]

Yet those losses pale in the face of the cumulative devastation that bad lending and fancy financial instruments wreaked across America. For cities like Cleveland, Stockton, Miami, Las Vegas, and others, recovery may be decades away. Foreclosures hit a record 1.2 million in 2010.[14] At least 11 million Americans and up to 25 percent of homeowners were underwater, owing more on their mortgages than their homes were worth.[15]

Canadian Banks Are Still Healthy, Eh?

Over 350 American banks failed between 2008 and April 2011.[16] Not a single Canadian bank failed.[17] Major Canadian banks remained profitable throughout the financial crisis. Because Canada's Liberal Party refused to give in to calls to deregulate its banking system to compete with American deregulation in the late 1990s, Canadian banks had little exposure to the complex toxic asset mortgage bundles.[18] While more than 25 percent of American housing loans were subprime, only 3 percent of Canadian housing loans were subprime.

Canada, often criticized for overregulating banking, maintained vigilant oversight. Canadian banks are protected from foreign competition and focused on Canadian markets. They have a higher reserve requirement and thus greater liquidity to weather any crisis. Canadian bank CEOs are compensated far less than their U.S. counterparts yet have performed demonstrably better. Canadian banks have more public shareholders focused on investment over speculation. Canadian banks needed no rescue. Evidently, an ounce of prevention is worth a trillion pounds of bailout.

In 2010, the World Economic Forum (WEF) ranked Canada as having the soundest, safest banking system in the world. The United States ranked 111th.[19] Interestingly, the WEF ranked Canada lower in "competitiveness" than the United States.

Snoring Treasury Department Awakes to Push Panic Button

Investors that had gobbled up mortgage bundles like chocolates discovered them to be poisonous. The greediest banks keeled over, insolvent. Hedge funds shrank like wet cotton candy. Lehman Brothers, after cooking up many of the derivative chocolates, was caught neck deep in unsold mortgage bundles, just like WaMu. Worried investors pulled their money out, and Lehman Brothers headed for bust. Lehman CEO Richard Fuld made a desperate and personal appeal to Treasury Secretary Henry Paulson (previously the CEO of competitor Goldman Sachs) to be saved.

Paulson wasn't buying. Lehman threw itself up for sale at the mercy of the market. No buyers. Electronic withdrawals quickly exceeded cash on hand, and Lehman Brothers went bankrupt. At the time, Lehman Brothers was holding over nine hundred thousand derivative contracts with more than eight thousand separate firms. That did not include more complex commodity, currency, and credit default swap trades needing to be "unwound." Legal claims against collapsed Lehman topped $1 trillion.[20] Two years later, it has cost over $1 billion in legal fees (one lawyer charged $990/hour) just to partially unwind the mess.[21]

The conservative *Economist* magazine warned of capitalism's potential collapse. Without apology, Treasury Secretary Paulson belatedly stormed into Congress warning of economic conflagration and asking permission to write checks of any size for anything he deemed necessary within a $700-billion budget to save the banking system, with no accountability to Congress.

The bailout vote failed. Congress couldn't accept *no* accountability. The news tanked the stock market. Investors, including retirement funds, lost trillions. Spooked, Congress passed an amended bill. Over $700 billion was provided to bail out more than 450 crumbling American banks. Layoffs hit Wall Street. As AIG siphoned taxpayer money in 2009, it also paid out $180 million in bonuses to the very executives who had previously received bonuses for insuring the mortgage bundles that demolished the company.

Consumers stopped spending. Demand dried up. Businesses stocked up inventory, cutting orders. Housing construction froze. Businesses and government laid people off. Unemployment surged. Both unemployed and employed purchased less. Automobile sales crashed. Chrysler and GM faced bankruptcy. Incomes, sales, and housing values fell. Local, state, and federal government tax revenues shrank. Governments, firms, and consumers cut spending. Demand fell further. Prices fell (deflation), reducing business income. Talk of recession turned to talk of depression.

Perhaps more than anything else, the collapsing economy guaranteed the election of Democrat Barack Obama.

The U.S. Financial Tsunami Slams the World

Let's consider a few cases here.

China built a financial war chest totaling over $2 trillion in reserves, a precaution after the 1997 Asian financial crisis. Buying U.S. bonds, China helped finance American debt, the bank bailout, and the stimulus package, rescuing the dollar from greater devaluation. The Chinese government maintained a set exchange rate with the U.S. dollar (pegged as opposed to flexible exchange rate) so that the Chinese yuan could not appreciate against the dollar. This policy ensured that Chinese exports would remain cheap and flowing to the United States. With no independent unions, depressed wages, weak environmental standards, and huge investment flows from Wall Street, Europe, and Japan, China's communist/capitalist economy surpassed Japan as the world's second largest in 2010 and stands to surpass the United States in size by 2020. Still, the crisis reduced demand for Chinese goods and left Chinese workers without production jobs. Without unemployment benefits, millions of them left coastal cities to return to their poor farming villages.

Iceland's prime minister David Oddsson, a Ronald Reagan admirer, privatized the nation's three national banks, which had financed a prosperous nation. The banks were purchased by the "New Vikings," a handful of aggressive Icelandic entrepreneurs.[22] Oddsson, with faith in unregulated markets, did not regulate, monitor, or guarantee the private banks. Offering high interest rates, the New Vikings brought in international capital and bought banks in Britain, Scandinavia, and the Netherlands, also luring deposits from pension funds, companies, schools, and individuals. They also gobbled up toxic derivatives. By 2008, there was a run on the Icelandic banks, and they collapsed.

The government seized the banks to save Iceland. The three banks held the deposits of virtually every Icelandic citizen. It was like a sardine trying to swallow a whale. The banks were nine times the size of the entire Icelandic government; a full bailout was impossible. Iceland only guaranteed Icelandic citizen's deposits. Depositors in northern European countries faced a 1930s, lose-your-shirt banking failure. The United Kingdom and other countries covered portions of the debts, demanding that Iceland repay over time. Iceland's parliament voted to dutifully pay the debt, but President Olafur Grimsson refused to sign the bill.

Iceland held the first referendum since 1944, on whether to pay the privately generated banking debt owed outside the country. It was equivalent to over $400,000 per person or $1.6 million in debt for a family of four. The vote was 93 percent no. Icelanders rejected a second referendum to pay the defunct private banks' debts in April 2010.[23] When Dave visited Iceland in December 2009, the University of Iceland economics professor Brynhildur Davidsdottir described the discussion there:

> We realized this was not the economy Icelanders wanted. We had a national dialogue with meetings in every Icelandic town about what kind of economy people want. It was clear that Ice-

landers don't want an economy that makes a few people wealthy while risking everyone else's well-being. We found that Icelanders want stable, safe, healthy communities, education, health care, and a fair, sustainable economy.[24]

Ireland collapsed as a real estate bubble, shaky banks, low taxes, and deregulation delivered insolvency to banks and the government. The Irish left for opportunities elsewhere, as they had after the potato famines of the nineteenth century. Irish finance minister Brian Lenihan announced a colossal government bailout of private Irish banks on September 30, 2010. The bailout, funded by the European Union and International Monetary Fund, included government purchase of "toxic" loans. It proportionally dwarfed the American bailout; as the BBC reported, "In other words, more than half of Ireland's GDP has now been devoted to keeping its banks afloat."[25]

Stimulate the Economy!

President Barack Obama inherited one of the biggest economic disasters in modern history. Since few people relish recession, it was an opportune time for change. As President Bush was packing to exit the White House in January 2009, the United States lost 779,000 jobs—the highest monthly job loss since employment record keeping began in the 1930s.[26] Overall, 7.8 million jobs were lost between January 2008 and October 2010.[27]

President Obama laid out a stimulus spending plan of over $700 billion to revive the economy. He successfully ended the economic freefall that Bush's team had created. Obama's economic team held solidly to the Keynesian economic view that recession is a problem of falling demand for goods and services that in turn results in a downward spiral of business and worker income, job loss, and shrunken money supply.

The Keynesian solution is government deficit spending to stimulate sagging demand. Stimulating demand is the key to getting a flat economy back on its feet. Keynesian economists hoped that the money would be spent on worthy projects, but if none were available, paying people to dig and then refill holes would still put money in workers' pockets, expand consumption, increase demand for other products, strengthen the banking system, and get the economy moving. Deficit spending is the Keynesian solution.

This has been accepted economic policy since the New Deal. Every president experiencing an economic downturn has used it since the 1930s, including Reagan and both Bushes. While deficit spending is possible at the federal level, many states have constitutional constraints that bind them to balanced budgets. This means that when tax revenues shrink, so do expenditures, exactly the path Keynes advised against.

The American Recovery and Reinvestment Act of 2009 approved $787 billion in spending; including $275 billion in grants, contracts, and loans for projects, $224 billion for supporting state and local governments, and $288 billion in tax breaks. Certainly, without this package, potentially millions of additional jobs would have been lost. Stimulus grants supported public schools, private companies, and more at the height of the recession. The program reported funding 750,000 jobs in the first three months.[28]

For many Keynesians, the stimulus was too small. To fundamentally improve the economic and employment picture would have taken a larger stimulus package estimated by the economist Dean Baker at $1.8 trillion over two years.[29] Congress was not ready for that. While the stimulus, combined with reform for banks and Wall Street, would have shifted both public and private investment, dramatic Wall Street reform was not to be. Big surprise.

It did not help that Obama's top economic adviser, Larry Summers, was ill equipped for his job. As chief economist at the World Bank, Summers infamously said that the World Bank should support the export of toxic waste to poor countries. A friend of Wall Street, Summers made millions after joining the hedge fund D. E. Shaw Group as managing director in 2006. He received $135,000 for a single speaking appearance at Goldman Sachs.[30] There is a conflict of interest when economic policymakers are in bed with Wall Street. Little wonder that the United States resists European demands for greater regulation of banks and hedge funds. Summers left the administration in 2010.

Fundamentally, the hastily prepared stimulus was geared more to bring back 2007 than to dramatically shift private and public investment to build a twenty-first-century economy. The goal was to revive GDP growth, not to achieve the greatest good for the greatest number over the longest run. In contrast, the 1930s New Deal was not designed to simply rebuild a 1920s economy; instead, it focused on dramatic new goals, measures, policies, and institutions to build a middle class and new economy. The New Deal used the new macroeconomics to build a new U.S. economy.

Obama's stimulus did arrest the economic collapse. It repaired buildings, instituted energy efficiency, funded state and local budgets, gave corporations tax relief, and restored corporate profitability as never before. American corporations chalked up the highest annualized profits in recorded history in late 2010 at $1.659 trillion.[31] However, the stimulus did not build a fundamentally better economy or put in place changes necessary to avoid another meltdown.

What Should We Do Now?

It's clear that our financial system is not working properly despite enormous and rising profitability. In 1950, the financial sector comprised 9 percent of total U.S. corporate profits. Notwithstanding the financial crisis, the finance sector comprised 29 percent of total American corporate profits in 2010.[32] This occurred while toxic instruments drove our economy into the ground and while providing obscene salaries and bonuses for its chieftains. We should immediately take far more serious steps than those contained in the financial regulation legislation of 2010, though that legislation, and especially the Consumer Protection Agency it created, was a step in the right direction.

But we need more.

- *Financial transaction taxes.* While we pay transaction taxes in our everyday lives, such as sales and excise taxes on just about everything bought and sold, financial transactions are not taxed. We suggest a small transactions tax, (of 0.05 percent), which would be inconsequential to *investors* who buy futures, stocks, or bonds with the idea of keeping them and using them to create wealth and employment. But it would eliminate much of the manipulative speculation we see today. For example, the trader that caused the "flash crash" in 2009 by dumping $4 billion in value, trading twenty-seven thousand shares in 0.2 seconds, would pay significantly.

  It would eliminate events like the flash crash caused by the lightning-fast turnover of stocks and futures. Speculators skimming profits by trading massive amounts of stock, unconcerned with real economic productivity, would pay. Investors would face no appreciable cost increases. Financial transaction taxes would not solve all Wall Street's problems, but they would lend greater market stability and resilience, raise tax revenues from speculators, and make taxation fairer across all transactions in the economy.

Switzerland, Sweden, Brazil, and the United Kingdom have financial transaction taxes, and London remains one of the world's great financial hubs. As proposed by European countries, these taxes would be most effective when imposed at the same rate across nations within a multilateral global agreement. Brazil's former president, Lula da Silva, proposed a 1 percent financial transaction tax for the entire global economy, with the money raised to be used to lift up the poor and combat global warming.

- *Currency trading tax.* Over $4 trillion is traded in currency exchanges every day.[33] Most of this is pure speculation. Currency speculation supports few jobs, cannot provide goods or services, and redistributes wealth from people who produce it to speculators who do not. Profits from currency trading rely on micromargins earned from vast trading volumes. A currency tax of $0.005 percent would not burden travelers, trade, or honest international business and would raise an estimated $33 billion globally each year.[34] It would reduce currency speculation, pressing these vast funds toward real investment. This proposal also is best applied in a multilateral framework. In a globalized world, we need some global rules.

- *Restructuring the Federal Reserve System of the United States.* A central bank is an essential part of a national economy. The U.S. system has had little fundamental change in almost one hundred years. Banks have far too much control over the Federal Reserve System. No other industrialized nation has such an antiquated system. Yet the Federal Reserve System still fills an important role. Those who advocate simply eliminating it are nostalgic for the nineteenth century. No nation with a modern economy can do without a central bank. The Fed has an essential role in promoting public-minded economic policy. But it needs to be revamped for the twenty-first century, so that it serves all Americans and not just the banks. We recommend the creation of an advisory committee that would consider ways to reform the Federal Reserve System.

- *Raising reserve requirements, reducing leverage, limiting derivatives.* The reserve requirements for banks operating in the United States should be raised from 10 percent to 20 percent, providing greater security from bankruptcies and less need for bailouts. Legal limits to leveraging should be imposed to reduce the impact of private risk-taking on taxpayers. The unregulated derivatives market is still wildly out of control, especially where insurance derivatives (so-called credit default swaps) are concerned. The United States is still at risk of a larger derivatives catastrophe, leaving the taxpayer as the ultimate insurer.

- *Bringing back usury laws.* In 1979, charging interest over 8 percent on loans or credit cards would land you in jail in Washington State and many other U.S. states. Even before there were laws, usury was a biblical sin. At one time, all U.S. states had usury laws to prevent individuals, banks, and institutions from charging unfair rates of interest. Legal rates of interest must be flexible so as to respond to high inflation, but there should be limits to the real rates that can be charged.

- *Regulating hedge funds.* Many people are determined to see hedge funds as an enemy, and we, too, think they should be regulated. Yet what hedge funds do is exactly what is needed. Nimble investment funds can shift sufficient capital to bring good ideas to market quickly. We live in a world of 7 billion people. Building a twenty-first-century economy must shift trillions of dollars from unproductive activities to productive investment quickly. There is an important role for hedge funds to play. The regulation needed should penalize speculative investment and encourage productive investment.

Like the groundhog's shadow, financial crises can herald either spring or a longer winter. They can catalyze a spirit of working together to improve the economy and everyone's lot, or they can bring scapegoating, back-biting, and greater misery. In 2011, Wisconsin governor Scott Walker attacked school teachers as pampered union members with unaffordable benefits, in an effort to eliminate their collective bargaining rights. He used some of the same arguments employed by opponents of restrictions on child labor eighty years ago.

The rights and benefits Walker sought to eliminate are all taken for granted in Europe, Japan, and neighboring Canada, and are increasingly common in developing nations as well. Yet rather than presenting a program to extend benefits to greater numbers of people, Governor Walker and other laissez-faire politicians work to eliminate the framework of legislation that helped build a strong middle class and strong economy.

But they have overreached. Citizens have awakened, and from chilly Wisconsin, prolonged protests and recall efforts may bring a new spring once again.

The financial crisis is far from over. But solving it, like all the other issues brought up in this book, requires a holistic approach and a much clearer understanding of our goals for an economy that provides the greatest good for the greatest number over the longest run.

CHAPTER 13

Building a Twenty-first-Century
Economy of Life, Liberty, and Happiness

We the People of the United States, in Order to form a more perfect Union, *establish Justice*, insure domestic Tranquility, provide for the common defence, *promote the general Welfare*, and secure the Blessings of Liberty to ourselves and our Posterity, do ordain and establish this Constitution for the United States of America.

—PREAMBLE OF THE U.S. CONSTITUTION

Congratulations! You've made it to chapter 13! It's been a long and bumpy ride—to the edge of a cliff: Americans fought and rejected laissez-faire economic policy a century ago, and there is a concerted effort to bring it back. The New Deal accomplished huge strides, securing a better quality of life, greater fairness, and the world's largest middle class, all under attack by the let-the-market-rule policies pursued over the last three decades, culminating in economic decline. Growing environmental threats, such as peak oil and climate change, are forcing an economic transition in any event. From happiness to debt, Americans now face the most significant economic challenges in generations. Yet we haven't bothered to ask ourselves what the economy is really for.

There is a ready status quo answer. You need to:

- Work harder at a job you don't like, for lower wages and less vacation.
- Be more competitive with people who earn a dollar a day.
- Glug down more caffeinated, alcoholic, or sugary drinks, and save

time by washing down TV-advertised antidepressants in the same gulp.

- Tough out sickness and go to work anyway.
- Stuff the kids and grandparents in 24/7 day care.
- Mortgage your life to pay for education and housing.
- Substitute TV, video games, and trash-the-planet (and your body) consumption (charged to the hilt on credit cards) for the family and friends you just don't have time for, because you're too busy working and maintaining your mountain of stuff.
- Forget retirement.
- Focus on helping corporations earn new record profits while just hoping Wall Street doesn't nuke the economy again.
- Understand that no one ever said the economy was here to make *you* happy.

That's the new American Dream, according to pudgy pundits and bailed-out CEOs.

But most Americans we talk to don't agree with that worldview. They, and we, think it's time to share some of the corporate wealth and time savings generated by higher worker productivity with the workers who generate it. What a concept!

We live in a remarkable time in human history. We don't have to chase woolly mammoths, make our own clothes, or live in fear of Viking raiders. Today's Vikings are friendly, relaxed, well-vacationed people—the happiest folks on the planet, actually. Life has really changed. A century ago, the American Dream was "a chicken in every pot." When many Americans were hungry, it made sense to measure how many more chickens were sold to know if we really were better off. Today, there is growing hunger in America, but more of us are overfed and we are starving for time. America once led the world with the shortest working hours, most free time, and highest labor productivity. Making some of us work sixty-five hours a week despite high unemployment just doesn't make sense.

Our quality of life, and that of our children, grandchildren, and great-grandchildren, really does depend on what kind of economy we build. We've had enough of work more, enjoy less, pollute more, eat toxics, get cancer, and increase the GDP. How about we work less, enjoy more, have more friends and time for them, consume less, pollute less, destroy less, owe less, live better, longer, and more meaningfully? Sounds positively revolutionary, doesn't it?

We need a twenty-first-century economy that provides the greatest good for the greatest number over the longest run. Americans *can* have more free time, more time for family and friends; infants can have more time with their parents. Getting that time will take individual change. As U.S. history shows, it will also require changing national policy. Freedom cannot be advanced by working more hours, borrowing more, and consuming more empty products. Spending more time as active citizens building a nation would be revolutionary.

The solutions to our economic problems exist. There's not enough room in this chapter for even a condensed version of an Encyclopedia of Solutions, though you can read *Solutions Journal* (www.thesolutionsjournal .com). But we're going to offer a few big ideas we think could make a world of difference.

An Economic Bill of Rights

Addressing a nation at war and still recovering from the Great Depression, President Franklin Roosevelt stated most clearly the economic *goals* of his administration and the New Deal on January 11, 1944.[1]

> It is our duty now to begin to lay the plans and determine the strategy for the winning of a lasting peace and the establishment of an American standard of living higher than ever before known. We cannot be content, no matter how high that general standard of living may be, if some fraction of our people—whether it be one-third or one-fifth or one-tenth—is ill-fed, ill-clothed, ill-housed, and insecure.
>
> This Republic had its beginning, and grew to its present strength, under the protection of certain inalienable political rights—among them the right of free speech, free press, free worship, trial by jury, freedom from unreasonable searches and seizures. They were our rights to life and liberty.
>
> As our nation has grown in size and stature, however—as our industrial economy expanded—*these political rights proved inadequate to assure us equality in the pursuit of happiness* [emphasis ours].

We have come to a clear realization of the fact that true individual freedom cannot exist without economic security and independence. "Necessitous men are not free men." People who are hungry
and out of a job are the stuff of which dictatorships are made.

In our day these economic truths have become accepted as
self-evident. We have accepted, so to speak, a second Bill of Rights
under which a new basis of security and prosperity can be established for all—regardless of station, race, or creed.

Among these [rights] are:

- The right to a useful and remunerative job in the industries
  or shops or farms or mines of the nation;
- The right to earn enough to provide adequate food and
  clothing and recreation;
- The right of every farmer to raise and sell his products at a
  return which will give him and his family a decent living;
- The right of every businessman, large and small, to trade in
  an atmosphere of freedom from unfair competition and
  domination by monopolies at home or abroad;
- The right of every family to a decent home;
- The right to adequate medical care and the opportunity to
  achieve and enjoy good health;
- The right to adequate protection from the economic fears of
  old age, sickness, accident, and unemployment;
- The right to a good education.

All of these rights spell security. And after this war is won we
must be prepared to move forward, in the implementation of
these rights, *to new goals of human happiness and well-being* [em-
phasis ours].

Roosevelt spoke of a standard of living higher than ever before. Of
course, 1944 was an earlier time when greater access to material things
was essential for many millions of Americans. Roosevelt did not include
"The right to a clean, safe, and accessible natural environment." We have
every reason to believe he would if speaking today. And that he might
have spoken of a *"quality of life* higher than ever before." But in the end,
he spoke, as Jefferson had, of "happiness" and well-being. He did not
suggest that our goal was growth or a higher GDP. He said they were
new goals of "human happiness and well-being."

These are still the right goals, the goals we should be striving for today and tomorrow. To achieve them, we suggest a holistic pattern of policy changes. They are not exhaustive, and they are only meant to be suggestions. But we think it's necessary to propose some first steps in an effort to rethink our economy so it can give all of us what we need in this new era.

You might think of our ideas as an economy of life, liberty, and happiness. Some of what follows includes the very ideas our founding fathers and Roosevelt spoke of, unfinished business that, after massive increases in our national wealth, remains to be won. But some of them are new and could not have been imagined earlier in our history. So here we go . . .

1. *Give us time*
    a. Mandate three weeks of paid vacation time for every working American, prorate for part-timers.
    b. Implement work-sharing systems, such as *Kurzarbeit*, to reduce unemployment without increasing working hours.
    c. Require hourly pay parity and prorated benefits for part-time workers, as in Europe.
    d. Ensure the right of workers to reduce their hours without losing their jobs, hourly pay, promotion opportunities, or health care, as in the Netherlands. Other benefits would be prorated.
    e. Ban compulsory overtime and provide double-time pay for overtime, as in Finland.
    f. Make federal holidays mandatory for all workers, or give greater compensation to those who must work on those holidays.
    g. Provide tax credits and other incentives to allow small businesses to make these changes without suffering financially.
2. *Improve life possibilities from birth*
    a. Provide prenatal and other care to all parents-to-be.
    b. Give six months of mandatory paid parental leave when a child is born, at a minimum of half the current salary levels, to be paid for by government, as in Canada, through small graduated payroll deductions rather than directly by the employer.

3. *Build a healthy nation*
   a. Provide basic single-payer health care for all Americans, with private insurance providing additional coverage, as in Canada.
   b. Offer tax incentives for healthy behavior, while raising taxes on unhealthy foods and activities.
   c. Carefully shift subsidies to encourage local, organic, and sustainable food production and away from unhealthy food and unsustainable agriculture.
   d. Ensure physical education classes for students.
   e. Protect children by banning television advertising aimed at those under twelve, as in Sweden and Quebec.

4. *Enlarge the middle class*
   a. Create a more progressive tax structure with fewer loopholes for the wealthy and corporations. (General Electric paid zero taxes on a profit of $14 billion in 2010.)
   b. Establish a national living wage with variations for cost-of-living in different states and cities.
   c. Restore limits on usury—restrict interest charged on loans to a certain percentage above the rate of inflation.
   d. Provide greater government support to reduce the cost of education and make college tuition easily affordable.
   e. Give more generous benefits to those losing employment while retaining business flexibility, as in Denmark.
   f. Strengthen the Social Security system by ending the income limit for taxation and tax breaks for private pension programs, while increasing benefit levels to the European average.

5. *Value natural capital*
   a. Change accounting rules and economic analysis to bring the value of natural capital into government and corporate investment decisions.
   b. Adopt physical sustainability measures to inform decision making for air, water, land, and climate resources.
   c. Set aside and restore sufficient natural lands for ecosystem services.
   d. Use tools to identify, value, map, and model ecosystem services for land use planning and environmental impact

statements, and create regional watershed investment districts to more efficiently invest in restoring natural systems and coordinate investment for potable water, flood protection, storm water, biodiversity, ports, navigation, and other water-related investments.

e. Reestablish the Civilian Conservation Corps to restore natural capital and our environmental commons and provide a portion of public works jobs.

6. *Fix taxes and subsidies*

   a. Increase the marginal income tax rate to 45 percent for the highest tax bracket.

   b. Make work pay by ensuring that money made from money (e.g., capital gains) is taxed at a rate at least as high as that made from employment.

   c. Use the tax system to correct market distortions, with new taxes on "bads," which inflict externalized costs on individuals, communities, or the environment, and by removing taxes on "goods" with positive social benefits.

   d. Remove subsidies for consumers and producers of nonrenewable resources and move these subsidies to renewable and nonpolluting or non-climate-changing industries.

7. *Strengthen the financial system*

   a. Reregulate the financial sector (and enforce those regulations).

   b. Implement financial and currency transaction taxes to shift money from risky speculation into productive investment.

   c. Restore the separation between savings and loans, commercial banks, and investment banks.

   d. Break up the largest banks and investment firms to achieve greater competition and provide public savings institutions at the state or local level—a public banking option.

8. *Build a new energy infrastructure*

   a. Ramp up $1 trillion in public and private investments shifting to local, low-carbon, renewable energy and off fossil fuels, funded by a carbon tax.

   b. Aggressively promote energy efficiency in policy and low-
       interest financing to improve existing and new infrastruc-
       ture and products.
   c. Utilize lower-grade energy (e.g., cooling steam from a data
       center to warm greenhouses or provide district heating).

9. *Strengthen community and improve mobility*
   a. Tax sprawl (which requires the extension of public ser-
       vices) and excessive home sizes, while incentivizing
       green building, small homes, public transportation, and
       pedestrian/bicycle infrastructure.
   b. Fund a modern railway system and increase the cost of
       driving autos to pay for it. Deprioritize road construction.
   c. Electrify our transportation system with electric buses,
       trains, and other vehicles.

10. *Improve governance*
    a. Ban corporate campaign contributions through an amend-
        ment to the U.S. Constitution. Limit television advertis-
        ing in campaigns.
    b. Require corporations to include codetermination policies,
        with at least one third of directors elected by the workers.

Good Governance

Democratic, transparent governance is essential to healthy and happy
societies. Economic progress in the United States has often followed on
the heels of improved governance. Markets cannot function without trust,
regulations, and the enforcement that brings cheaters to justice. Effective
competition requires a level playing field and a strong set of rules. If you
doubt this, think of what would happen in a football game if one team
were allowed to come out with brass knuckles and there were no penalties. Such games would be woefully one-sided, and spectators would
quickly lose interest. Setting and enforcing rules for markets, human
health, ecological sustainability, and other important goals are necessary
to ensure the greatest good for the greatest number over the longest run.
This is the role of government. And because the economy is never static,
governance must change and adapt lest new threats weaken the economy.

At times in American history, the Supreme Court, with its justices
appointed for life, has made harmful decisions favoring the rich and

powerful. The Court supported slavery in the Dred Scott decision. It supported monopolies until 1911. It struck down attempts to regulate child labor until 1938, and ruled in favor of the internment of Japanese Americans and legal segregation. The present Supreme Court has done it again, deciding in the *Citizens United* case (and by the slimmest 5–4 majority) that there should be no limits to corporate contributions during elections.[2] Perhaps the most important and urgent priority for improving governance is passing an amendment to the Constitution sharply limiting corporate spending in election campaigns.

Limit the State and the Market

Subsidiarity is the idea that the level of government closest to the people and sufficiently effective in scale should set economic rules for the market. In other words, the activities of local businesses should be overseen by local governments, while large corporations need a larger government watchdog in the service of the people. This seems like a reasonable idea to us. This is not the same as saying "the smaller the government, the better." There is no question that, in the United States, at least, pollsters find more confidence in local government than in the state or federal governments, although in many times and cases this has not been true. (For example, blacks in the Jim Crow South had little reason to trust local officials, some of whom put on white sheets while not in office. The federal government, however, was required to deliver equality and to protect African Americans from retribution and intimidation.) *Subsidiarity* still works. Americans are far more able, generally, to effectively exert their influence on decision making at the local level than in Washington, D.C. The more decisions that can be effectively made in this way, the better.

Conservatives fear the rise of a larger and, ultimately, all-powerful state, or *mega state*. (Much of the attack on President Obama is based on the idea that he is trying to create such an all-powerful federal government.) But, as the economist Stefano Bartolini points out in his powerful Italian bestseller *Manifesto for Happiness*, the rise of the megastate is a response to the rise of the megamarket.[3] A market invading all aspects of life for purposes of private profit and composed of monolithic corporations requires a powerful vigilant regulator. Otherwise Wall Street, the phone companies, or credit card firms steal us blind. Bartolini's case (mirroring the billionaire George Soros's words: "We want a market economy, but not a market society") supports our call for a different kind of economy.

In less regulated capitalist economies, like the United States, the market tends to expand into all areas of life—everything becomes for sale. Commercial messages increasingly litter the visual and auditory world. The average American now sees more than one thousand advertising messages every day.[4] Even conservative economists worry about this assault on beauty by commercialism and huckstering, warning that the market would destroy itself by entering all areas of life—that is, by putting everything up for sale.

Limiting the market's reach is hardly a new idea. The story of Jesus throwing the moneychangers out of the temple was recorded in all four gospels. Jesus expelled the market from the temple not because he universally opposed trade and commerce, but because the temple was a place for spiritual relationships and activities, separate from market activities. The moneychangers degraded "the house of prayer" into a "den of thieves."

"Money talks," goes the old adage, and if allowed, the market crowds out activities that cannot be bought and sold. Goods once commonly provided either by friends, neighbors, or family, or as ecosystem services from the environmental commons, are displaced and increasingly must be purchased. Groundwater is poisoned or depleted and demonstrably more expensive, and lower-quality bottled water is sold. As parents and grandparents must work to make ends meet, week-old infants are sent to day care, expanding the market but providing lower-quality care, lower educational achievement, greater crime, less enjoyment, reduced family cohesion, and requiring increased regulation of day care. How many Americans would rather work than have paid leave to care for their new infants? It does not "cost too much"; other countries have proven the policy successful.

Work more, hurry more, worry more, bond less with others, grow more lonely, and buy your escape from loneliness with more work and more "growth." No wonder economics has been called *the dismal science*—this treadmill is getting grimmer in the world's wealthiest nation.

There is an answer to this dilemma: limit both market *and* state through policies that free people's time. The economy should provide greater *freedom for life*, a freedom in part from overreaching markets.

A society with strong local economies and communities, with many activities provided by local nonprofits, a focus on local small businesses and banking, on farmers' markets and urban gardens, on urban design that favors shared walks instead of isolated commutes, on public spaces for social interaction, and circumstances in which buyers know sellers, sellers donate and volunteer for local activities, salary differences are not vast, and citizens build a better world together, is the kind of society that makes for health, happiness, true prosperity, and sustainability. We know how to create such a society; what we need is the determination to keep the market, no matter how useful it is, within useful boundaries, and the political will to make change happen.

The Happiness Initiative

"Political will?" You say. "Suuure, good luck. The gridlocked, partisan, polarized, corrupt morass of American politics makes all these proposals, policies, and programs from chapter 1 to 13 practically impossible. Dream on."

You have a point.

But despite bad politics and pervasive corruption throughout our nation's history, progress has been made. No idea here is a silver bullet, but collectively, we think their pursuit can realign American politics and bring a fractured progressive movement into sufficient constructive harmony to actually see these ideas through to implementation and clear economic progress. Some Americans have vehemently opposed every step toward progress, whether it was the vote for women, civil rights, or protection of endangered species. This rancorous minority has lost when progressives unite.

Pursuing quality of life, or happiness, over GDP growth is bitterly criticized by economists on the Left and the Right, yet we find that Americans of all political perspectives like the idea. Above all, moving forward requires greater citizen involvement in the shaping of our democracy, laws, and future.

We believe the solutions to America's economic problems are spread before us like puzzle pieces waiting for the support, leadership, effort, and skill to put them all together. It is stunning how much knowledge we actually have about dealing with everything from reduced infant mortality to effective education, reduced prison recidivism, renewable energy, lower carbon emissions, and a host of other problems.

We believe the catalyst for change in America is the economy. And economic transformation is the hub that turns progress and on a wide wheel of issues. A pragmatic economic vision for a better economy builds political momentum by bringing Americans together across issues, parties, and ideologies to enact a broad progressive agenda. While implementing solutions, we Americans need to be engaged in a process for setting out our goals for the economy (what we want from it) as opposed to the economy's goals (what it demands from us). We Americans are constantly told that what we want is more *economic growth*. Yet in hundreds of discussions the two of us have had across the United States, Americans haven't told us that they want more economic growth. They say they want more time with their families, they want health care, secure jobs, college for their kids, a healthy environment, and less debt. Most Americans are saying not that they want more stuff, but that they want a secure and happy life.

So we need a real national dialogue. Let's ditch the pundits and talk with our neighbors. City by city, town by town, state by state, we deserve a national discussion of what Americans actually want out of the economy. Are our current economic goals, measures, policies, and institutions reflective of what Americans want? The two of us don't think so.

Polling has a place, but most of it is superficial—your momentary position on this issue or politician, et cetera. The outcome of a real American dialogue would be different and far more valuable. (What if the only input to formulate the U.S. Constitution had been polls, rather than months of heated discussion? One shudders at the thought.) But is a national dialogue possible?

Iceland did it. And found it highly valuable. Shockingly, its politicians were out of touch with what people wanted! Our bet is that Americans can have a constructive national dialogue too.

Let's start with assessing the well-being of citizens. A survey tool developed in Bhutan and now used in several other countries provides a good starting point. This process is not prescriptive. It does not start out by telling people what they need to do, and it does not ask them their position on "issues." Instead, through a series of questions, it assesses their relative well-being in the nine happiness domains developed in Bhutan.

As part of the Happiness Initiative (www.sustainableseattle.org/sahi), Sustainable Seattle, the first organization in the world to establish regional indicators of well-being, has been using a shortened version of this survey tool. You can take that survey yourself at: www.sustainableseattle.org/sahi. You will find your individual scores for each domain, and you may think about what you can do to improve your scores where they are low. Sustainable Seattle plans to couple the subjective data from these surveys with objective measurements. For example, a score for self-reported health might be coupled with data on life expectancy, child mortality, or obesity.

Once the scores are made public, the question becomes: What kinds of economic policies are most likely to improve areas of concern without damaging others? If people are economically insecure and there is high unemployment, yet at the same time, levels of stress and "time poverty" are high, the best economic policy would not be the creation of more sixty-hour-a-week jobs; it would be policies that help increase the amount of reasonable income part-time work with benefits, so that work can be shared, creating both jobs and more leisure time. This would also benefit employers, since many studies show that overwork reduces productivity and endangers worker safety. Bhutan actually provides a good model. Investment did not stop while citizens filled out Gross National Happiness surveys and discussed policy. At the same time they built schools, clinics, and provided electricity to 80 percent of the population in just a few decades. In fact, the process of national dialogue and physically implementing economic solutions has proceeded simultaneously.

Toward Life, Liberty and Happiness

America can have a better economy in the twenty-first century, but it requires reallocating labor, technology, resources, and capital. There must be both private and public investment for research and implementation. For example, solving the Sustainability Paradox requires public and private investment, job creation, scaling back overconsumption, new technology, wiser uses of resources and time. Oil reserves are declining, while the climate is heating up. Displacing oil with conservation and renewable resources and reducing carbon dioxide emissions to eventually check climate change require the investment of trillions of dollars. Fortunately, the U.S. economy has trillions of investment dollars available. Much of it is currently rolling the dice of wealth redistribution without providing any actual goods or services. Bold action to regulate and tax speculation is needed. Policies that dramatically shift the incentives governing private capital investment toward solutions are also needed. Economic conversion requires public investment, and that will require higher taxes, particularly for the wealthiest Americans and corporations.

Every industrial process needs to be improved. American agriculture needs to be improved. Fortunately, the know-how for those improvements is at hand for every industry. We will have to forgo some profits and consumption for long-term investment and improvement, but achieving a better economy is well worth it.

The point is that there are many solutions out there, but getting to them requires answering the question: What is the economy for, anyway? It requires citizen engagement in assessing real well-being as a substitute for the failed gods of GDP and economic growth. It requires the physical transformation to a sustainable economy by shifting investment on a grand scale and creating new jobs.

Shouting "I'm number one" never made anyone number one. That takes paying attention to what works better in other countries and what's not working well now in the United States. It's time for a *solidarity* economy, one that recognizes we're all in this together. We can learn from Europe and other parts of the world and from the "best policies" in our own American states. We can begin improving and redesigning markets to reflect real costs and to serve human needs. We can make personal changes as well, living more healthfully, simplifying our lifestyles so as to work less, pollute less, use fewer resources, and have more time for each other and our communities. You could call it *capitalism with a human face*.

What's the economy for, anyway, if not life, liberty, and happiness? Together, we can organize our economy to secure the greatest good for the greatest number over the longest run. We can build a twenty-first-century economy and achieve a new American Dream.

Acknowledgments

No book is the simple product of a writer . . . or two. Both John and Dave are indebted to many people for the ideas in this book and for their support during its writing.

From John

Thanks, first, to the folks who helped inspire this project and found me the resources to begin developing its first products: Nancy Folbre and James Boyce, both faculty in the University of Massachusetts Department of Economics, Mike Conroy of the Rockefeller Brothers Fund, and Laura Pacheco, my colleague for the first stage of the project.

Thanks, also, to Tim Jones, my co-faculty for the University of Washington "What's the Economy for, Anyway?" summer school class, to Lance Bennett and Gael Tarleton, who helped make that class possible, and to my intern, Atanas Grozdev. I am indebted to Nancy Parkes, my colleague for a class of the same name at the Evergreen State College, and to Lloyd Jansen, who helped Tim Jones create the www.citizenecon omy.org Web site for the original project.

David Fox and Diana Wilmar provided great production work on the film, *What's the Economy For, Anyway?* Thanks also go to our distributor, Bullfrog Films, and to everyone who helped support that film.

I want to acknowledge my board members at Take Back Your Time, especially Cecile Andrews, who offered many creative ideas; my partner for the Happiness Initiative, Laura Musikanski, executive director of Sustainable Seattle; Vicki Robin and Susan Andrews, who helped get me to Brazil; and the many people I met there, including my new friends from Bhutan, who taught me about Gross National Happiness. Thanks to all the faculty and students I have learned from at the many colleges where I have spoken over the years.

Thanks to all my colleagues at KCTS-TV, who help keep me informed, to all the authors whose ideas informed me, and especially to Paula and David, for putting up with my travels and my hypocritical overwork, as I urge others to work less. Life is never simple. And finally, thanks to my colleague, Dave Batker, for his patience whenever I ranted.

From Dave

A book takes time outside normal demands; I could not have accomplished this without the kind patience and wonderful support of my family. My gorgeous journalist wife, Isabel de la Torre, improved my writing through the years and helped improve parts of this book. Our wonderful children, Rafael and Gabriel, my amazing parents, Ken and Nell Batker, and my dear sister, Carol, were all astoundingly supportive throughout this project.

It has been a pleasure for me to work with John de Graaf on the film and book. *What's the Economy For, Anyway?* was John's idea. When he asked me to work on the film, I immediately liked the idea and dove in. Thanks to the Cosman Family Foundation, Mountaineers Foundation, and Glaser Progress Foundation, which provided funding for the film. Thanks also to Annie Leonard, who encouraged me and, with her example, showed me that this project could be done.

I was warned that writing a book would be incompatible with my work as executive director of Earth Economics (www.eartheconomics .org), but the staff and board were outstandingly supportive in allowing me to take time to complete this book: Jennifer Harrison-Cox, Tedi Dickinson, Maya Kocian, Rowan Schmidt, Yvonne Snider, Joshua Reyneveld, Ingrid Rasch, David Cosman, and Joshua Farley. Earth Economics is stronger today; I am deeply privileged to work with them all.

Many academic colleagues assisted with work that is reflected in this book: my mentor, Herman E. Daly, and colleagues Sarah Anderson, Robert Costanza, John Erikson, Roel Boumans, Ferdinando Villa, Ken Bagstad, Marta Ceroni, Jack Santa Barbara, John Day, and Paul Kemp.

We both thank our agent, Melissa Flashman, who cheerfully opened doors we could not have. Peter Ginna of Bloomsbury immediately understood the project. Both he and Pete Beatty edited the manuscript and gave excellent suggestions that strengthened the book. Thanks also to Maya and Jan Kocian, who provided the visuals, and to our production editor, Laura Phillips. The errors and omissions in this book should be blamed only on us.

Notes

INTRODUCTION

1. Nathaniel Popper, "Ikea's U.S. Factory Churns Out Unhappy Workers," *Seattle Times*, April 12, 2011.
2. Michael I. Norton and Dan Ariely, "Building a Better America—One Wealth Quintile at at a Time," *Perspectives on Psychological Science* 6 (2011): 9–12.

1: THE GROSSEST DOMESTIC PRODUCT

1. Quoted in David Jolly, "G.D.P. Seen as Inadequate Measure of Economic Health," *New York Times*, September 14, 2009.
2. Carmen DeNavas-Walt, Bernadette D. Proctor, and Jessica C. Smith, "Income, Poverty, and Health Insurance Coverage in the United States: 2009," U.S. Census Bureau, September 2010, p. 33, http://www.census.gov/prod/2010pubs/p60-238.pdf.
3. James E. Hanson, "The Need for an International Moratorium on Coal Power," *Bulletin of the Atomic Scientists*, January 21, 2008.
4. Bureau of Economics Analysis Web site, mission page, http://www.bea.gov/about/mission.htm, accessed on September 15, 2010.
5. David M. Kennedy, *Freedom from Fear: The American People in Depression and War, 1929–1945*, p. 11.
6. Simon Kuznets, "National Income, 1929–1932: Letter from the Acting Secretary of Commerce Transmitting in Response to Senate Resolution No. 220 (72D CONG.). A Report on National Income, 1929–1932," 73rd U.S. Congress, 2d session, Senate document no. 124 (Washington, D.C.: U.S. Government Printing Office, 1934), p. 7.
7. Robert Kennedy, "Remarks of Robert F. Kennedy at the University of Kansas, March 18, 1968," John F. Kennedy Presidential Library and Museum Web site, http://www.jfklibrary.org/Historical+Resources/Archives/

Reference+Desk/Speeches/RFK/RFKSpeech68Mar18UKansas.htm, accessed on September 16, 2010.

8. Carrie Holba, "Exxon Valdez Oil Spill: Facts, Links and Unique Resources at ARLIS," Alaska Resources Library and Information, Anchorage, AK, June 2010; and John Harper, Ann Godon, and Alan A. Allen, "Costs Associated with the Cleanup of Marine Oil Spills," Coastal & Ocean Resources, British Columbia, Canada, 1994.

9. Matt DeLisi, "ISU Team Calculates Societal Costs of Five Major Crimes; Finds Murder at $17.25 Million," http://www.news.iastate.edu/news/2010/sep/costofcrime, accessed on March 14, 2010.

10. Federal Trade Commission, "FTC Releases Reports on Cigarette and Smokeless Tobacco Sales and Marketing Expenditures," http://www.ftc.gov/opa/2009/08/tobacco.shtm, accessed on March 24, 2011.

11. National Cancer Institute, "Cancer Trends Progress Report: 2009/2010 Update," figure LCO2, Estimates of National Expenditures for Cancer Care in 2006, National Cancer Institute Web site, http://progressreport.cancer.gov/doc_detail.asp?pid=1&did=2007&chid=75&coid=726&mid, accessed on March 20, 2010.

12. Stephanie Coontz, "Separate Peace," *Wall Street Journal*, June 6, 2008.

13. Credit.com, "Consumers Paying More to File Bankruptcy," http://www.credit.com/news/credit-debt/2010-08-31/consumers-paying-more-to-file-for-bankruptcy.html, posted on August 30, 2010, accessed on March 24, 2011.

14. Sara Murray, "Consumer Bankruptcies Trend Down," *Wall Street Journal*, April 4, 2011.

15. Steve Goldstein, "AIG Reports Fourth-quarter Loss of over $61 Billion," MarketWatch, *Wall Street Journal*, March 2, 2009, http://www.marketwatch.com/story/aig-reports-fourth-quarter-loss-over, accessed on August 14, 2010.

16. Michael G. Palumbo, and Jonathan A. Parker, "The Integrated and Real Systems of National Accounts for the United States: Does It Presage the Financial Crisis?" Bureau of Economic Analysis Web site, http://www.bea.gov/about/pdf/PalumboParke_2009.pdf, accessed on March 12, 2010.

17. Michael Janofsky, "Million Years of Safety Are Sought for A-Waste," *New York Times*, August 10, 2005.

18. Jonathan Rowe, "Our Phony Economy," *Harper's*, June 2008.

19. World Bank, "Saving Species and Ecosystems Through Greener Economic Planning," http://web.worldbank.org/WBSITE/EXTERNAL/NEWS/0,,contentMDK:22743902~pagePK:64257043~piPK:437376~theSitePK:4607,00.html, accessed on March 22, 2011.

20. Jolly, "G.D.P. Seen as Inadequate Measure of Economic Health."

21. Joseph Stiglitz, Amartya Sen, and J. Fitoussi, "The Measurement of Economic Performance Revisited: Reflections and Overview," Commission on the Measure of Economic Performance and Social Progress, 2010.

22. Ibid., p. 9.

23. Ibid., p. 7.

24. Jonathan Rowe, "Looking Backward: Economics and the Cult of Yesterday," *Yes! Magazine*, December 2009.

25. Stiglitz, Sen, and Fitoussi, "The Measurement of Economic Performance Revisited."

26. Christopher Hoening, "Working Toward a Key National Indicator System," http://www.stateoftheusa.org, accessed on August 14, 2010.

2: THE PURSUIT OF HAPPINESS

1. Char Miller, *Gifford Pinchot and the Making of Modern Environmentalism*, p. 155

2. Ibid.

3. Derek Bok, *The Politics of Happiness*, p. 1.

4. Karma Ura, speech, Foz do Iguaçu, Brazil, November 18, 2009.

5. Karma Tshiteem, speech, Seattle Green Festival, June 2010.

6. Kuenga Tshering, interview with David K. Batker, March 31, 2011.

7. Bok, *Politics of Happiness*, p. 5.

8. Ibid., p. 63.

9. Richard Layard, *Happiness*, p. 55.

10. Lauren Sherman, "World's Happiest Places," Forbes.com, May 5, 2009.

11. Ibid.

12. John Helliwell, interview with John de Graaf, August 2009.

13. Line Kikkenborg Christensen, interview with John de Graaf, June 2010.

14. Jennifer Lail, interview with John de Graaf, August 2009.

15. John Helliwell, interview with John de Graaf, August 2009.

16. Bok, *Politics of Happiness*, p. 28.

17. Tim Kasser, interview with John de Graaf, April 2009.

18. Karma Tshiteem, speech to Seattle EPA, June 7, 2010.

19. Michael Pennock, interview with John de Graaf at Vancouver Island Health Authority, April 2010.

20. Susan Andrews, speech, Foz do Iguaçu, Brazil, November 2009.

21. See http://www.sustainableseattle.org.

22. Bok, *Politics of Happiness*, p. 26.

23. John Graham, "Baseball and the Anger of America," *Huffington Post*, August 12, 2010.

24. Bok, *Politics of Happiness*, p. 134.

25. Charles Barber, *Comfortably Numb: How Psychiatry is Medicating a Nation*.

26. See http://gnhusa.org/wp-content/uploads/2010/05/bernanke20100508a.pdf.

27. Arthur Brooks, *Gross National Happiness*.

28. Bruce Bartlett, "Liberaltarians," Forbes.com, May 29, 2009.

29. Arthur Brooks, *The Battle*, p. 88.

30. The sources for the polls are as follows: vacation poll, Opinion Research Corporation, June 23, 2008; paid family leave poll, Family-Friendly Policies: What the Federal Government Can Do, March 3, 2009, testimony of Eileen Appelbaum, Center for Economic and Policy Research; sick days poll, Paid Sick Days: A Basic Labor Standard for the 21st Century Prepared by Dr. Tom W. Smith at the National Opinion Research Center.

31. Arthur Brooks, *Gross National Happiness*, p. 201.

32. Bill McKibben, *Deep Economy* (New York: Henry Holt, 2008), p. 105.

3: PROVISIONING THE GOOD LIFE

1. Manfred A. Max-Neef, *Human Scale Development: Conception, Application and Further Reflections*.

2. Ibid., p. 32.

3. Abraham H. Maslow, "A Theory of Human Motivation," *Psychological Review* 50 (1943): 370–96.

4. Amanda W. Vemuri and Robert Costanza, "The Role of Human, Social, Built and Natural Capital in Explaining Life Satisfaction at the Country Level: Toward a National Well-Being Index (NWI)," *Ecological Economics* 58, issue 10 (June 2006): 119–33.

5. Herman E. Daly and Joshua Farley, *Ecological Economics* (Washington, D.C.: Island Press, 2004), p. 107.

6. United Nation's Food and Agriculture Organization, *The State of Food Insecurity in the World: Addressing Food Insecurity in Protracted Crises*, p. 4.

7. Franco Sassi, *Obesity and the Economics of Prevention: Fit not Fat* (Paris: OECD, 2010), p. 60.

8. U.S. Department of Agriculture Economic Research Service (ERS), "Food Availability (Per Capita) Data System," http://www.ers.usda.gov/Data/Food Consumption, accessed on August 21, 2010.

9. Ibid.

10. All data at http://www.michaelpollan.com.

11. Mary Duenwald, "An Appetite Killer for a Killer Appetite? Not Yet," *New York Times*, April 19, 2005.

12. Amy Goldstein, "America's Economic Pain Brings Hunger Pangs: USDA Report on Access to Food 'Unsettling,' Obama Says," *Washington Post*, November 17, 2009.

13. Richard Wilkinson and Kate Pickett, *The Spirit Level*, p. 25.
14. Ibid.
15. Michael Ableman, interview with John de Graaf, November 1999.
16. Benjamin Somers, "News: Antibiotic Use in Agriculture Is Helping Drive Antibiotic Resistance in Humans, Experts Say," the American Association for the Advancement of Science, March 13, 2009, http://www.aaas.org/news/releases/2009/0313antibiotic.shtml, accessed on April 6, 2011.
17. U.S. Department of Agriculture Research Service, "Sugar and Sweeteners Yearbook: Tables Excel Spreadsheets," table 27, Use of Field Corn, by Crop Year, http://www.ers.usda.gov/Briefing/Sugar/Data.htm, accessed March 9, 2011.
18. David Pimentel, Alison Marklein, Megan A. Toth, Marissa N. Karpoff, Gillian S. Paul, Robert McCormack, Joanna Kyriazis, and Tim Krueger, "Food Versus Biofuels: Environmental and Economic Costs," *Human Ecology* 37, no. 1 (January 29, 2009): 1–12.
19. Douglas McIntyre, "The 10 Worst Real Estate Markets in the U.S.," *Daily Finance*, July 31, 2010, http://www.dailyfinance.com/story/real-estate/the-10-worst-real-estate-markets-in-the-u-s-where-foreclosure/19573907/?icid=sphere_copyright, accessed on August 10, 2010.
20. Alex Kotlowitz, "All Boarded Up," *New York Times Magazine*, March 4, 2009.
21. Paul Carlson, interview with John de Graaf, April 2010.
22. Many companies advertise bulk clothing sales. These prices came from the Web site of America's Best Closeouts, http://www.abcloseouts.com/Used_Winter_Clothing.html, accessed on April 4, 2011.
23. Annie Leonard, *The Story of Stuff*, 45–51.
24. Ibid., 50.
25. Juliet Schor, *Plenitude: The New Economics of True Wealth*, p. 29.

4: UNHEALTHY AT ANY COST

1. Quoted in James Lardner and David Smith, *Inequality Matters*, p. 103.
2. Stephen Bezruchka, interview with John de Graaf, August 2010.
3. Andrew Sisko et al., "Health Care Projections Through 2018," *Health Affairs* 2 (2009).
4. Stephen Bezruchka, interview with John de Graaf, August 2010.
5. T. R. Reid, *The Healing of America*, p. 9
6. World Health Organization, "Health Systems: Improving Performance," June 21, 2000.
7. Country Comparison: Life Expectancy at Birth, *CIA World Factbook*, 2010.

8. "US Life Expectancy Lags Behind 41 Nations," *USA Today*, August 11, 2007.

9. David Brown, "Life Expectancy Drops for Some US Women," *Washington Post*, April 22, 2008.

10. Thandi Fletcher, "Adult Mortality Rate Figures Put Canada Ahead of US," *Vancouver Sun*, April 30, 2010.

11. Lisa Girion, "Europe Healthier than US," *Los Angeles Times*, October 2, 2007.

12. "New Study Finds 45,000 Deaths Annually Linked to Lack of Health Coverage," *Harvard Gazette*, September 17, 2009.

13. Vicente Navarro, "The Inhuman State of US Health Care," *Monthly Review*, September 2003.

14. Elizabeth Warren, "Sick and Broke," *Washington Post*, February 9, 2005.

15. Stephen Bezruchka, speech, Olympia, Washington, August 2010.

16. "The Case for Paid Family Leave," *Newsweek*, August 3, 2009.

17. Sharon Lerner, "Why Unpaid Maternity Leave Isn't Enough," *Washington Post*, June 13, 2010.

18. Jody Heymann and Alison Earle, *Raising the Global Floor*.

19. "US, Britain Ranked Last in Child Welfare," Associated Press, February 14, 2007.

20. Richard Knox, "Too Fat to Fight: Obesity Threatens Military Recruiting," National Public Radio, April 20, 2010.

21. Sarah Speck, speech to National Vacation Matters Summit, August 2009.

22. Stephen Bezruchka, speech, Olympia, Washington, August 2010.

23. National Highway Traffic Safety Administration, http://www-fars.nhtsa .dot.gov/Main/index.aspx, accessed on January 1, 2011.

24. Richard Wilkinson and Kate Pickett, *The Spirit Level*, p. 67.

25. Kristen Hallam, "Working Ten Hours or More a Day Raises Health Risks, Study Finds," *Bloomberg News*, May 11, 2010.

26. Robert Putnam, "You Gotta Have Friends," *Time*, June 25, 2006.

27. Joanne Silberner, "Study Finds English Are Healthier than Americans," National Public Radio, May 3, 2006.

28. Rachel Sladja, "Ensign: Our Health System Is Way Better than Europe's," *PTM Livewire*, September 29, 2009.

29. Greg Kaufmann, "The Nation: Sick and Tired of No Sick Leave," National Public Radio, October 8, 2010.

30. Steven Greenhouse, "Most Americans Support Paid Sick Leave, Poll Finds," *New York Times*, June 22, 2010.

31. Christopher Ruhm, interview, http://www.richmondfed.org/publications/research/region_focus/2008/winter/pdf/interview.pdf, accessed April 10, 2011.

32. Stephen Bezruchka, "The Effect of Recessions on Population Health," *Canadian Medical Association Journal*, 2009.
33. Ibid.

5: Risky Business

1. John Helliwell, interview with John de Graaf, August 2009.
2. "Bush Offers Up Ownership Society, " Associated Press, February 2, ,2005.
3. http://www.realclearpolitics.com/video/2010/11/16/bush_you_can_spend_your_money_better_than_the_government.html, accessed April 10, 2011.
4. http://www.everychildmatters.org/homelandinsecurity/index.html.
5. Ailis Aaron Wolf, "'Blue' State Kids are Healthier," *Boston Edge*, January 26, 2007.
6. Ibid.
7. Jacob Hacker, *The Great Risk Shift*, p. 1.
8. Ibid., p. 2.
9. Ibid., p. 8.
10. Ibid., p. 13.
11. Ibid.
12. Ibid., p. 14.
13. Ibid., p. 19.
14. Ibid., p. 27.
15. Ibid., p. 25.
16. See Steven Hill, *Europe's Promise*; T. R. Reid, *The United States of Europe*; Jeremy Rifkin, *The European Dream*; Thomas Geoghegan, *Were You Born on the Wrong Continent?*
17. Jody Heymann and Alison Earle, *Raising the Global Floor.*
18. http://en.wikipedia.org/wiki/Flexicurity, accessed April 20, 2011.
19. http://en.wikipedia.org/wiki/List_of_minimum_wages_by_country, April 20, 2011.
20. Richard Layard, *Happiness*, p. 69.
21. Dean Baker, http://www.huffingtonpost.com/dean-baker/unemployment-solution-pay_b_359008.html.
22. "The Ten Things the Government Could Do to Cut Unemployment In Half," http://finance.yahoo.com/career-work/article/110572/the-10-things-the-government-could-do-to-cut-unemployment-in-half, accessed April 20, 2011.
23. Nicole Woo, "Reducing Unemployment with Work-Sharing," Center for Economic and Policy Research, August 20, 2010.
24. Hacker, *The Great Risk Shift*, p. 14.
25. Ibid., p. 126.

26. Ibid., p. 122.
27. Michael Pennock, interview with John de Graaf, October 5, 2010.
28. Steven Hill, http://www.huffingtonpost.com/steven-hill/dont-cut-social-security_b_718988.html.
29. Wilkinson and Pickett, *The Spirit Level*, p. 135.
30. Fran Mainella, interview with John de Graaf, August 2010.
31. Wilkinson and Pickett, *The Spirit Level*, p. 149.
32. "Rough Justice in America," *Economist*, July 22, 2010.
33. Homeland Insecurity, http://www.everychildmatters.org/homelandinsecurity/index.html, accessed April 20, 2011.
34. OECD Factbook, 2009, p. 249.
35. Boyce Watkins, "U.S. Prisons More Racist Than South Africa During Apartheid," Black Spin, April 4, 2010.
36. "Rough Justice," *Economist*.
37. http://www.time.com/time/nation/article/0,8599,2064468,00.html.
38. Dwight David Eisenhower, http://mcadams.posc.mu.edu/ike.htm.
39. David Beckmann, interview with John de Graaf, Bread for the World, June 2003.

6: THE TIME SQUEEZE

1. "How Long Should a Man's Vacation Be?" *New York Times*, July 31, 1910.
2. "Running Out of Time," PBS documentary, September 1994.
3. Juliet Schor, *The Overworked American*, p. 29.
4. See John Robinson and Geoffrey Godbey, *Time for Life: The Surprising Ways Americans Use Their Time.*
5. For much of this history, see Benjamin Hunnicutt, *Work Without End.*
6. See Benjamin Hunnicutt, *Kellogg's Six-Hour Day.*
7. William McGaughey, http://www.progressiverepublicans.org/debtdriven.html.
8. William McGaughey, http://www.shorterworkweek.com/swwhistory.html, accessed on April 22, 2011.
9. Ibid.
10. Schor, *The Overworked American*, p. 126.
11. Edward Prescott, http://www.minneapolisfed.org/publications_papers/pub_display.cfm?id=3346, accessed on April 20, 2011.
12. http://www.the9billion.com/2011/01/31/too-many-working-hours-at-the-expense-of-overall-happiness/, accessed on April 20, 2011.
13. Anders Hayden, *Sharing the Work, Sparing the Planet*, p. 50; see also http://en.wikipedia.org/wiki/Wassenaar_Agreement, accessed on April 20, 2011.
14. Quoted in Hayden, *Sharing the Work, Sparing the Planet*, p. 36.

15. Anders Hayden, "Europe's Work-Time Alternatives," in John de Graaf, *Take Back Your Time*, p. 206.

16. Anmarie Widener, *Sharing the Caring*, Ph.D. dissertation, Leiden University, Netherlands.

17. UNICEF, 2005, http://www.npr.org/templates/story/story.php?storyId= 7407245, accessed on April 20, 2011.

18. Annette van der Feltz, personal communication with John de Graaf, September 2010.

19. *Time*, March 14, 2011, p. 33.

20. Jon Messenger, *Decent Working Time.*

21. John de Graaf, "Shorter Work-Time as a Path to Sustainability," Worldwatch, State of the World, 2010.

22. CEPR study, http://www.cepr.net/index.php/press-releases/press-releases/ long-us-work-hours-are-bad-for-the-environment-study-shows, accessed on April 22, 2011.

23. Jörgen Larsson, http://jorgenlarsson.nu/wp-content/uploads/Would-shorter- work-hours-reduce-greenhouse-gas-emissions-100326.pdf.

24. Olga, phone conversation with John de Graaf.

25. Heymann and Earle, *Raising the Global Floor*, p. 106.

26. Opinion Research poll on vacation time, June 23, 2008.

27. Arnold Pallay, personal conversation with John de Graaf, August 2008.

28. Robin Pallay, personal conversation with John de Graaf, August 2008.

29. Donald Worster, *A Passion for Nature*, p. 227.

30. Heymann and Earle, *Raising the Global Floor*, pp. 23–70.

31. Leslie Perlow and Jessica Porter, "Making Time Off Predictable and Required," *Harvard Business Review*, October 2009.

7: The Greatest Number

1. Michael Abramowitz and Lori Montgomery, "Bush Addresses Income Inequality," *Washington Post*, February 1, 2007. For inequality figures see Pew mobility, p. 3, http://www.economicmobility.org/assets/pdfs/PEW_EMP_ AMERICAN_DREAM.pdf, accessed on April 24, 2011.

2. John Hamilton, "What Tea Party Activists Should Really Be Upset About," *Seattle Times*, March 10, 2011.

3. John Schmitt, "Inequality as Policy," Center for Economic and Policy Research paper, 2009.

4. For full data, see http://sociology.ucsc.edu/whorulesamerica/power/wealth .html.

5. Hamilton, "What Tea Party Activists should Really Be Upset About."

6. http://www.brandeis.edu/legacyfund/bio.html, accessed on April 23, 2011.

7. Lardner and Smith, *Inequality Matters*, p. 36.

8. Ibid., p. 39.

9. Ibid., p. 21.

10. Joan Williams, http://www.huffingtonpost.com/joan-williams/the-gender-pay-gap-grossl_b_687779.html, accessed on April 23, 2011.

11. http://www.economicmobility.org/assets/pdfs/EMP%20American%20Dream%20Report.pdf, accessed on April 23, 2011.

12. http://www.nytimes.com/2006/11/26/business/yourmoney/26every.html, accessed on April 23, 2011.

13. All Pietilä quotes are from *YES!* magazine, December 31, 2002, http://www.nytimes.com/2006/11/26/business/yourmoney/26every.html, accessed on April 23, 2011.

14. http://www.weforum.org/issues/global-competitiveness, accessed on April 23, 2011.

15. http://www.usatoday.com/money/perfi/taxes/2010-05-10-taxes_N.htm, accessed on April 23, 2011.

16. http://www.timesonline.co.uk/tol/money/tax/article1996735.ece, accessed on April 23, 2011.

17. See David Cay Johnston, "The Great Tax Shift," in Lardner and Smith, *Inequality Matters*, pp. 165–77.

18. http://abcnews.go.com/Politics/general-electric-paid-federal-taxes-2010/story?id=13224558, accessed on April 23, 2011.

19. http://www.economicmobility.org/assets/pdfs/EMP%20American%20Dream%20Report.pdf, accessed on April 23, 2011.

8: THE CAPACITY QUESTION

1. Arthur Brooks, *The Battle*, p. 71.

2. Ibid.

3. Ibid, p. 89.

4. Ibid, p. 75.

5. Ibid, p. 77.

6. http://ppc.uiowa.edu/uploaded/Forkenbrock/BalancedLives/Slides/Kasser.pdf, accessed on April 24, 2011.

7. Brooks, *The Battle*, p. 81.

8. See Steven Hill, *Europe's Promise*.

9. Joan Blades and Kristin Rowe-Finkbeiner, *The Motherhood Manifesto*, p. 167.

10. http://www.nytimes.com/imagepages/2011/02/19/opinion/19blowch.html?ref=opinion, accessed on April 24, 2011.

11. Anya Kamenetz, *DIY U*, p. 50.

12. http://www.nytimes.com/2008/12/03/world/americas/03iht-03college
.18352687.html, accessed on April 24, 2011.

13. http://completionagenda.collegeboard.org/, accessed on April 24, 2011.

14. Kamenetz, *DIY U*, p. 56.

15. Thomas Geoghegan, *Were You Born on the Wrong Continent?*

16. http://www.citizen.org/documents/Citizens-United-20110113.pdf, accessed
on April 24, 2011.

17. http://www.well-beingindex.com/, accessed on April 24, 2011.

18. http://en.wikipedia.org/wiki/Co-determination, accessed on April 24, 2011.

19. http://www3.weforum.org/docs/WEF_GlobalCompetitivenessReport_
2010-11.pdf, accessed on April 24, 2011.

20. http://en.wikipedia.org/wiki/Mondragon_Corporation, accessed on April
24, 2011.

21. http://triplecrisis.com/letter-from-flint-michigan/, accessed on April 24, 2011.

22. Dean Fortin, interview with John de Graaf, January 2011.

23. Lyle Grant, http://firstmonday.org/htbin/cgiwrap/bin/ojs/index.php/bsi/
article/viewFile/2789/2576.

9: THE LONGEST RUN: SUSTAINABILITY

1. U.S. Census Bureau, "World Population," http://www.census.gov/ipc/www/
popclockworld.html, accessed on September 18, 2010.

2. NOAA, *2009 State of the Climate Report*.

3. United Nations Environment Program, *Millennium Ecosystem Assessment,
Ecosystems and Human Well-Being*, p. 3.

4. Ibid., p. 6–8. The UN Food and Agriculture Organization reports peak
catch in 2000. However, this is based on over-reporting by China, as Daniel
Pauly has shown. See Reg Watson and Daniel Pauly, "Systematic Distortions in World Fisheries Catch Trends," *Nature* 414 (2001): 534–36.

5. U.S. Agency for International Development, *The Global Water Crisis*, http://
www.usaid.gov/our_work/environment/water/water_crisis.html, accessed on
November 24, 2010.

6. U.S. Department of Energy, *International Energy Statistics*, Total Oil Supply 1980–2010, http://www.eia.doe.gov, accessed on February 14, 2011.

7. United Nations Environment Program, *Millennium Ecosystem Assessment*,
p. 25.

8. Ibid., p. 32.

9. EPA, "Montreal Protocol on Substances That Deplete the Ozone Layer,"
http://www.epa.gov/ozone/intpol/, accessed on March 15, 2011.

10. United Nations Environment Program, *Millennium Ecosystems Assessment*, p. 4.

11. Kerry Emanuel, "Increasing Destructiveness of Tropical Cyclones over the Past Thirty Years," *Nature* 436 (July 2005): 686–88.

12. Chemical Body Burden, http://www.chemicalbodyburden.org, accessed on March 22, 2011.

13. Ariana Eunjung Cha and Stephanie McCrummen, "Financial Meltdown Worsens Food Crisis," *Washington Post*, http://www.washingtonpost.com/wp-dyn/content/article/2008/10/25/AR2008102502293.html, accessed on November 24, 2010.

14. Global Footprint Network, "Living Planet Report," 2010, http://www.footprintnetwork.org/en/index.php/GFN/page/world_footprint/.

15. Ibid., accessed on March 27, 2011.

16. National Academy of Sciences, http://www.nationalacademies.org/includes/StabilizationTargetsFinal.pdf, accessed on March 27, 2011.

17. David Brower, see http://www.wildernesswithin.com, accessed on November 5, 2010.

18. Based on Herman E. Daly and Joshua Farley, *Ecological Economics: Principles and Applications*, p. 105; and Rudolf de Groot, Matthew Wilson, and Roelof Boumans, "A Typology of Classification, Description, and Valuation of Ecosystem Functions, Goods, and Services," *Ecological Economics* 41: 393–408.

19. Pavan Sukhdev et al. *The Economics of Ecosystems and Biodiversity: Mainstreaming the Economics of Nature: A Synthesis of the Approach, Conclusions and Recommendations of TEEB.*

20. Herman E. Daly, "Uneconomic Growth: In Theory, in Fact, in History and in Relation to Globalization" (lecture, Saint John's Universtiy, October 25, 1999).

21. David Batker, Isabel de la Torre, Robert Costanza, Paula Swedeen, John Day, Roelof Boumans, and Kenneth Bagstad, *Gaining Ground* (Tacoma, Washington: Earth Economics, 2010), http://www.eartheconomics.org, accessed on August 1, 2010.

22. Ibid., p. 45.

23. Ibid., pp. 75–76.

24. "Timeline: Gulf Oil Spill Lasted Three Months," Reuters, April 15, 2011, http://www.reuters.com/article/2011/04/15/us-oil-spill-timeline-idUSTRE73E3EG20110415, accessed on April 15, 2011.

25. Byron Grote, "2010 Results and Investor Presentation: 1 February 2011," http://www.bp.com/liveassets/bp_internet/globalbp/STAGING/global_assets/downloads/B/bp_fourth_quarter_2010_results_presentation_transcript.pdf, accessed on April 15, 2011.

26. Seattle Public Utilities Web page, http://www.cityofseattle.net/util/About_SPU/Management/History_&_Overview/SPUHISTOR_200312020817523.asp, accessed on August 1, 2010.

27. Seattle Public Utilities Web page, http://www.seattle.gov/util/About_
    SPU/Water_System/History_&_Overview/WATERSYST_2003120209
    08156.asp, accessed on August 1, 2010.
28. Earth Economics, "Workshop: Accounting for Natural Capital: The Es-
    sential Economics of a 21st Century Utility," November 5, 2010 (sum of resi-
    dents served by all six water utilities).
29. David Batker, Maya Kocian, Jennifer McFadden, and Rowan Schmidt,
    "Valuing the Puget Sound Basin: Revealing Our Best Investments, 2010,"
    Earth Economics (2010): 46.
30. Ibid., p. 47.
31. E-mail communication with David Batker, March 8, 2011.
32. Peter Barnes, Robert Costanza, Paul Hawken, David Orr, Elinor Ostrom,
    Alvaro Umaña, and Oran Young, "Creating an Earth Atmospheric Trust,"
    Science, February 8, 2008, p. 724, DOI:10.1126/science.319.5864.724b.
33. Ibid.
34. Roscoe Bartlett, "Peak Oil," U.S. House of Representatives Congressional
    Record, February 28, 2008, H1177.

10: Ancient History

1. H. H. Kohlsaat, "National Affairs: Extracts from Kohlsaat" quoted from Khol-
   saat, *From McKinley to Harding* in *Time*, March 24, 1923, http://www.time
   .com/time/magazine/article/0,9171,726975-1,00.html, accessed on April 12, 2011.
2. Department of Labor, Children's Bureau, "Child Labor, Facts and Figures:
   Bureau Publication No. 917" (Washington, D.C.: U.S. Government Printing
   Office, 1933), http://www.mchlibrary.info/history/chbu/20648-1933.PDF, accessed on January 25, 2011.
3. Ibid.
4. The President's Research Committee on Social Trends; Weasley Michell,
   chair, "Recent Social Trends in the United States; Report of the President's
   Research Committee on Social Trends, 1933" (Washington, D.C.: U.S.
   Government Printing Office, 1933).
5. See descriptions of Dr. Bonnor's and other patent medicines at http://www
   .knowledgerush.com/kr/encyclopedia/Patent_medicine/, accessed on September 6, 2010.
6. Columbia University professor Kevin Murphy provides a more in-depth
   discussion at http://www.kevincmurphy.com/harveywiley.htm, accessed on
   January 25, 2011.
7. Upton Sinclair, *The Jungle*.
8. The Federal Meat Inspection Act and Pure Food Act are discussed in detail
   at http://www.fda.gov, accessed on July 20, 2009.

9. See *Lochner v. New York* (1905) at http://www.law.cornell.edu/supct/html/ historics/USSC_CR_0198_0045_ZD1.html, accessed on August 22, 2010.

10. See *Standard Oil Co. of New Jersey v. United States* for further information at http://supreme.justia.com/us/221/1/case.html, accessed on August 22, 2010.

11. Speech on the trusts at Music Hall, Cincinnati, Ohio, September 20, 1902, in *The Works of Theodore Roosevelt Roosevelt*, memorial edition, http://www .theodore-roosevelt.com/images/research/txtspeeches/28.txt, accessed on March 2, 2011.

12. Ibid.

13. For the rise in education and reduction in illiteracy, see the National Center for Education Statistics: http://nces.ed.gov/naal/lit_history.asp, accessed on May 18, 2011.

14. David M. Kennedy, *Freedom from Fear*, p. 21.

15. There are many good sources for information on the history of the Fed. A brief version is provided at http://www.federalreserveeducation.org/about %2Dthe%2Dfed/history, accessed on May 18, 2011.

16. The University of Colorado American Studies department provides an overview of the women's suffrage movement at http://www.colorado.edu/ AmStudies/lewis/2010/suffrage.htm, accessed on May 18, 2011.

17. Richard N. Current, T. Harry Williams, and Frank Freidel, *American History: A Survey*, p. 683.

18. David M. Kennedy, *Freedom from Fear*, p. 30.

19. Ibid.

20. John Maynard Keynes, *The General Theory of Employment Interest and Money*, p. v.

21. Joan Robinson, *Essays in the Theory of Unemployment*, p. 73.

22. Lyndon B. Johnson, "The 'Great Society' Speech, President Lyndon Johnson, University of Michigan Commencement, 1964," Bentley Historical Library, University of Michigan, 1964, http://bentley.umich.edu/exhibits/lbj1964/, accessed on April 13, 2011.

11: When (or How) Good Went Bad

1. http://www.americanrhetoric.com/speeches/ekennedytributetorfk.html, accessed on April 15, 2011.

2. Andrei Sakharov, *Memoirs*, p. 288.

3. http://www.infoplease.com/t/hist/state-of-the-union/183.html, accessed on April 15, 2011.

4. http://comm-org.wisc.edu/papers2009/dreier.htm, accessed on April 15, 2011.

5. http://www.democracynow.org/2009/3/24/thomas_geoghegan_on_infinite_
   debt_how, accessed on April 15, 2011.

6. http://www.theatlantic.com/magazine/archive/2009/05/the-quiet-coup/
   7364/, accessed on April 15, 2011.

7. http://www.pbs.org/wgbh/americanexperience/features/primary-resources/
   carter-crisis/, accessed on April 15, 2011.

8. John de Graaf, David Wann, Thomas Naylor, *Affluenza*, p. 152.

9. http://www.rightwingnews.com/quotes/reagan2.php, accessed on April 15,
   2011.

10. For a full explanation of these trends, see Kevin Philips, *The Politics of Rich
    and Poor.*

11. De Graaf, Wann, and Naylor, *Affluenza*, p. 28.

12. For a full explanation of the over-leveraged banks, see Joseph Stiglitz,
    Freefall.

13. All Born quotes from PBS Frontline documentary, *The Warning*, http://
    www.pbs.org/wgbh/pages/frontline/warning/view/, accessed on April 15,
    2011.

14. http://www.msnbc.msn.com/id/6902224/ns/politics-state_of_the_union/,
    accessed on April 15, 2011.

15. http://www.economicmobility.org/assets/pdfs/EMP%20American
    %20Dream%20Report.pdf, accessed on April 15, 2011.

16. http://money.cnn.com/2008/08/27/news/economy/state_of_working_amer
    ica/, accessed on April 15, 2011.

12: The Housing, Banking, Finance, Debt, Bankruptcy, Foreclosure, Unemployment, Currency . . . Hell-of-a-Mess Crisis

1. Paul Krugman, *The Return of Depression Economics and the Crisis of 2008*,
   p. 165.

2. Herman E. Daly, *Beyond Growth* p. 178.

3. Neva R. Goodwin (lead author), Global Development and Environment
   Institute (content partner), and Cutler J. Cleveland (topic editor), "Capital,"
   in *Encyclopedia of Earth*, ed. Cutler J. Cleveland (Washington, D.C.: Environmental Information Coalition, National Council for Science and the
   Environment, 2006). First published in the *Encyclopedia of Earth*, April 1,
   2007; last revised November 6, 2006; retrieved September 16, 2010, http://
   www.eoearth.org/article/Capital.

4. Peter S. Goodman and Gretchen Morgenson, "Saying Yes, WaMu Built
   Empire on Shaky Loans," *New York Times*, December 27, 2008.

5. Ibid.

6. U.S. Senate, Permanent Subcommittee on Investigations, Committee on Homeland Security and Governmental Affairs, Exhibits: Hearing on Wall Street and the Financial Crisis: The Role of High Risk Home Loans, Exhibit #1a, April 13, 2010), p. 6.

7. Ibid., p. 6.

8. Ibid., p. 3.

9. Bureau of Labor Statistics, "Productivity Change in the Non-farm Business Sector, 1947–2010," ftp://ftp.bls.gov/pub/special.requests/opt/lpr/nfbbardata .txt, accessed on April 11, 2011.

10. Carmen DeNavas-Walt, Bernadette D. Proctor, and Jessica C. Smith, "Income, Poverty, and Health Insurance Coverage in the United States: 2009," U.S. Census Bureau, September 2010, p. 33, http://www.census.gov/prod/ 2010pubs/p60-238.pdf, accessed on February 23, 2011.

11. U.S. Senate, Permanent Subcommittee on Investigations, Committee on Homeland Security and Governmental Affairs, Exhibits: Hearing on Wall Street and the Financial Crisis: The Role of High Risk Home Loans, Exhibit #1a, p. 5.

12. Goodman and Morgenson, "Saying Yes."

13. Ellen Rosen, "State Street, Novartis, WaMu, Vivendi, BP, Societe Generale in Court News," *Bloomberg*, September 30, 2010, http://www.bloomberg. com/news/2010-10-01/state-street-novartis-wamu-vivendi-bp-societe-generale-in-court-news.html, accessed on February 23, 2011.

14. Amy Hoak, "More Foreclosures, Home-Price Drops on Tap in 2011, MarketWatch, *Wall Street Journal*, December 13, 2010, http://www.marketwatch .com/story/more-foreclosures-home-price-drops-on-tap-in-2011-2010-12-13300,000 foreclosers/month, X million underwater, ref, accessed on February 18, 2011.

15. Keith Gumbinger, "How to Help Underwater Homeowners," Reuters, October 12, 2010.

16. Federal Deposit Insurance Corporation, "Failed Bank List," http://www .fdic.gov/bank/individual/failed/banklist.html, accessed on April 9, 2011.

17. Kevin G. Hall, "Few Foreclosures, No Bank Failures: Canada Offers Lessons," McClatchy Newspapers, January 11, 2011. And Canadian Deposit Insurance Corporation Web site: http://www.cdic.ca/e/index.html, accessed on April 9, 2011.

18. "How Canadian Banks Sidestepped the Financial Crisis," CBS Weekend Journal, April 18, 2009, http://moneywatch.bnet.com/economic-news/video/ how-canadian-banks-sidestepped-the-financial-crisis/289843/, accessed on July 15, 2010.

19. Klaus Schwab, ed., *The Global Competitiveness Report: 2010–2011, Global*

Competitiveness Index 2010–2011 Rankings and 2009–2010 Comparisons, Table 8.07, Soundness of Banks (Davos, Switzerland: World Economic Forum, 2011), p. 460.

20. Linda Sandler and David McLaughlin, "Lehman Defies Bankruptcy to Become a Business Again," *Bloomberg,* September 15, 2010.

21. Clair Zillman, "Legal Fees Pile Up in Recession's Biggest Bankruptcies," *AmLaw Daily,* February 25, 2011, http://amlawdaily.typepad.com/amlawdaily/2011/02/legalfeesnlj.html, accessed on April 9, 2011.

22. Roger Boyes, *Meltdown Iceland: How the Global Financial Crisis Bankrupted an Entire Country,* p. 7.

23. Charles Forelle, "Icelanders Reject Deal to Repay U.K., Netherlands," *Wall Street Journal,* April 11, 2011.

24. Brynhildur Davidsdottir, interview with David K. Batker, December 15, 2009.

25. Robert Preston, "Make or Break for Ireland Finances," BBC Web page: http://www.bbc.co.uk/blogs/thereporters/robertpeston/2010/09/make_or_break_for_ireland_fina.html, accessed on September 30, 2010.

26. Megan M. Barker and Adam A. Hadi, "Payroll Employment in 2009: Job Losses Continue," *Monthly Labor Review,* Bureau of Labor Statistics, March 2009, http://www.bls.gov/opub/mlr/2010/03/art2full.pdf, accessed on September, 24, 2010.

27. Chris Isadore. "Recession Job Losses: Worse than First Thought," CNN Money.com, October 12, 2010, http://money.cnn.com/2010/10/12/news/economy/jobs_revisions/index.htm, accessed on October 15, 2010.

28. "Overview of Funding," http://www.recovery.gov/Pages/home.aspx, accessed on October 1, 2010.

29. Dean Baker, *False Profits: Recovering from the Bubble Economy,* p. 103.

31. Michael Powell, "Profits Are Booming. Why Aren't Jobs?" *New York Times,* January 8, 2011.

32. Bureau of Economic Analysis, "National Income and Product Accounts Table: Corporate Profits by Industry," tables 6.16B, 6.16C and 6.16D, http://www.bea.gov/national/nipaweb/TableView.asp?SelectedTable=237&ViewSeries=NO&Java=no&Request3Place=N&3Place=N&FromView=YES&Freq=Year&FirstYear=1950&LastYear=1970&3Place=N&Update=Update&JavaBox=no#Mid, accessed on April 9, 2011.

33. Tom Lauricella and Dave Kansa, "Currency Trading Soars: Market Hits $4 Trillion a Day as Investors Chase Profit in Growing Economies," *Wall Street Journal,* August 31, 2010, http://online.wsj.com/article/SB10001424052748704421104575463901973510496.html, accessed on February 15, 2010.

34. Rodney Schmidt, "The Currency Transaction Tax: Rate and Revenue Estimates," North-South Institute, Ottawa, October 2007, http://www.nsi-ins.ca/english/pdf/CTT%20revenue.pdf, accessed on February 15, 2011.

13: BUILDING A TWENTY-FIRST-CENTURY
ECONOMY OF LIFE, LIBERTY, AND HAPPINESS

1. Franklin D. Roosevelt, "The Economic Bill of Rights," in *The Public Papers and Addresses of Franklin D. Roosevelt*, ed. Samuel Rosenman, vol. 13 (New York: Harper, 1950), pp. 40–42. Accessed through the Franklin D. Roosevelt American Heritage Center, http://www.fdrheritage.org/bill_of_rights .htm, on April 17, 2011.
2. Supreme Court of the United States, *Citizens United v. Federal Election Commission*, U.S. Supreme Court Web site: http://www.supremecourt.gov/ opinions/09pdf/08-205.pdf, accessed on April 17, 2011.
3. Stefano Bartolini, *Manifesto per la Felicita*.
4. Louise Story, "Anywhere the Eye Can See, It's Likely to See an Ad: Add This to the Endangered List: Blank Spaces," *New York Times*, January 15, 2007, http://www.nytimes.com/2007/01/15/business/media/15everywhere .html, accessed on January 3, 2011.

IMAGE CREDITS

p. 23 GDP and GPI: 1950–2002 Per Capita in 2000 USD
Source: John Talberth, Clifford Cobb, and Noah Slattery, *The Genuine Progress Indicator: A Tool for Sustainable Development*. Oakland: Redefining Progress, 2007.

p. 45 Fundamental Human Needs
Source: Manfred Max-Neef, *Human Scale Development: Conception, Application and Further Reflections*.

p. 47 Maslow's Pyramid
Source: A. H. Maslow, "A Theory of Human Motivation," *Psychological Review* 50 (1943): 370–96.

p. 85 Prison Population Rates
Source: OECD Country Statistical Profiles, 2010.

p. 120 Share of Total U.S. Income Received by Top 1 Percent of Americans
Source: Robert Reich, Great Switch by the Super Rich, 2011, www.robertreich .org.

p. 139 College Graduation Rates, 2007
Source: OECD Country Statistical Profiles, 2010.

p. 156 Ecological Footprint
Source: WWF, Living Planet Report, 2010.

p. 158 Incorrect World View
Source: Industrial Revolution.

p. 158 Correct World View
Source: Modern Science.
p. 160 Ecosystem Goods, Services and Benefits
Source: Modified from de Groot et al., "A Typology of Classification, Description, and Valuation of Ecosystem Functions, Goods, and Services."
pp. 166–167 Solutions
Source: Authors.

Bibiliography

Ableman, Michael. *Fields of Plenty*. San Francisco: Chronicle, 2005.

———. *From the Good Earth*. New York: Abrams, 1993.

———. *On Good Land*. San Francisco: Chronicle Books, 1998.

Ackerman, Frank, and Lisa Heinzerling. *Priceless: On Knowing the Price of Everything and the Value of Nothing*. New York: New Press, 2004.

Ackerman, Sherry. *The Good Life*. Mt. Shasta, CA: Hermitage House, 2010.

Andrews, Cecile. *The Circle of Simplicity*. New York: HarperCollins, 1997.

———. *Slow Is Beautiful*. Gabriola Island, B.C.: New Society, 2006.

Andrews, Cecile, and Wanda Urbanska (eds.). *Less Is More*. Gabriola Island, B.C.: New Society, 2009.

Anielski, Mark. *The Economics of Happiness*. Gabriola Island, B.C.: New Society, 2007.

Aron, Cindy. *Working at Play*. New York: Oxford University Press, 1999.

Aronowitz, Stanley, and William DiFazio. *The Jobless Future*. Minneapolis: University of Minnesota, 1994.

AtKisson, Alan. *Believing Cassandra*. White River Jct., VT: Chelsea Green, 1999.

Baker, Dean. *False Profits: Recovering from the Bubble Economy*. Sausalito, CA: PoliPointPress, 2010.

————. *The United States Since 1980*. Cambridge, UK: Cambridge University Press, 2007.

Barber, Benjamin R. *A Place for Us*. New York: Hill and Wang, 1998.

————. *Consumed*. New York: Norton, 2007.

Barber, Charles. *Comfortably Numb: How Psychiatry Is Medicating a Nation*. New York: Pantheon, 2008.

Barnes, Peter. *Capitalism 3.0*. San Francisco: Berrett-Koehler, 2006.

————. *Who Owns the Sky? Our Common Assets and the Future of Capitalism*. Washington, D.C.: Island Press, 2001.

Bartlett, Bruce. *The New American Economy*. New York: Palgrave Macmillan, 2009.

Bartlett, Donald, and James Steele. *America: What Went Wrong?* Kansas City, MO: Andrews and McNeal, 1992.

————. *America: Who Really Pays the Taxes?* New York: Touchstone, 1994.

Bartolini, Stefano. *Manifesto for Happiness*. Siena, Italy, 2010. (Manuscript as yet unpublished in English).

Bellah, Robert et al. *The Good Society*. New York: Knopf, 1991.

————. *Habits of the Heart*. Berkeley: University of California Press, 1985.

Bernstein, Jared. *All Together Now*. San Francisco: Berrett-Koehler, 2006.

————. *Crunch*. San Francisco: Berrett-Koehler, 2008.

Blades, Joan, and Kristin Rowe-Finkbeiner. *The Motherhood Manifesto*. New York: Nation Books, 2006.

Bok, Derek. *The Politics of Happiness*. Princeton, NJ: Princeton University Press, 2010.

Bollier, David. *Silent Theft: The Private Plunder of Our Common Wealth*. New York: Routledge, 2002.

Boulin, Jean-Ives, Michael Lallement, Jon Messenger, and Francois Michon. *Decent Working Time*. Geneva: ILO, 2006.

Boyes, Roger. *Meltdown Iceland*. New York: Bloomsbury, 2009.

Boyte, Harry. *The Citizen Solution*. St. Paul, MN: Minnesota Historical Society, 2008.

————. *Everyday Politics*. Philadelphia: University of Pennsylvania, 2004.

Boyte, Harry, and Nancy Kari. *Building America*. Philadelphia: Temple, 1996.

Brandt, Barbara. *Whole Life Economics*. Philadelphia: New Society, 1995.

Brekke, Kjell Arne, and Richard B. Howarth. *Status, Growth and Environment: Goods as Symbols in Applied Welfare Economics*. Cheltenham, UK: Edward Elgar, 2002.

Brooks, Arthur. *The Battle*. New York: Basic Books, 2010.

————. *Gross National Happiness*. New York: Basic Books, 2008.

Brower, Michael, and Warren Leon. *The Consumer's Guide to Effective Environmental Choices*. New York: Three Rivers Press, 1999.

Brown, Marvin. *Civilizing the Economy*. Cambridge, UK: Cambridge University, 2010.

Buettner, Dan. *Blue Zones*. Washington, D.C.: National Geographic, 2008.

————. *Thrive*. Washington, D.C.: National Geographic, 2010.

Bunting, Madeline. *Willing Slaves*. London: HarperCollins, 2004.

Cacioppo, John T., and William Patrick. *Loneliness*. New York: Norton, 2008.

Cheney, George. *Values at Work*. Ithaca, NY: ILR, 2002.

Childs, James. *Greed*. Minneapolis, MN: Fortress, 2000.

Chiras, Dan, and David Wann. *Superbia*. Gabriola Island, B.C.: New Society, 2003.

Chouinard, Yvon. *Let My People Go Surfing*. New York: Penguin, 2006.

CIA World Factbooks. Langley, VA: Central Intelligence Agency, 2007–2010.

Clapp, Rodney (ed.). *The Consuming Passion*. Downer's Grove, IL.: Intervarsity, 1998.

Cobb, Clifford W. "Roads Aren't Free." Working Paper Number 3. San Francisco: Redefining Progress, July 1998.

Cobb, Clifford W., Gary Sue Goodman, and Joanne Kliejunas. *Blazing Sun Overhead and Clouds on the Horizon: The Genuine Progress Report for 1999*. San Francisco: Redefining Progress, December 2000.

Cohen, Joel. *How Many People Can the Earth Support?* New York: Norton, 1995.

Cohen, Robert. *Freedom's Orator*. New York: Oxford University Press, 2009.

Colburn, Theo, Diane Dumanoski, and John Peterson Myers. *Our Stolen Future*. New York: Dutton, 1996.

Collins, Chuck, and Mary Wright. *The Moral Measure of the Economy*. Maryknoll, NY: Orbis, 2007.

Collins, Robert M. *More: The Politics of Growth in Postwar America*. New York: Oxford University Press, 2000.

Cosby, Arthur et al. *About Children*. Washington, D.C.: American Academy of Pediatrics, 2005.

Costanza, Robert, John Cumberland, Herman Daly, Robert Goodland, and Richard Norgaard. *An Introduction to Ecological Economics*. Boca Raton, FL: St. Lucie Press, 1997.

Cross, Gary. *An All-Consuming Century*. New York: Columbia University Press, 2000.

Current, Richard N., T. Harry Williams, and Frank Freidel. *American History: A Survey.* New York: Knopf, 1964.

Czech, Brian. *Shoveling Coal for a Runaway Train.* Berkeley: University of California, 2000.

Daly, Herman. *Beyond Growth.* Boston: Beacon, 1996.

———. *Steady-State Economics.* Washington, D.C.: Island Press, 1991.

Daly, Herman, and John Cobb. *For the Common Good.* Boston: Beacon, 1994.

Daly, Herman, and Joshua Farley. *Ecological Economics: Principles and Applications.* Washington, D.C.: Island Press, 2004.

De Bell, Garrett (ed.). *The Environmental Handbook.* New York: Ballantine, 1970.

De Graaf, John (ed.). *Take Back Your Time.* San Francisco: Berrett-Koehler, 2003.

De Graaf, John, David Wann, and Thomas Naylor. *Affluenza.* San Francisco: Berrett-Koehler, 2005.

Devall, Bill. *Living Richly in an Age of Limits.* Salt Lake City, UT: Gibbs Smith, 1993.

Diamond, Jared. *Collapse: How Societies Choose to Fail or Succeed.* New York: Penguin: 2005.

Drago, Robert. *Striking a Balance.* Boston: Dollars and Sense, 2007.

Draut, Tamara. *Strapped.* New York: Anchor, 2005.

Durning, Alan. *How Much Is Enough?* New York: Norton, 1992.

Durning, Alan, and John C. Ryan. *Stuff: The Secret Lives of Everyday Things.* Seattle: Northwest Environment Watch, 1997.

Eisler, Riane. *The Real Wealth of Nations.* San Francisco: Berrett-Koehler, 2007.

Elkind, David. *The Hurried Child*. Reading, MA: Addison-Wesley, 1988.

Elwood, J. Murray. *Not For Sale*. Notre Dame, IN: Sorin, 2000.

Etzioni, Amitai. *The Spirit of Community*. New York: Crown, 1993.

Faludi, Susan. *Stiffed*. New York: Morrow, 1999.

Farley, Tom, and Deborah Cohen. *Prescription for a Healthy Nation*. Boston: Beacon, 2005.

Fassel, Diane. *Working Ourselves to Death*. San Francisco: Harper San Francisco, 1990.

Folbre, Nancy. *The Invisible Heart*. New York: New Press, 2001.

———. *The New Field Guide to the U.S. Economy*. New York: New Press, 1995.

Food and Agriculture Organization. *Global Forest Resources Assessment 2005*. Rome: FAO, 2006.

———. *World Review of Fisheries and Aquaculture*. Rome: FAO, 2006.

Fox, Matthew. *The Reinvention of Work*. San Francisco: Harper San Francisco, 1994.

Frank, Robert. *Luxury Fever*. New York: Free Press, 1999.

Frank, Thomas. *One Market Under God*, New York: Doubleday, 2000.

Fromm, Erich. *The Anatomy of Human Destructiveness*. Greenwich, CT: Fawcett, 1973.

———. *The Heart of Man*. New York: Harper and Row, 1964.

———. *The Sane Society*. New York: Rinehart, 1955.

———. *To Have or To Be?* New York: Bantam, 1982.

Galbraith, John Kenneth. *The Affluent Society*. Boston: Houghton Mifflin, 1998.

Gates, William H., and Chuck Collins. *Wealth and Our Commonwealth*. Boston: Beacon, 2002.

Geoghegan, Thomas. *Were You Born on the Wrong Continent? How the European Model Can Help You Get a Life*. New York: New Press, 2010.

Goldberg, M. Hirsh. *The Complete Book of Greed*. New York: William Morrow, 1994.

Goodell, Jeff. *Big Coal*. Boston: First Mariner Books, 2007.

Goodwin, Neva, Frank Ackerman, and David Kiron (eds.). *The Consumer Society*. Washington, D.C.: Island Press, 1997.

Gore, Al. *Earth in the Balance*. Boston: Houghton Mifflin, 1992.

Gornick, Janet, and Marcia Meyers. *Families That Work*. New York: Russell Sage, 2007.

Greenhouse, Steven. *The Big Squeeze*. New York: Knopf, 2008.

Hacker, Jacob. *The Great Risk Shift*. New York: Oxford University Press, 2006.

Hamilton, Clive. *Growth Fetish*. London: Pluto, 2003.

Hammond, Jeff et al. *Tax Waste, Not Work*. San Francisco: Redefining Progress, 1997.

Hawken, Paul. *The Ecology of Commerce*. New York: Harper Business, 1993.

Hawken, Paul, Amory Lovins, and Hunter Lovins. *Natural Capitalism*. Boston: Little, Brown, 1999.

Hay, Peter. *Main Currents in Western Environmental Thought*. Boston: Beacon Press, 2002.

Hayden, Anders. *Sharing the Work, Sparing the Planet*. London: Zed Books, 1999.

Hayden, Tom. *Reunion*. New York: Random House, 1988.

Heal, Geoffrey. *Nature and the Marketplace: Capturing the Value of Ecosystem Services*. Washington, D.C.: Island Press, 2000.

Henderson, Hazel, and Simran Sethi. *Ethical Markets*. White River Junction, VT: Chelsea Green, 2006.

Henwood, Doug. *After the New Economy*. New York: New Press, 2003.

Hertsgaard, Mark. *Earth Odyssey*. New York: Broadway Books, 1998.

Heymann, Jody, and Christopher Beem. *Unfinished Work*. New York: New Press, 2005.

Heymann, Jody, and Alison Earle. *Raising the Global Floor*. Palo Alto, CA: Stanford University, 2010.

Hill, Steven. *Europe's Promise*. Berkeley: University of California, 2009.

Hochschild, Arlie Russell. *The Time Bind*. New York: Metropolitan, 1997.

Hoffman, Edward. *The Right to Be Human: A Biography of Abraham Maslow*. Wellingborough, UK: Crucible Press, 1989.

Honore, Carl. *In Praise of Slowness*. San Francisco: Harper San Francisco, 2004.

Hunnicutt, Benjamin. *Kellogg's Six-Hour Day*. Philadelphia: Temple, 1996.

———. *Work Without End*. Philadelphia: Temple, 1988.

Illich, Ivan. *Energy and Equity*. New York: Perennial, 1974.

———. *Shadow Work*. Boston: Marion Boyars, 1981.

———. *Tools for Conviviality*. New York Harper and Row, 1973.

Jackson, Tim. *Prosperity Without Growth*. London: Earthscan, 2009.

Jacobson, Michael, and Laurie Ann Mazur. *Marketing Madness*. Boulder, CO: Westview, 1995.

Johnston, David Cay. *Perfectly Legal*. New York: Portfolio, 2005.

Josephson, Eric, and Mary Josephson (eds.). *Man Alone*. New York: Dell, 1970.

Judt, Tony. *Ill Fares the Land*. New York: Penguin, 2010.

Kamenetz, Anya. *DIY U*. White River Junction, VT: Chelsea Green, 2010

Kasser, Tim. *The High Price of Materialism*. Cambridge, MA: Bradford/MIT, 2002.

Kasser, Tim, and Allen Kanner (eds.). *Psychology and Consumer Culture*. Washington, D.C.: American Psychological Association, 2004.

Kawachi, Ichiro, and Bruce Kennedy. *The Health of Nations*. New York: New Press, 2002.

Kelley, Linda. *Two Incomes and Still Broke*. New York: Times Books, 1996.

Kennedy, David M. *Freedom from Fear: The American People in Depression and War, 1929-1945*. Oxford, UK: Oxford University Press, 2005.

Keynes, John Maynard. *The General Theory of Employment, Interest and Money*. New York: Harcourt, Brace, 1936.

Klein, Naomi. *No Logo*. New York: HarperCollins, 2000.

Kohut, Andrew, and Bruce Stokes. *America Against the World*. New York: Times Books, 2006.

Korten, David. *The Post-Corporate World*. San Francisco: Berrett-Koehler, 1999.

————. *When Corporations Rule the World*. San Francisco: Kumarian/Berrett-Koehler, 1995.

Krugman, Paul. *The Conscience of a Liberal*. New York: Norton, 2007.

————. *The Return of Depression Economics and the Crisis of 2008*. New York: Norton, 2009.

Lakoff, George. *Don't Think of an Elephant*. White River Junction, VT: Chelsea Green, 2004.

————. *Whose Freedom?* New York: Picador, 2006.

Lane, Robert. *The Loss of Happiness in Market Democracies*. New Haven, CT: Yale University Press, 2000.

Lardner, James, and David Smith (eds.). *Inequality Matters*. New York: New Press, 2005.

Lasch, Christopher. *The Culture of Narcissism*. New York, Norton, 1978.

———. *The Minimal Self.* New York, Norton, 1984.

———. *The Revolt of the Elites*. New York: Norton, 1995.

———. *The True and Only Heaven*. New York, Norton, 1991.

Latouche, Serge. *Farewell to Growth*. Cambridge, UK: Polity, 2009.

Layard, Richard. *Happiness: Lessons from a New Science*. New York: Penguin, 2005.

Lee, Sangheon et al. *Working Time Around the World*. London: Routledge, 2007.

Leonard, Annie. *The Story of Stuff.* New York: Free Press, 2010.

Lerner, Michael. *The Politics of Meaning*. Reading, MA: Addison-Wesley, 1996.

Levine, Madeline. *The Price of Privilege*. New York: HarperCollins, 2006.

Lewis, Michael. *The Big Short*. New York: Norton, 2009.

Linden, Eugene. *The Future in Plain Sight*. New York: Simon and Schuster, 1998.

Linder, Staffan. *The Harried Leisure Class*. New York: Columbia University Press, 1970.

Louv, Richard. *Childhood's Future*. New York: Houghton Mifflin, 1990.

———. *The Last Child in the Woods*. Chapel Hill, NC: Algonquin, 2006.

———. *The Web of Life*. Berkeley, CA: Conari Press, 1996.

Luttwak, Edward. *Turbo-Capitalism*. New York: HarperCollins, 1999.

Macy, Joanna, and Molly Young Brown. *Coming Back to Life: Practices to Reconnect Our Lives, Our World*. Gabriola Island, B.C.: New Society Publishers, 1998.

Maniates, Michael, and John Meyer (eds.). *The Environmental Politics of Sacrifice*. Cambridge, MA: MIT Press, 2010.

Manning, Robert. *Credit Card Nation*. New York: Basic Books, 2000.

Marchard, Roland. *Advertising the American Dream*. Berkeley: University of California, 1985.

Marcuse, Herbert. *An Essay on Liberation*. Boston: Beacon, 1969.

————. *One Dimensional Man*. Boston: Beacon, 1964.

Martineau, Pierre. *Motivation in Advertising*. New York: McGraw Hill, 1971.

Maslow, Abraham. *Motivation and Personality*. New York: Harper and Row, 1970.

Max-Neef, Manfred A. *Human Scale Development: Conception, Application and Further Reflections*. New York: Apex Press, 1991.

McCarthy, Eugene, and William McGaughey. *Non-Financial Economics*. New York: Praeger, 1989.

McElvaine, Robert. *What's Left?* Holbrook, MA: Adams Media, 1996.

McKenzie, Richard. *The Paradox of Progress*. New York: Oxford University Press, 1997.

McKenzie-Mohr, Doug, and William Smith. *Fostering Sustainable Behavior*. Gabriola Island, B.C.: New Society Publishers, 1999.

McKibben, Bill. *The Age of Missing Information*. New York: Random House, 1992.

————. *The Comforting Whirlwind*. Grand Rapids, MI: Eerdmans, 1994.

————. *Deep Economy*. New York: Henry Holt, 2007.

————. *Hope, Human and Wild*. New York: Little, Brown, 1995.

Meadows, Donella, Dennis Meadows, and Jorgen Randers. *Beyond The Limits*. Post Mills, VT: Chelsea Green, 1992.

Medoff, James, and Andrew Harless. *The Indebted Society*. Boston: Little, Brown, 1996.

Meffe, Gary et al. *Ecosystem Management: Adaptive Community-Based Conservation*. Washington, D.C.: Island Press, 2002.

Menzies, Heather. *No Time*. Vancouver, B.C.: Douglas and McIntyre, 2005.

Messenger, Jon C. *Decent Working Time*. Geneva: International Labor Organization, 2005.

————. *Working Time and Workers' Preferences in Industrialized Countries*. London: Routledge, 2006.

Miller, Char. *Gifford Pinchot and the Making of Modern Environmentalism*. Washington, D.C.: Island Press, 2001.

Miller, Matt. *The Tyranny of Dead Ideas*. New York: Times Books, 2009.

Myers, David. *The American Paradox*. New Haven, CT: Yale University Press, 2000.

Nabhan, Gary, and Stephen Trimble. *The Geography of Childhood*. Boston: Beacon, 1994.

Nadeau, Robert, L. *The Wealth of Nature: How Mainstream Economics Has Failed the Environment*. New York: Columbia University Press, 2003.

Napoli, Lisa. *Radio Shangri-La*. New York: Crown, 2011.

National Conference of Catholic Bishops. *Economic Justice for All*. Washington, D.C.: National Conference of Catholic Bishops, 1986.

National Oceanic and Atmospheric Administration. *2009 State of the Climate Report*. Washington, D.C.: NOAA, 2009.

National Research Council. *Abrupt Climate Change: Inevitable Surprises*. Washington, D.C.: National Academies Press. 2002.

———. *Nature's Numbers: Expanding the National Income Accounts to Include the Environment*. Washington, D.C.: National Academies Press, 1999.

Needleman, Jacob. *Money and the Meaning of Life*. New York: Doubleday Currency, 1991.

Nevarez, Leonard. *Pursuing Quality of Life*. New York: Routledge, 2011.

New Road Map Foundation and Northwest Environment Watch. *All-Consuming Passion* (pamphlet). Seattle: New Road Map Foundation and Northwest Environment Watch, 1998.

New York Times. *The Downsizing of America*. New York: Times Books, 1996.

OECD Factbooks. Paris: Organization for Economic Cooperation and Development, 2007–2010.

O'Hara, Bruce. *Working Harder Isn't Working*. Vancouver, B.C.: New Star, 1993.

Oldenburg, Ray. *The Great Good Place*. New York: Paragon House, 1991.

Orr, David. *Earth in Mind: On Education, Environment and the Human Prospect*. Washington, D.C.: Island Press, 2004.

———. *The Last Refuge: Patriotism, Politics, and the Environment in an Age of Terror*. Washington, D.C.: Island Press, 2004.

Packard, Vance. *The Hidden Persuaders*. New York: Pocket, 1973.

———. *The Status Seekers*. New York: Pelican, 1961.

———. *The Waste Makers*. New York: McKay, 1960.

Partnoy, Frank. *Fiasco*. New York: Penguin, 1999.

Perucci, Robert, and Earl Wysong. *The New Class Society*. Lanham, MD: Rowman and Littlefield, 1999.

Phillips, Kevin. *The Politics of Rich and Poor.* New York: Random House, 1990.

Postman, Neil. *Amusing Ourselves to Death.* New York: Viking, 1986.

———. *Conscientious Objections.* New York: Vintage, 1988.

Princen, Thomas. *The Logic of Sufficiency.* Cambridge, MA: MIT, 2005.

Putnam, Robert D. *Bowling Alone.* New York: Simon and Schuster, 2000.

Rampton, Sheldon, and John Stauber. *Trust Us, We're Experts.* New York: Tarcher/Putnam, 2001.

Reid, T. R. *The Healing of America.* New York: Penguin, 2009.

———. *The United States of Europe.* New York: Penguin, 2004.

Rifkin, Jeremy. *The Age of Access.* New York: Tarcher/Putnam, 2000.

———. *The Empathetic Civilization.* New York: Tarcher/Penguin, 2009.

———. *The End of Work.* New York: Tarcher/Putnam, 1995.

———. *The European Dream.* New York: Tarcher/Penguin, 2004.

———. *Time Wars.* New York: Simon and Schuster, 1987.

Robbins, John. *Diet for a New America.* Tiburon, CA: H. J. Kramer, 1998.

Robin, Vicky, Joe Dominguez, and Monique Tilford. *Your Money or Your Life.* London: Penguin, 2008.

Robinson, Joan. *Essays in the Theory of Unemployment.* London: Macmillan, 1937.

Robinson, Joe. *Don't Miss Your Life.* Hoboken, NJ: Wiley, 2011.

———. *Work to Live.* New York: Pedigree, 2003.

Robinson, John, and Geoffrey Godbey. *Time for Life: The Surprising Ways Americans Use Their Time.* University Park: Pennsylvania State University Press, 1997.

Ropke, Wilhelm. *A Humane Economy*. Indianapolis, IN: Liberty Fund, 1971.

Rosenblatt, Roger (ed.). *Consuming Desires*. Washington, D.C.: Island Press, 1999.

Ross, Andrew. *Nice Work If You Can Get It*. New York: New York University Press, 2009.

Rubens, Jim. *Oversuccess*. Austin, TX: Greenleaf Book Group, 2009.

Rybczynski, Withold. *Waiting for the Weekend*. New York: Viking, 1991.

Sakarov, Andrei. *Memoirs*. New York: Knopf, 1990.

Sapolsky, Robert. *Why Zebras Don't Get Ulcers*. New York: Henry Holt, 2004.

Schlosser, Eric. *Fast Food Nation*. Boston: Houghton Mifflin, 2001.

Schor, Juliet. *The Overspent American*. New York: Basic Books, 1998.

———. *The Overworked American*. New York: Basic Books, 1992.

———. *Plenitude*. New York: Penguin, 2010.

Schut, Michael (ed.). *Money and Faith*. Denver, CO: Morehouse, 2008.

———. *Simpler Living, Compassionate Life*. Denver, CO: Living the Good News, 1999.

Scurlock, James. *Maxed Out*. New York: Scribner, 2007.

Segal, Jerome. *Graceful Simplicity,* New York: Henry Holt, 1999.

Sessions, George (ed.). *Deep Ecology for the 21st Century*. Boston: Shambala Press, 1995.

Shames, Lawrence. *The Hunger for More*. New York: Times Books, 1989.

Sieber, Sam. *Second-Rate Nation*. Boulder, CO: Paradigm, 2005.

Sinclair, Upton. *The Jungle*. New York: Doubleday, Page, 1906.

Slater, Philip. *The Pursuit of Loneliness.* Boston: Beacon Press, 1970.

Smith, J. W. *The World's Wasted Wealth 2: Save Our Wealth, Save Our Environment.* Cambria, CA: Institute for Economic Democracy, 1994.

Speth, James Gustave. *The Bridge at the Edge of the World.* New Haven, CT: Yale University Press, 2008.

Speth, James Gustave, and Peter Haas. *Global Environmental Governance.* Washington, D.C.: Island Press, 2006.

Stein, Herbert, and Murray Foss. *The New Illustrated Guide to the American Economy.* Washington, D.C.: The American Enterprise Institute, 1995.

Stiglitz, Joseph. *Freefall.* New York: Norton, 2010.

———. *The Roaring Nineties.* New York: Norton, 2003.

Stiglitz, Joseph, Amartya Sen, and Jean-Paul Fitoussi. *Mis-Measuring Our Lives: Why GDP Doesn't Add Up.* New York: New Press, 2010.

Stiles, Paul. *Is the American Dream Killing You?* New York: HarperCollins, 2005.

Sukhdev, Pavan, Heidi Wittmer, Christoph Schröter-Schlaack, Carsten Nesshöver, Joshua Bishop, Patrick ten Brink, Haripriya Gundimeda, Pushpam Kumar, and Ben Simmons. *The Economics of Ecosystems and Biodiversity: Mainstreaming the Economics of Nature: A Synthesis of the Approach, Conclusions and Recommendations of TEEB.* Malta: Progress Press for the United Nations Environment Program, 2010.

Swenson, Richard. *Margin.* Colorado Springs, CO: Navpress, 1992.

———. *The Overload Syndrome.* Colorado Springs, CO: Navpress, 1998.

Talbott, John. *Obamanomics.* New York: Seven Stories, 2008.

Thompson, William Irwin. *The American Replacement of Nature.* New York: Doubleday Currency, 1991.

Thornton, Joe. *Pandora's Poison.* Cambridge, MA: MIT Press, 2000.

Thurow, Lester. *The Future of Capitalism*. New York: Penguin, 1996.

Tietenberg, Tom. *Environmental Economics and Policy*. Boston: Pearson Addison Wesley. 2004.

United Nations Environment Programme. *Global Environment Outlook 3*. London: Earthscan, 2002.

———. *Millennium Ecosystem Assessment, Ecosystems and Human Well-Being: Synthesis*. Washington, D.C.: Island Press, 2005.

United Nation's Food and Agriculture Organization. *The State of Food Insecurity in the World: Addressing Food Insecurity in Protracted Crises*. Rome: UN-FAO, 2010.

Wachtel, Paul. *The Poverty of Affluence*. New York: Free Press, 1983.

Wackernagel, Mathis, and William Rees. *Our Ecological Footprint*. Gabriola Island, B.C.: New Society, 1996.

Wallis, Jim. *The Soul of Politics*. New York: New Press, 1994.

Walljasper, Jay. *All That We Share*. New York: New Press, 2010.

Walsh, David. *Designer Kids*. Minneapolis, MN: Deaconess, 1990.

———. *Selling Out America's Children*. Minneapolis, MN: Fairview Press, 1995.

Wann, David. *Biologic*. Boulder, CO: Johnson Books, 1994.

———. *Deep Design*. Washington, D.C.: Island Press, 1996.

———. *The New Normal*. New York: St. Martin's, 2011.

Wattenberg, Ben. *Values Matter Most*. Washington, D.C.: Regnery, 1995.

Weiner, Eric. *The Geography of Bliss*. New York: Twelve, 2008.

Wexler, Sarah Zoe. *Living Large*. New York: St. Martin's, 2010.

White, Curtis. *The Spirit of Disobedience*. Sausalito, CA: Polipoint, 2006.

Wilkinson, Richard, and Kate Pickett. *The Spirit Level*. New York: Blooms-bury, 2010.

World Health Organization. *Climate Change and Human Health*. Geneva: WHO, 2003.

Worldwatch Institute. *State of the World*. New York: Norton, 1995–2010.

———. *Vital Signs 1995–2000*. New York: Norton, 2000.

Worster, Donald. *A Passion for Nature: The Life of John Muir*. New York: Oxford University Press, 2008.

Index

A Note on the Authors

John de Graaf is the executive director of Take Back Your Time (www .timeday.org) and a director of the Happiness Initiative (www.sustain ableseattle.org). He is a documentary television producer with fifteen national PBS specials and more than one hundred filmmaking awards. He is the coauthor of *Affluenza: The All-Consuming Epidemic* and the editor of *Take Back Your Time: Fighting Overwork and Time Poverty in America*. He has taught at the Evergreen State College in Olympia, Washington, and lives in Seattle.

David K. Batker is the executive director of Earth Economics and a native of Tacoma, Washington. Earth Economics (see www.eartheconomics .org) is a pragmatic nonprofit organization that helps identify, value, map, and model ecosystem services. He is a cofounder of Myoonet, a private company developing next-generation data centers for the integration of education, health, and sustainability. He has worked in the coal industry and for Greenpeace International. David has also worked in over forty countries solving a wide variety of practical environmental problems, including improving policies for international finance.